CHICAGO BY DAY AND NIGHT

CHICAGO

BY DAY AND NIGHT

The Pleasure Seeker's Guide
to the Paris of America

Edited by

PAUL DURICA  BILL SAVAGE

NORTHWESTERN UNIVERSITY PRESS

EVANSTON, ILLINOIS

Northwestern University Press
www.nupress.northwestern.edu

Printed in the United States of America

10 9 8 7 6 5

Library of Congress Cataloging-in-Publication Data
Chicago by day and night : the pleasure seeker's guide to the Paris of
    America / edited by Paul Durica and Bill Savage.
        p. cm.
    Republication with annotations of the title previously published by
Thomson and Zimmerman, 1892.
    Includes bibliographical references.
    ISBN 978-0-8101-2909-2 (pbk. : alk. paper)
    1. Chicago (Ill.)—Description and travel. 2. World's Columbian
Exposition (1893 : Chicago, Ill.) 3. Chicago (Ill.)—Social life and customs—
19th Century. I. Durica, Paul. II. Savage, Bill.
F548.5.C5247 2013
917.73'110441—dc23

                                                    2012046390

For Tim Samuelson,
who has the rare gift of making
the past feel present

—Paul Durica

For Colleen

—Bill Savage

LILLIAN RUSSELL.

CHICAGO

BY

DAY <small>AND</small> NIGHT.

THE

PLEASURE SEEKER'S GUIDE

TO THE

PARIS OF AMERICA.

———

300 PAGES.

69 ILLUSTRATIONS.

———

CHICAGO:

THOMSON AND ZIMMERMAN,

234 AND 236 LA SALLE ST.,

1892.

The Gist of it.

THE CITY OF CHICAGO.

THE GREAT WORLD'S FAIR.

Being a Complete History of the Stupendous Exposition that will be Thrown Open in 1893, when the Peopled World Will be Called Upon to View the Progress of the Future Metropolis — How the Exposition will be Opened in the Fall of the Present Year — The Colossal Buildings and Their Contents — Hints for the Wayfarer to Follow in His Strolls About the City During Fair Time.

Introduction

Chicago by Day and Night, Then and Now
PAUL DURICA AND BILL SAVAGE

The World's Columbian Exposition of 1893 has shaped Chicago's image more than any historical event, apart from the Great Chicago Fire and Prohibition-era gang violence. Chicago won a blustery contest against other American cities that hoped to host the exposition to commemorate the four hundredth anniversary of Christopher Columbus's landing—as well as mark the ascension of the United States to a world power by outshining the 1889 fair in Paris. Chicagoans (with help from architects imported from, cough, New York) managed to design and build the fairgrounds, what came to be called the White City, in an impossibly short period of time. After a rocky start, the event that Chicagoans informally dubbed "the Fair" became a national and worldwide sensation. Manufacturers and inventors showed off such futuristic innovations as Cracker Jack and the first Ferris wheel, thrilled crowds with Wild West shows, or introduced exotic belly dancers to shocked yet oddly steady audiences. Visitors from across the globe and from American farms, towns, and cities flocked to the Fair to ponder the future promised there, a future that seemed as wide open as the New World Columbus had "discovered" four centuries earlier.

The Fair also provided an excuse for all these visitors to enjoy Chicago beyond the White City and the Midway. Clearly, Chicagoans would be remiss in their duties as hosts if they failed to guide out-of-towners to the city's many attractions: hence, *Chicago by Day and Night: The Pleasure Seeker's Guide to the Paris of America*. This small volume (sized to fit the front inner pocket in a fashionable gentleman's suit coat), would help visitors to the city discover whatever they might seek away from the fairgrounds proper (or improper)—provided what they were after was a good time, with perhaps some atonement at church or temple services the next morning. Recent best sellers such as Erik Larson's *The Devil in the White City* and Karen Abbott's *Sin in the Second City* have introduced readers to the Fair and the chaotic city that hosted it. This annotated edition of *Chicago by Day and Night* will, we hope, bring our audience back to that moment.

◉◦—

Most popular nonfiction books about Chicago can be roughly divided into three broad genres: boosterism, reformism, and exposé, and all speak a portion of truth about the city. Boosters are convinced that Chicago is simply the greatest city ever, and they set out to prove that case by selectively emphasizing Chicago's accomplishments in urban design, architecture, engineering, or the arts. (Such writers are fond, lately, of the adjective "world-class.") Daniel Burnham and Edward Bennett's 1909 *Plan of Chicago* did indeed shape how we think about cities, and we did invent skyscrapers and raise the grade of the streets to put in sewers before making the Chicago River flow uphill. Chicagoans have a lot to boast about. Reformers were convinced that Chicago was, and is, a sinkhole of corruption, crime, violence, and depravity. Writers like W. T. Stead, in *If Christ Came to Chicago*, set out to reform the sinful city by selectively emphasizing Chicagoans' aptitude for organized crime, serial murder, vice, graft, and bribery. Exposés combine these two genres: instead of calling for reform and excoriating Chicago for its failings, writers of exposés glory like boosters in the telling of lurid tales of the city. Herbert Asbury, in his 1943 book *Gem of the Prairie* (later retitled *The Chicago Underworld*, then re-retitled *Gangs of Chicago*), recounted tales of crimes large and small, claiming that Chicago was unparalleled in vice. In 1951, Jack Lait and Lee Mortimer's *Chicago Confidential* covered much of the same ground, though with a greater emphasis on strippers. Unlike muckraking journalists, or novelists like Upton Sinclair, exposé writers weren't much interested in reform: they just wanted lurid stories to tell, stories that would in turn sell books or newspapers or magazines, or guidebooks.

Chicago by Day and Night combines all three genres: it's a booster's exposé, with a reformer's veneer. The writer or writers brag about Chicago's legitimate cultural attractions beyond the Fair with that superlative overconfidence that secretly insecure Chicagoans specialize in. (We wouldn't compare ourselves to Paris so often if we didn't secretly think we had more in common with Des Moines.) They tell tales of spectacular crime and quotidian criminality that would do any exposé writer proud. And much of the book could guide Stead and his reforming ilk right to the free and easy shows where drinking, dancing, and mixing between the sexes so scandalized them. The writer, and presumably the publisher, avoid censure for providing such information by making repeated disclaimers that such entertainments are, of course, to be avoided. But if one has an inclination for liquid refreshments of the alcoholic variety, well, here are some of the beer gardens you might check out. And if you like the sort of show where scanty costuming is a key part of the aesthetic appeal, well, Sam T. Jack's Burlesque might be right up your alley. And if you'd like perhaps to buy an actress a postshow drink, Engel's might be your destination.

This wink-and-a-nod approach to gambling, drinking, drugs, and sexual freedom (and/or prostitution) is part and parcel of our forgotten past. Vice districts such as the Levee, the Tenderloin, or Cheyenne thrived in Chicago, with the tacit or explicit approval of politicians, not because of some depravity peculiar to Chicagoans but due to the widespread attitude about morals at the time. Human beings, especially men, the thinking went, were morally weak and inherently prone to vice. Carter Harrison Sr., mayor during the Fair, famously said, "You cannot legislate morality." Although their era has a reputation for prudery, the Victorians' attitude toward sin was actually more complicated than mere suppression. Many people believed that since immorality was inevitable, it was better to have it concentrated in one part of town, where the police could contain it, than to have it all over the city. This arrangement also made it more convenient for corrupt police and politicians to collect their payoffs from madams and other executives of the vice trades. Reformers wanted to stamp out such vice entirely, of course. Boosters ignored, minimized, or excused its existence. Exposé writers wanted to profit off the prurient interest of its audience. In this way, *Chicago by Day and Night* perhaps lands more firmly in the urban-exposé genre, as it was published to make money off credulous tourists who were looking for a good time. Or trouble. Or both. The *Pleasure Seeker's Guide* can be understood as a product of what was known as "flash" press—weekly newspapers such as the *Chicago Sporting Gazette* or *Chicago Street Gazette*, which featured stories about horse races, the theater, and nightlife for men-about-town.

These papers resembled today's tabloid press or trash television with their emphasis on celebrity gossip and inside dope about the underworld of the city, news of a famed criminal's release from jail, or a popular prostitute's relocation to a different "resort."

Chicago by Day and Night also shares literary attitudes with fictional representations of cities in this era. Literary standards of the late nineteenth century required a very particular spin on depictions of sin, especially sexual immorality. A book could tell the lurid, or instructive, story of a fallen woman, say, but the tale would be considered proper (and immune from prosecution for obscenity, depending on its degree of directness) only if the heroine sees the error of her ways or, better yet, dies in some manner fitting her debased moral status. In 1879, Henry James's Daisy Miller gets malaria because she has the temerity to parade about in public with disreputable Italians; as late as 1903, Stephen Crane's Maggie drowns herself in despair. Theodore Dreiser, who attended the Fair and in whose meaty hands it's easy to picture this volume, began to change that with his 1900 novel *Sister Carrie,* in which he depicts the realistic notion that sometimes good things happen to ostensibly bad people. For fans of Dreiser, *Chicago by Day and Night* is the sort of tome Charles Drouet, Carrie's initial seducer, would have read with interest; George Hurstwood, Carrie's second seducer, would have had his saloon, Fitzgerald and Moy's, featured in it, based as it was on Chicago's Hannah & Hogg saloon.

But in 1893, literature still required morality. In this book, the textual atonement takes two forms: first, the inclusion of a lengthy chapter on the city's prominent churches and synagogues, as well as the clergy who man their pulpits. The reviews of the churches are fascinating, both because many of these churches survive today (though with very different congregations) and because the clergy are treated as show-men, with the length and quality of their sermons judged for how they entertain as well as enlighten. Second, an entire chapter is devoted to "A Complete Refutation of the Libelous Assertion that Chicago is the Wickedest City in the World." This chapter lists various good works done by Chicago orga-nizations, but given how the majority of the book stresses "free and easy" entertainments, these chapters doth protest too much, we think.

Cities are patterns of persistence and change. The urban landscape of Chicago has been built, broken, and rebuilt in the 120 years since *Chicago by Day and Night* went on sale at the newsstands and cigar stores of the city in 1893. Newsstands are now almost as rare as wood-paved streets, and smoking in public is practically illegal. But where once "bloods" sought the company of comely "soubrettes" at "free and easy shows," today's "players" frequent "gentlemen's clubs." This book is both a ticket to this past Chicago and a reminder of how little, really, things change. They were driving horse-drawn carriages rather than Crown Vics, but cabdrivers were no more trusted or popular in 1893 than they are today, and chapter 15, "Hackmen and Their Ways," advises visitors how to avoid being taken for a ride in more ways than one. Theater had its large downtown venues, with expensively produced spectacles, and smaller neighborhood venues with cheaper and more down-to-earth productions. People flocked to the boulevards, parks, and lakefront for rec-reation and to cool off on hot days.

But 1893 was a different world in other ways. Most theatrical productions would not be straightforward plays in one genre or another but rather what we would now consider vaudeville or variety shows, mixing comedy, clowning, song and dance, magic, and other diversions. Forms of entertainment that no longer exist—or have become marginal—were all the rage. Saloonkeepers would set up carousels in their beer gardens, and young men and women would seek out these novelties, now relegated to small-scale traveling carnivals as larger amusement parks emphasize high-tech roller coasters. Modern museums are now serious cultural endeavors, sites of scholarship as much as exhibition, but such places as the Libby Prison Museum retained the cabinet of curiosities or freak show roots of our museums, along with the political sensationalism of post–Civil War waving of the bloody shirt. Panoramas—nineteenth-century versions of IMAX—offered patrons a vicarious experience of the Great Chicago Fire or the Battle of Gettysburg on painted canvases that moved like an animated film around the viewer. Panoramas are nearly defunct, forgotten, replaced by the movies.

The repeated emphasis in various chapters on forms of entertainment where men and women would mix in public seems odd today, but in the nineteenth century such mixing was seen as an inherent moral threat, and not without cause. Women who freely went to any public place, much less saloons, or performed in the theater or otherwise led public lives, were assumed to be sexually available, if not outright prostitutes. Young women who came to Chicago looking for work would be vulnerable not just to seduction but to being forced into prostitution, and the procurers who did that horrific work frequented any place where an unescorted young woman might be found in public. In Ernest Bell's reformist book *Fighting the Traffic in Young Girls, or, War on the White*

Slave Trade (1910), the frontispiece depicts the dangers posed to virtue not by the saloon—but by the ice cream parlor. Many thousands of young women came to Chicago seeking freedom and excitement, but with that freedom inevitably came danger.

Attitudes toward race in this book also show both continuity and change. The overtly racist assumptions that inform much of chapter 24, "Cheyenne—A Unique Spot in the City's Centre that it is Safer to Read About than to Visit," would be unthinkable today in any sort of guidebook. But Chicago remains the most segregated big city in the United States, and problems of violent crime in ghettos defined in no small part by race dominate news coverage of the city. At the same time, the inclusion of Italian immigrants in this chapter's depiction of depraved and inherently criminal groups of people reminds twenty-first-century readers how our understanding of different forms of identity has shifted; what we now consider ethnicities, subclassifications of whiteness, were once considered as distinct as race, and prejudices against Italian immigrants now sound as offensive as those against African Americans.

Some of the subtler differences between then and now are also both entertaining and instructive, such as how the writer treats the economic activity of the Chicago Board of Trade. Today, making a fortune by buying and selling things that don't yet exist, to be traded at some future date, at prices set by shouting traders in a pit, is considered one of the bedrock foundations of America's free-market financial services economy. But back in 1893, the writer of chapter 10, "The Tiger and its Haunts," saw such futures trading as a form of gambling no different than a hand of poker in the back of a saloon or a game of craps in an alley. As that chapter's subtitle puts it, "Gambling Games Great and Small wherein the Process of Parting the Fool and his Money is Carried on with Facility and Dispatch." The writer neither condemns nor promotes "playing the market"; he just describes how futures trading works in language that Economics 101 textbooks might do well to emulate. It's also interesting to learn that when *Chicago by Day and Night* was written, the U.S. Congress was under pressure to make futures trading illegal since market manipulation was making a few people very rich while impoverishing farmers and other workers. Given the recent great recession, caused in part by reckless trading in impossibly complex financial markets, perhaps our anonymous economist had greater insight into the American system than might at first seem to be the case.

Some of the matters that concerned the writers are still central to Chicagoans and visitors to the city today, including architecture. But it's fascinating to note some of the different attitudes of the late nineteenth century. For instance, while the writer brags about the Auditorium Building, he never once mentions Dankmar Adler and Louis Sullivan, the architects. Daniel Burnham and John Wellborn Root were certainly prominent men-about-town, movers and shakers for both the Fair and the emergent skyscraper city. None of these great men are mentioned once in this text. Apparently, writers, publishers, and their audience had yet to develop the attitude of reverence for the architect-as-artist expressed by contemporary outfits like the Chicago Architecture Foundation. The Auditorium is still there, albeit altered: a saloon in the former south lobby is now a sidewalk, to allow for the widening of Congress Parkway called for by Burnham and Bennett's Plan. But what Chicagoans value about the building has changed. Statistics about its construction materials or the view from its deck matter less than the artistry of Adler and Sullivan. Some things change, some things stay the same, and this book reminds us of both transformations and continuity.

In the endnotes of this volume, we have tried to do two things. First, we hope to contextualize people, places, events, and forms of entertainment in the period around the Fair to make more arcane references clearer and to illuminate the obscure (including annotations for slang and archaic Americanisms). Second, we try to connect people, places, and events to Chicago in the twenty-first century: how places, neighborhoods, and cultural practices have changed or endured. Our annotations, we hope, will make this fascinating historical document more alive to contemporary readers, perhaps even to serve as a *Pleasure Seeker's Guide* to the contemporary city.

Formally, we've tried to strike a balance between re-creating the book as it originally appeared and making it modern. We've retypeset it from the first edition but have chosen to include design aspects from the original, including illustrations and one striking bit of typography: the title on the table of contents page, "The Gist of It." Beyond the odd terminology, the curvaceous lettering seems more at home as a title for a 1960s pop art poster than a headline in a book from generations before. But all of *Chicago by Day and Night* is like this, a combination of gaslit Chicago (open prostitution, panoramas, and rented horse-drawn carriages) and seemingly fresh as this morning's newspaper (con men, cabdrivers who might want to overcharge unwary tourists, theater, and shopping).

In its original publication, *Chicago by Day and Night* was

not edited with the level of care that the *Chicago Manual of Style* would prescribe. For example, the title of chapter 16 is "The City's Moral Code" in the table of contents and "The City's Moral Side" in the chapter itself. The lists of illustrations were inaccurate and incomplete, so we have cut them. (When the titles for the illustrations were not identical or very similar to the title of the chapter where they appear, we have added the title as a caption.) When the writer describes places where a visitor might watch a play, the term varies from "Play Houses" to "Playhouses." And that's just in the table of contents; a third variation, "play-houses," appears in the text. Sometimes "pleasure seekers" find a hyphen, other times they lose it. Sometimes "the Fair" is capitalized, sometimes it isn't. Sometimes one goes to a "theater," other times to a "theatre." Usage is mostly American, but sometimes British spellings appear; sometimes foreign words are italicized, sometimes not; sometimes dollar amounts or the dimensions of buildings are expressed numerically, sometimes those numbers are spelled out. And these variations often take place on the same page or even in the same sentence. One consistency amid this relative chaos is the lack of accents and other diacritical marks for French words; perhaps the typesetter just didn't have any at hand. So while *cafe* might or might not be italicized, it will never be a proper *café*. We decided to leave these inconsistencies for historical purposes. We have corrected obvious errors in spelling, and we have modernized punctuation and some usage (capitalization of "Street" or "Park," for instance). But to retain the flavor of the original *Pleasure Seeker's Guide*, we've mostly left the text as it was originally published. In other words, when in doubt, think: [*sic*].

And welcome to Chicago, home of the World's Columbian Exposition. We hope you enjoy your visit.

THE CITY OF CHICAGO.

INTRODUCTORY.

AT a Time when the attention of the world is concentrated upon Chicago, as it is at present, it is fitting that the stranger within its gates, as well as the uninitiated native, should be made aware of the various attractions, of all sorts and conditions, possessed by the future metropolis of the United States. Chicago has been called the Paris of America, that title having been bestowed upon it by some bright-minded and discerning person who evidently knew whereof he spoke. That the title is indisputable goes without saying. In no other city of its size on the continent is the same variety of amusements to be found as in this one. All tastes may be promptly satisfied, all preferences catered to. If, when confronted by the marvelously variegated array of recreations and pursuits that this great city has to offer, the stranger or the periodical visitor should turn away dissatisfied, imagining that he has failed to discover anything especially suited to his fancy, his mental and physical organism must be sadly askew. It is his fault and not Chicago's.

From now on, and for the next year or so, this mighty city by the lake will swarm with myriads of men and women of all races, tribes, and languages, being brought hither by the Great Exposition that is destined to be the marvel of all nations. That some of this floating mass will remain here is beyond question. In that case the population will swell until the two million mark is passed, and in the proportion that the population increases, so also will increase the attractions of the city that harbors it.

It is the purpose of the present work to set forth, in a terse but comprehensive manner, the various sorts of entertainment offered by the Coming Metropolis. The Author, while sufficiently modest to keep his identity a secret, makes bold to assert that no person who scans the pages of this book will be able, after he has done so, to lay claim to ignorance of the means whereby to procure entertainment or solace for such hours of idleness as he may find on his hands during his stay in this city. The present area of Chicago is a fraction over 180 square miles. What its area will be next year, or ten years hence, nobody can predict. For the present it is sufficient to know that within that area of 180 square miles there dwells a community active, energetic, mercurial — eager in business and therefore keen in its thirst for recreation outside of business hours.

The present work is undertaken in no spirit of levity or thoughtlessness. Its author is a man-of-the-world who, recognizing the desire of the average man to be amused when the cares of business are done, and being fully cognizant of the qualifications of this city in the amusement line, aims to instruct the uninitiated wayfarer in the paths he may follow with the most satisfaction to himself and the greatest benefit to his system. If but one reader confesses his indebtedness to this work for enlightenment in the smallest degree, its purpose will have been achieved.

With renewed assurances, therefore, that the seeker after light upon a great city's manner of amusing itself will not seek in vain, the Author makes his bow to the reader and tenders him an invitation to accompany him through the following pages.

CHAPTER I.

WHERE TO STAY.

THE GUEST REGISTERING.

THE question of location must of course be decided by the individual taste of the visitor. It would be strange indeed if, with a transient population roughly estimated at 200,000, the city did not possess hotels of all grades and descriptions, from which the most captious-minded person might take his choice and procure satisfaction. Chicago, at the present writing, contains at least 1,500 hotels, with constant additions each year. There is no more difficult task than to tell a man with any accuracy what hotel will suit him best. A caravansary that would delight one man would disgust another and vice versa. The most satisfactory plan, therefore, and the safest, is to give a brief pen-sketch of the leading hotels, with some idea of the special characteristics of each and the style of entertainment they afford.

The Lake Front hotels — the Richelieu, Auditorium, and Leland — enjoy the cream of the new transient patronage. By "new" is meant those people who have never before visited

Chicago and who naturally select the houses with the prettiest sites. The Auditorium (Michigan Avenue and Congress Street), despite its gorgeousness and the flourish of trumpets with which it was opened, does not indulge in ruinous rates. It is a very large hotel, and accommodations may be had therein from $4 per day up. Perhaps it is this moderate charge that makes it so great a favorite with the theatrical profession, the more prosperous members of which enjoy the comfort it affords. Well-to-do managers, famous stars, and sometimes interrogatively opulent soubrettes and chorus girls seek lodging at the Auditorium, and some very pretty romances are narrated of flirtations more or less interesting which the "blooded" habitues of this swell hotel "strike up" with the fair footlight favorites who enjoy its hospitality. It is worth the price of a day's board, or at least a dinner, sometimes, to take a stroll in the corridors and catch the fragments of delicious lays that are being caroled forth by the song birds who are practicing their chosen art in the sanctity of their various chambers. Especially is this the case during a season of grand or light opera in the great theater adjoining the hotel, in which case the latter is sure to be thronged with singers of both sexes and of all grades of artistic and professional prominence. There is a roomy balcony over the entrance to the Auditorium which, on pleasant days, is thronged with gaily dressed people of both sexes, who sit there and enjoy the dual delight of drinking in the balmy air and watching the cavalcade on the broad avenue below.

A block north of the Auditorium is the Richelieu, the famous hostelry the destinies of which are presided over by the renowned "Cardinal" Bemis. For people of means, to whom money is less of an object than the engagement of luxuries, the Richelieu, they say, is the place par excellence at which to stop. Some notable people have honored the Richelieu with their presence, and one is just as liable to run plumb against a real, live English Lord or Italian Marquis within its doors as against a plain, everyday American citizen. Sara Bernhardt selects the Richelieu when in the city; so does Mrs. Langtry when the confines of her private car become too narrow for comfort. The Richelieu is famous for the rare pictures that adorn its walls, some of which are worth small fortunes, and also — whisper this with bated breath. Oh, ye irreverent! — for its wine cellars, which are stocked with some of the rarest and costliest vintages to be found on the entire continent. On state occasions, when the Cardinal is entertaining some choice party of notables, he is wont to disappear suddenly, absent himself for about fifteen minutes, and then reappear with a quaint-shaped bottle or two in either hand covered with cobwebs. Those who sample the contents of said bottles close their eyes, pat their stomachs softly as the divine liquid glides down their throats, and then shed tears of joy and gratitude to the Cardinal for having given them the happiest moment of their lives. If you are a connoisseur of wines and wish to test your art in judgment thereof, cultivate the acquaintance of the Cardinal, and perhaps he will go down into the cellar for you.

Mr. Warren Leland, who recently sold the hotel of that name, always said he had the prettiest house in Chicago, and there are some people who agree with him. The Leland rates, on the American plan, are from $3 to $5 per day up; the European, $1.50 up. The Leland is known as the "home hotel" of Chicago, and there is a tradition abroad to the effect that people who once patronize it never go elsewhere.

"THE BLOODED DISTRICT" — Before proceeding to the consideration of other prominent hotels, it may be interesting

to inform the reader that the district which we are about to leave, and of which the three hostelries enumerated form the nucleus, has achieved some fame in the annals of the town as "the blooded district" — so-called for the reason that the "high-rolling" young men of the city have made it a sort of headquarters or rendezvous, both before and after the hours when sober-minded and steady-going folk are fast asleep. The Auditorium, Richelieu, and Leland Cafes, together with Devine's wine-room on the other side of Jackson Street, and Colonel John Harvey's "Wayside Inn" in the alley, form a sort of circuit or beat, which these "rapid" young men (i.e., the "bloods") travel at all times, including such hours as the sale of cheering beverages is forbidden by city ordinance. Of these, Harvey's is perhaps the most unique resort, though if one cannot find his friends in one of the places named after midnight, he is tolerably certain to encounter them in one of the others. Colonel Harvey is the father of the pert little soubrette, Hattie Harvey, of whom the great diva, Patti, became so desperately enamored as to invite her to her castle in Wales, and admirers of the young lady are fond of dropping in to discuss her merits with her papa, the Colonel, who, it goes without saying, is the most devoted of her admirers. If you praise Hattie's beauty to the Colonel, he will mix for you, with his own hands, one of his choicest drinks; if you swear on your honor that she is destined to become the greatest actress of the century, he will probably crack a bottle. The door of Harvey's "Wayside Inn" is tightly closed at midnight, but the initiated may gain ready admittance by learning the pass-word of the night and roaring it, in tones more or less musical, through the keyhole. You can always tell whether there is any fun going on in Harvey's by the galaxy of hack men who stand in line at the curb, waiting for the "boys" to emerge in the small hours of the morning. But we may now leave the "blooded district" and take a glance at other South side hotels.

The venerable Palmer House stands like a bulwark at the corner of State and Monroe Streets, its vast expanse stretching away for half a block. The Palmer enjoys a steady

HARVEY'S "WAYSIDE INN."

patronage from people who have been "putting up" there for years. It has a large clientele of the better class of commercial travelers. The wits of the town crack jokes at the expense of the Palmer on the score of the number of guests of Hebraic extraction it shelters. Be that as it may, the Palmer welcomes all who pay their bills, and those who patronize it generally possess that admirable qualification. The Palmer's rates are $3 to $5 per day.

There is a little room on the sixth floor of the Palmer which is an environ of romantic interest, it having been the scene of one of the most famous tragedies in Chicago's history. In the summer of 1882, it was occupied by Charles Stiles, the popular and high-living "caller" of the Board of Trade. Early one morning a veiled woman, whose tasteful but somber raiment revealed the outlines of an entrancing figure, took the elevator to the sixth floor and knocked at the door of Stiles' room. He came out scantily clad in response to the summons. There was a flash, the ringing report of a revolver, and in another instant the young man lay dead on the floor. The woman knelt down, kissed his forehead, and submitted to arrest without a murmur. She was an Italian, Teresa Sturlata by name, and the mistress of Stiles. His previous abuse of her, as testified to at the trial, so influenced the jury in her behalf that she received but the nominal punishment of one year in the penitentiary, though her great beauty doubtless had some influence on the leniency of the sentence. Many men went daft over the beautiful murderess. Some of the letters that she received while in jail were published, and precious epistles they were, too. They all contained protestations of affection, and several offers of marriage were included among them. The woman went to the penitentiary and served her sentence. When released she disappeared as completely as though the earth had swallowed her. Her present whereabouts is unknown, but the room made famous by the great tragedy is still pointed out to new guests at the Palmer.

The Grand Pacific, on South Clark Street, kept by Landlord Drake, is of the same class as the Palmer, enjoying a steady patronage all the year round. The rates are $3 to $5 per day. The Tremont, kept by Mr. Eden (Lake and Dearborn), and the Sherman, kept by Mr. Pierce (Clark and Randolph), are of the same grade as the Palmer and Grand Pacific.

These comprise the list of first-class down-town hotels, though several others are in progress of construction, with a view to caring for the thousands of strangers who will visit the World's Fair. Notable among these is the Great Northern, which, under the supervision of Mr. Eden, has just been pushed to completion. It is on Dearborn Street opposite the post office, between Jackson and Quincy, being situated, therefore, in the very heart of the business district.

The Victoria, the new hotel on the site of the building formerly known as the Beaurivage, Michigan Avenue and Congress Street, is a fashionable house, patronized by the best people. The same is true of The Wellington, corner of Jackson Street and Wabash Avenue.

The smaller hotels are much too numerous to particularize. They are scattered in all directions, and their rates for rooms vary from fifty cents upward per day. There is no street in the business part of the city without two or three such hotels, and the traveler must be hard to please who cannot suit himself at one or another among so many. The residence part of the city, particularly on the North and South sides, is thickly dotted with first-class family hotels, where persons contemplating an extended stay may obtain quiet accommodation in the exact ratio for which they care to pay. The two most magnificent family hotels are the Virginia, 78 Rush Street, and the Metropole, Michigan Avenue and Twenty-third Street. These two houses cannot be surpassed for style and elegance, and they are patronized exclusively by people of means.

CHAPTER II.

THE THEATERS.

THE Wayfarer having received some hints as to the quarters in which he may establish himself, one reaches the much more important question of how he shall amuse or divert himself while here. Before coming to the point of the more unique or unusual modes of diversion with which the city abounds, one's first thoughts naturally turn to the theaters.

Chicago is famous as a theatrical center, and the very best attractions are constantly to be found at one or another of the great play-houses. Just at this stage, therefore, it is meet to utter a few remarks on the leading theaters and the class of excellent entertainment they present to their patrons.

THE CHICAGO OPERA HOUSE. — This theater, one of the youngest in Chicago, is perhaps entitled to primary mention by reason of its virtual monopoly, except at stated intervals, of the cream of the city's theatrical business. It has a very large seating capacity; was first opened about seven years ago with the tragedian, Thomas Keene, as the attraction. The director of the Chicago Opera House, Mr. David Henderson, has achieved a wide popularity, both in and out of the profession, and is aided in his efforts by a corps of efficient assistants, notable among who are Messrs. Thomas W. Prior and Max Godenrath. While presenting to the public attention first-class attractions all the year around, the Chicago Opera House has earned the major part of its distinction by the superb extravaganzas it has been producing annually. These extravaganzas usually commence in May and run through the summer months, thus securing to the house a steady patronage during the "dog-days." It is beyond all question that the first of these spectacles, the "Arabian Nights," established Mr. Henderson's reputation as a purveyor of this class of entertainment (termed by the irreverent "leg shows"). The second production, the "Crystal Slipper," enhanced this reputation, and those succeeding — "Bluebeard Jr." and "Sinbad" — kept it going. This year (1892) the summer spectacle at The Chicago will be "Ali Baba, or the Forty Thieves," and if advance gossip is to be taken as evidence, it will transcend in magnificence anything of its kind that has ever been produced under Mr. Henderson's supervision. The libretto of "Ali Baba" is by Harry B. Smith, the distinguished wit and literateur, who has performed a like service for the pieces before mentioned. The Chicago Opera House is situated on the South side of Washington Street, between Clark and La Salle Streets, and is invariably thronged throughout the hot weather. Mr. Henderson manages to group upon his stage as choice a galaxy of feminine loveliness as is to be found in any climate, and the costuming (or rather the lack of it) is doubtless as gratifying to the performers as it is to the spectators, being constructed on the hot weather plan; light and airy. It is no uncommon sight to see a party of honest country folks appearing, gripsacks in hand, at the doors of the Chicago Opera House, having come straight from the train to the theater to witness the show, the fame of which had penetrated to their homes in the country; and which, after their return, they would rather die than let their families and the church folks know they had seen.

McVicker's Theater. — It is situated on the south side of Madison Street, between State and Dearborn, and is one of the oldest resorts of its kind in the city, though the present structure is quite new, having been reconstructed on the site of the old one, which was destroyed by fire in the spring of 1891. The attractions at McVicker's are usually of the solid, legitimate order, though the gray-haired proprietor occasionally is guilty of a lapse to a variety show. McVicker's, however, is the home of high-class drama and comedy, and the theater itself is perhaps without a rival on the continent in the way of magnificent decorations and comfortable furnishing. While Mr. McVicker is opposed to Sunday performances, he occasionally permits them, which enables the stranger, not infrequently, to encounter a first-class Sunday night show within a few paces of his hotel.

The Grand Opera House. — This admirable play-house is located on the east side of Clark Street, just north of Washington. It is another old-established theater enjoying a large patronage. The Grand is the home of Hoyt's farces, each of these fanciful productions having been produced successfully at Mr. Hamlin's temple. At the Grand also appear most of the German companies, though the latter will, it is to be presumed, go to the new edifice, Schiller theater, Randolph Street, near Dearborn.

HOOLEY'S THEATER. — Located conveniently on Randolph, between Clark and La Salle Streets, is devoted to all sorts of attractions, and is one of the handsomest theaters of its size in the country. The patrons of Hooley's may run the gamut from low comedy to grand opera; and Irish comedy drama often following immediately after one of the high-class engagements, such as that of the Madison Square or Lyceum Theater Companies.

COLUMBIA THEATER. — In the very heart of the business district, on the south side of Monroe, between Dearborn and Clark Streets. This theater is one of the oldest in the city and has passed through many managements, being at present under the direction of the Hayman Bros, and Mr. Will J. Davis, both of whom are gentlemen of the highest standing in the profession and thoroughly competent to cater to the desires of an amusement-loving public. The attractions presented at the Columbia are of a wide range, the properties of the house being suited to the production of grand or light opera more than anything else. Some of the first artists in the world have appeared at the Columbia, notably, Henry Irving and Ellen Terry, the latter having, on one memorable night, formally christened the theater which, prior to that time, was known as Haverley's; Sarah Bernhardt, Adelina Patti, Christine Nielsson, and others almost equally famous. The seating capacity of the Columbia is as large as that of any of the down-town theaters, and it possesses the advantage of large, comfortable seats, very liberally spaced, that other managers might do well to emulate.

THE "PROVINCIAL" THEATERS. — The houses mentioned are known as the "down-town" or high-priced theaters, the scale of prices ranging from 25 cents to $1.50 per seat. In addition to these, however, there are a number of houses, some of which are equally large, scattered about in the three sections of the city, which are known as the "second class" or "provincial" theaters, where the price of admission ranges from 15 cents to $1.00. Of these may be mentioned the following:

SOUTH SIDE. — Alhambra, State and Archer Ave.; Madison Street Opera House, 83 Madison Street; Olympic, 46 South Clark Street; Havlin's, Wabash and 19th Street; People's, 339 State Street. NORTH SIDE. — Clark Street Theater, Clark and Kinzie Streets; Criterion, 374 Sedgwick Street; Windsor, 459 North Clark Street. WEST SIDE. — Haymarket, 169 West Madison Street; Lyceum, 58 South Desplaines Street; Standard, 167 South Halsted Street; Halsted Street Theater, Halsted and West Congress Streets.

The outside, or provincial, theaters usually offer a more sensational type of plays, specimens of the wild and woolly border drama being usually presented for the edification of their mercurial patrons. The Park Theater, 335 State Street, ought not to rank with the other theaters but is often patronized by travelers whose tastes lead them to desire entertainment of the more democratic type. The accessories of tobacco smoke and liquid refreshment, which are to be indulged in at the Park, form an attraction that they find it impossible to resist, nor is it difficult for a patron, whose pocketbook enables him to indulge in such luxuries, to obtain an introduction through the influence of the manager to the more or less fascinating "fairies," who go through their performances on the stage. Further mention of the Park will be made later.

THE DIME MUSEUMS. — Chicago is probably more bountifully supplied than any other city in the Dime Museum line. It is not necessary to particularize as to the various houses of this character; they are scattered in all quarters of the city, and in them is to be found infinite material for entertainment and instruction at the modest admission fee of 10 cents. The freaks of all climes are to be found on exhibition, and most of the museums throw in a stage performance of some kind more or less meritorious. A favorite plan of a party, large or small, desirous of a little quiet fun, is to execute a "Dime Museum Raid," as it is called. They assemble at the hotel or other meeting place and start out on a tour of the various museums, visiting each in turn, with, of course, the usual intermission for drinks. The amount of fun to be obtained from such an excursion can easily be imagined. Aside from the entertainment to be derived from viewing the freaks on exhibition, it is a very easy matter to discover food for mirth in the freaks among the audience. There is a happy-go-lucky atmosphere in a Dime Museum which is not found elsewhere, and the Dime Museum "raiders" are in the habit of getting much more than their money's worth; but so long as their fun does not end in a fight, there need be no cause for complaint. A thing that should be looked into is the attendance at certain of these cheap shows of young girls whose tender youth leads one to marvel why their parents do not manage to keep them at home or, failing that, to box their ears and send them to bed for their contumacy. It is not the province of the writer, however, to purify the morals of this great and growing town, so let those "kick" who will.

THE CASINO. — This resort, formerly known as the Eden Musee, is a unique place of amusement, situated on the west side of Wabash Avenue just north of Jackson Street. Its leading feature is a magnificent wax-work exhibit, which good judges say almost equals the famous resort of Madame Tussaud in London. All the famous characters in history, past and present, are reproduced in life-like manner. There is also a "Chamber of Horrors," which may be visited by those who desire to feel their flesh creep. On the top floor is a roomy amphitheater, in which a good stage show is always in progress, and the rear part of which is filled with neat, round tables, where the patrons may indulge in light refreshments of various sorts. The admission fee to the Casino is 50 cents, which entitles the visitor to all the privileges of the house without extra charge.

POPULAR PLAYHOUSES.
Clockwise from top left: The Columbia; McVicker's; Hooley's Theatre; Chicago Opera House; The Schiller Theatre; Grand Opera House. *Center:* The Auditorium.

CHAPTER III.

THE AUDITORIUM AND THE NEW GERMAN THEATER.

DETAILED mention of the magnificent opera house in the Auditorium building has been reserved until now in order that it might take its proper place in the description of the mighty edifice which is the wonder and admiration of the United States, and a topic of comment to some extent in Europe.

The project of the Auditorium, three sides of which face Wabash Avenue, Congress Street, and Michigan Avenue, is said to have emanated from the brain of Mr. Ferd W. Peck, a capitalist, who, in a speech to the Commercial Club, outlined the advantages that would be likely to accrue to the city from the possession of such a building. As the Auditorium is one of the sights of the city, it deserves a special description.

The Auditorium Hotel, mention of which has been made in a previous chapter, fronts on Michigan Avenue and occupies the upper floor of the building, the colossal outlines and massive architecture of which, rivaling as they do the ancient Coliseum of Rome, strike the beholder dumb with admiration. The stock company that constructed the Auditorium was formed at Mr. Peck's suggestion in the spring of 1886, and in January of the following year work was commenced upon it. Less than eighteen months afterward the building had progressed to a stage that made it possible to hold the National Convention of 1888 under the roof of the great theater. On that occasion 12,000 people cheered the nomination of Harrison as the presidential candidate. The formal dedication of the great structure took place December 9, 1889. The star of the occasion was Adelina Patti, the world-famous singer, who, although she had dyed her hair a brilliant red, aroused a cyclone of enthusiasm by her time-honored rendition of "Home, Sweet Home." Speeches were made by Benjamin Harrison, President of the United States; by DeWitt C. Cregier, then Mayor of Chicago; by Ferd W. Peck, President of the Auditorium Company; and others. It required an expenditure of nearly $2,000,000 in hard cash to erect the Auditorium, and the men who invested their money in the project are drawing a fair interest on the amount of their wise venture. The building has a frontage of 187 feet on Michigan Avenue, 361 feet on Congress Street, and 161 feet on Wabash Avenue. The material used is mostly American granite from Maine and Minnesota; the ornamentation being largely in Mexican onyx. To the visitor who stands rapt in admiration at the sight of this superb edifice, a few figures may not be uninteresting. The main building is 144 feet in height; the tower on the Congress Street side, 225 feet, with lateral dimensions of 40 x 71 feet. The building weighs in its entirety 110,000 tons. There are 17,000,000 bricks in the building and 50,000,000 pieces of marble. The flooring is in Antique Mosaic.

Now for the theater itself, which is, after all, the main interior attraction of the Auditorium, the smaller halls and office suites which are contained in the main structure possessing only a commercial interest. The theater has a regular seating capacity of 4,000, though when it is arranged for a convention or a ball it will hold three times that number. The stage is ninety-eight feet in width and 6,862 square feet in area. The great lobby, with its massive pillars and porticos, prepares the visitor for the sublime magnificence of the immense audience chamber. The ceiling, which is decorated in white and gold, glitters with a myriad of electric lamps, and the spectacular effect, when the house is filled with a fashionable audience, the long tiers of boxes gleaming with the brilliant costumes and jewels of scores of handsome women, surpasses description. It must be seen to be appreciated. The Auditorium theater is equipped, among other things, with an organ that is said to be the finest and most complete in the world, possessing, as it does, 7,193 pipes.

But without question the tower is a stupendous feature of the Auditorium and is most popular with strangers; it may be said that no stranger should leave the city without visiting it. Enter from the Congress Street side and purchase a ticket at the box office, costing twenty-five cents. The elevator carries you up at rapid speed to the top. The final ascent is made by a small flight of iron stairs and the tower is reached. The splendor of the view from this tower can be imagined but not described. On a clear day the Michigan shore is discernible far away over the blue water of the lake, while on the east side, north and south the eye may penetrate to the furthest limits of the city. To stand there and look down on the mazes of buildings and the swarming thousands of your fellowmen produces a strange feeling of awe and wonderment. The popularity of the tower with sight-seers may be imagined from the fact that the attendance brings in an average of $120 per day to the company throughout the year.

Preparations are now in progress for the presentation at the Auditorium during the World's Fair year of a theatrical spectacle which shall eclipse anything of the kind ever before seen in any country. The plans are yet in embryo, but a rough outline has been drawn. The production, which is to be historical in character, will be under the direction of Managers Adams, Abbey, and Grau. It will open in the spring of 1893 and run through the World's Fair season.

The New German Theater on Randolph Street, between Dearborn and Clark, deserves special mention by reason of the fact that it will be the youngest of all Chicago first-class theaters, and because great promises have been made as to the magnificence of its furnishings and equipment. The structure is fire-proof, nine stories in height with a large square tower fifteen feet in height surmounted by a cupola. The main building fronts eighty-four feet on Randolph Street with a depth of 186½ feet. There will be a covered balcony in front from which street parades may be advantageously viewed. The cornices, balustrades, and other parts of the building are decorated with rich carvings. The construction is of steel columns and cross-beams, the outer walls being in terra cotta. The main entrance leading to the theater is thirty-two feet wide. All the floors and wainscoting are in polished marble. From the entrance to the theater foyer will extend two vestibules, in the inner one of which the box office is located. Four passenger elevators furnish access to the hotel and club rooms of which the main portion of the palatial structure will consist. Broad marble stairs lead from the foyer to the main floor, balcony, and gallery of the theater, the

Auditorium plan of seating the people having been decided upon. The theater will seat 1,300 people. The stage has a superficial area of 3,200 square feet, with a proscenium arch twenty-nine feet wide and thirty feet high.

Seven stories of the building are devoted to the hotel, which also deserves a word of description. There are 131 guest chambers, 39 bath rooms, a dining room 76 feet long by 49 wide, and other features. The hotel will of course have a separate entrance. Club, billiard, card, and other rooms occupy the tenth floor. The eleventh is devoted to a fine ball room, separate quarters being provided for the servants on the floors above.

The total cost of this fine structure is estimated at $600,000, inclusive of the price paid for the ground. The building is erected by a company of which the following well-known citizens are directors: A. C. Hesing, Theodore Arnold, Louis Wolff, Edward Eiblein, Franz Amberg, Charles Wacker, C. P. Dose, Louis Wampold, J. A. Orb, Joseph Scheurer, William Heineman, George E. Weiss, John M. Krause, C. Herman Plautz, and Theodore Oehne.

It goes without saying that this will be an attractive place for strangers to visit.

AUDITORIUM PROSCENIUM ARCH.
J. Manz & Co. Eng. Chi.

CHAPTER IV.

TWO UNIQUE PLAYHOUSES.

ASTRIDE OF THE MOON.

THE Madison Street Opera House and the Park Theater, which were briefly mentioned in the preceding chapter, are two resorts that may be regarded as occupying a unique position in the amusement roster. The Madison Street Opera House gives two performances daily, and its manager, the veteran Colonel Sam T. Jack, is reputed to be coining money. The size of the audiences that fill Col. Jack's theater twice a day is attributable, possibly, to the fact that the house is devoted entirely to the presentation of burlesque. Companies of more or less merit appear from week to week, and in order that they may secure a "date," it is necessary that they possess a number of shapely women in the cast. An artist would probably call the costumes of the ladies who appear at the Madison Street Opera House artistic. Certain it is that if they were constructed on any other plan than that of the present one, they could not possibly convey a more liberal view of "the female form divine." Indeed, there was one engagement that included the presentation of a series of classic tableaux, in which the complete suits of skintights that the ladies wore were if anything more attractive than no costumes at all. No drinks are served in the Madison Street Theater itself, but it is situated over a large saloon which is easy of access by means of a staircase leading directly into the parquet. It is needless to say, perhaps, that the nature of the spectacular gems to be seen on the Madison Street Opera House stages are strongly calculated to produce thirst — especially in a masculine audience. Not very long ago the Chicago "Mail" undertook to "roast" the Madison Street Opera House and to stigmatize its performances as improper. Mr. Jack at once sued the paper for libel. If a jury should have a notion to visit the theater, it might materially assist in the rendition of a verdict in accordance with the facts.

The Park Theater, situated on State Street, in the "Levee," or "Tenderloin" district, is even more democratic. Drinks are sold and consumed during the stage performance, and smoking is allowed. This is a favorite resort for "bloods" who, having come to town for fun, propose to see all there is in it. A party of three or four who purchase a box may, if they choose, enjoy the society of the actresses who will visit them between acts and have a pleasant, social time. It is within the bounds of decorum to invite the fair performers to drink, and if an acquaintance so auspiciously begun should be carried to even more agreeable lengths, why, who is going to complain so long as the City authorities permit its open programme? Not the manager, surely. He is there to see that his guests have a good time and will exercise all his efforts to the procurement of that end.

There are several wine-rooms upstairs, and in these one may enjoy a *tete-a-tete* and a bottle of champagne with his chosen charmer, if his inclinations (and his pocketbook) will permit him to go to that length. An amusing feature of the regime at the Park is the system whereby the actresses keep matters straight with "the house." Under the rules, each "lady" is allowed a percentage on the money received for drinks that she causes to be purchased. She carries a memorandum book and pencil, and jots down every cocktail or whiskey straight that her admirer (for the moment) may purchase. After the "show," when the audience departs, she goes to the bar and tallies up with the barkeeper. A balance is struck at the end of the week and the money paid over. An idea of the informality of the performances at the Park may be gathered from the fact that when James Owen O'Connor played there awhile ago, a lot of boys went about in the theater selling stale cats, cabbages and other garden produce to the audience — the same to be used

for the purpose of pelting the actor! Anyone who wishes to see a "tough" audience and a "tough" show will find what he wants at the Park, which seems to be entirely within the idea of police regulation, nevertheless.

CHAPTER V.

FREE AND EASY SHOWS.

UNDER this caption come the entertainments of a more or less unstilted character; that is to say, entertainments that, while being in no wise disreputable, are nevertheless arranged with a view of catering to the tastes of people of both sexes who do not care to spend the evening in the narrow confines and the matter-of-fact atmosphere of a regular theatre. The modern music hall, or *cafe chantant*, of which there are so many in Paris and London, has not yet been duplicated to any great extent in this city. There are, however, a few places of the kind, widely separated by distance, that resemble the "old country" music hall in some respects. The old beer dens of noisome character that formed a blot upon the city's escutcheon in earlier days have quite disappeared, and the few music halls that still flourish, besides being of a much more pretentious character, have in their management a much stronger claim to toleration. At any of these places an evening may be spent without serious prejudice to one's morals and without contamination of any sort. If the jokes are a little "rocky" and the antics of the actors and actresses just a shade off color when viewed from the standpoint of strict propriety, there is no reason why the spectator should go home convulsed with a sense of the depravity of the city that can suffer such things to be. The pleasure of the entertainment at these places is enhanced to a greater or less extent, according to the taste of the attendant, by the latter's ability to solace himself with such liquid refreshments as his system may crave during the progress of the show. He may also smoke like a chimney if he so desires.

The old Tivoli restaurant and concert hall on Dearborn Street, just below Madison, which was made famous by the assassination therein of Jim Elliott, the prize fighter, by Jere Dunn (the slayer being afterward acquitted on the ground of self-defense), has long since passed into oblivion, and on its site, the scene of so many wonderful revelries, a fine office building now stands. When the Tivoli passed away there was for a long time a dearth of music halls in Chicago. At present, however, there are at least three resorts of the kind that may be mentioned for the enlightenment of those who desire to investigate this class of entertainment.

Over on the North Side, on the west side of Clark Street, a few doors north of Division Street, there is an establishment which in some respects is unique. It is reached either by the North side cable cars or by hansom cab, the fare for the latter being fifty cents for each person. This resort is known as Engel's, and for several seasons past it has been the favorite with the blooded youth of the North side as well as of a large *clientele* of chance visitors. It was formerly kept by a man named Matthai, and adjoining it was a smaller resort kept by a Monsieur Andre. Andre is now dead and his place closed. On the site of Mr. Matthai's triumphs Mr. Engel now lives and flourishes.

Enter Engel's at any time between eight and nine in the evening, after having paid the modest admission fee of ten cents, and you will find the large hall, with its imposing array of polished tables and rows of seats, rather sparsely filled. The early part of the performance consists of a series of musical numbers rendered by the orchestra, the members of which now and then take a lay-off for drinks. By 10 o'clock, however, there is a perceptible increase in the attendance, and the white-aproned waiters are kept busy rushing to and fro supplying the wants of thirsty customers. The visitor, meanwhile, has been supplied with a printed programme which tells him what artists, ladies or gentlemen, are to appear that evening, and the manner in which they will endeavor to amuse the auditors. The curtain rises and a pert soubrette with a very gaudy complexion and abbreviated skirts trips to the foot-lights and sings a song of true love or something else equally interesting. She may awaken a hurricane of applause and then again she may not. The stars of the troupe are usually reserved for the latter part of the programme. Meanwhile more drinks are ordered by everybody, and by 11 o'clock a general spirit of hilarity prevails, which is testified to by the added enthusiasm with which the advancing and retiring favorites are greeted. The last hour of the entertainment, between 11 and 12 o'clock, is usually devoted to a more ambitious effort of some kind. It may be an opera in one act, a burlesque of the current follies of the day, or anything else that will give an opportunity for the singing of "catchy" songs, the execution of intricate dances, and, above and beyond all, the lavish display of feminine charms. It is a pleasant custom of the place for young men of means, possessed of more money than sense, to purchase bouquets, which are carried up and down the aisles on trays by attractive flower girls, and cast the same upon the stage at their especial favorites. When a more than usually attractive damsel sings an unusually taking song, the boards upon which she treads are often fairly deluged with flowers, and the degree of grace with which she stoops to pick them up enhances in just that ratio the warmth of the plaudits which she receives. It is perhaps unnecessary to say that during this latter part of the show the added attractions of the spectacle presented, together with the concentrated enthusiasm of the performers, all grouped on the stage at once, increases the general demand for refreshments. The waiters are fairly scurrying hither and thither, and the consumption of stimulating beverages is something enormous. During all this "Papa" Engel, as he is affectionately termed by his *coterie* of more youthful patrons, looks on with a bland and satisfied smile, noting with evident enjoyment the merry spirits of his guests and the rapidity with which they are enriching his coffers.

The ground floor of Engel's is exclusively devoted to the sterner sex. No ladies are allowed on that floor; up above, however, a roomy balcony runs around the hall, and lady patrons of all ages and grades of attractiveness sit at the tables with their escorts and enjoy the entertainment with the rest. No gentleman is allowed in the balcony unaccompanied by a lady, and no lady can enter it unescorted. The popping of corks and the sparkle of champagne are perpetual adjuncts to this part of the house, and the balcony itself, it is safe to say, forms no inconsiderable part of Mr. Engel's gold mine. Nobody who does not wish to buy anything, however, is ever requested to do so, the ten cents admission fee entitling the visitor to every privilege of the house. Occasionally, it is true, a bit of disorder may break out, caused by some indiscreet visitor imbibing not wisely but too well, but it is very speedily squelched, and there is no case on record where a person guilty of causing disorder in Engel's ever repeated the offense.

Another feature of Engel's, and many people find it an agreeable one, is the stage boxes. These boxes are located above the stage and behind the curtain, being arranged in such a way that persons seated therein may view all that is going forward on the stage itself and still remain invisible to the audience. With prominent citizens, or other people who like to keep their attendance at the music hall a secret, this is an advantage not to be denied. Occupants of stage boxes, far from being denied the privileges of quenching their thirst, are granted every facility for so doing. There is a neat table in the rear of the box, and an obsequious waiter stands steadily at the door ready to minister to the wants of patrons. It is quite permissible, if the occupant of a stage box desires, to send the waiter around behind the scenes to inquire whether this or that fair actress will not deign to imbibe something at your expense, an attention which she duly acknowledges by stepping daintily up beneath the box and, as she quaffs the soothing beverage, nodding her thanks to the donor. A spirit of good nature prevails throughout the entire performance, and when it is all over nobody has been hurt very much by his contact with this strange element of life in a great city.

There is another feature of Engel's which merits a word or two of mention. Promptly at 12 o'clock, in obedience to the mandate of the city fathers, the front doors of the place are closed as tight as a drum. Adjoining the bar, however, is a commodious *café* where parties of friends, from two to ten in number, may sit down and enjoy any sort of a repast that their appetites may crave, with all the liquid accessories thrown in.

You, young man, who may have become interested in an especially charming member of Mr. Engel's *corps de ballet*, may, if you stay in this *cafe* long enough, possibly be rewarded by a sight of your charmer for a moment, emerging from behind the scenes in her street clothes after the performance. You are tolerably safe from giving her offense if you offer her refreshment at your expense, though if it happens that she is accompanied by a stalwart cavalier who appears to exert a proprietory influence over her, it is just as well to reserve your attention for some more appropriate season. Some of Mr. Engel's cory-

TYPES AT ENGEL'S.

phees take supper regularly every night in his *cafe*, the costs of such meals presumably being charged against their salary, unless some outside devotee at their various shrines should feel an inclination to pay the bills. Mr. Engel himself, animated by we know not what generous impulse, has been known to sit at the head of a long table, around which were grouped a dozen or so of the lady members of his troupe, and cheerfully invite them to eat or drink their fill at his expense. Some wag, who noticed this spectacle on one occasion, made an observation to the effect that Mr. Engel seemed to be having a good time with his harem, and for that reason, possibly, it has been customary among the flippant and irreverent young men who frequent the place to jocosely refer to it over their wine as "Engel's harem."

All in all, it is not such a bad sort of place to visit, especially if the visitor is desirous of seeing something a little unusual in a place where he will not be bothered by a demand for a too strict observance of the proprieties. In any event it is a good place to go if you happen to be in that part of the town after midnight and are possessed of a thirst of the sort that only some of the choice alcoholic liquids dispensed by Mr. Engel and his aids can quench.

On the South side are two well-patronized resorts that, while resembling Engel's in some respects, differ from it in others. Baum's Pavilion, situated at the point where 22d Street and Cottage Grove and Indiana Avenues merge together in a sort of triangle, has been famous for many years as a concert hall, *cafe,* and dance house. It is a large structure of two stories, and adjoining the building is an open air expanse or beer garden, dotted with trees, which is always crowded on summer nights. The pavilion is reached from three sides; the main door faces north and entrance can be had either through the beer garden on Cottage Grove Avenue or through the restaurant on Indiana Avenue. The style of entertainment presented at Baum's varies from week to week. Sometimes it is a first-class variety show, at other times Mr. Baum grows more ambitious and puts on a full-fledged comic opera troupe as an additional divertissement. The admission fee is 25 cents, and the visitor may select his seat according to his fancy. If it is the summer season (that is when Baum's pavilion is best patronized), the open air garden is only separated from the hall where the opera is in progress by open arches, and one may sit at his table and smoke and drink with nothing but the blue vault of heaven for a roof and at the same time have wafted to his ears the exhilarating music from the stage within.

While the stage show is, of course, the principal feature of Baum's and the one from which the establishment draws its steady patronage, the dances that are given there usually every Saturday and Sunday night, at the nominal admission fee of fifty cents per couple, are always numerously attended. In the winter season, when the garden is too frosty to be agreeable and is closed up in consequence, the dances are held in the hall above the saloon; but in the radiant summer, when dancing is at best a fatiguing pleasure, they take place on the ground floor. Between the dances the revelers may adjoin to the open air and partake of whatever refreshments their hearts and souls most desire. It is a "free and easy" spot but, as in all other places of the kind, the best of order is always maintained, the least semblance of unruly conduct being sternly checked by the management. Anyone who violates a second time the system of etiquette that governs the place is promptly pitched into the street and never again admitted to the hallowed precincts unless he manages to conceal his identity.

The crowd that attend the summer night dances afford excellent opportunity for study; all classes of men and women are represented there. The well-to-do club man who stays at a distance and sips his lemonade in peace and quiet is content to find his share of amusement in watching the antics of the throng; the hard-working and respectable mechanic, who works his best at his trade for six days in the week, is evidently enjoying the bit of recreation that is yielded to him there. Scattered in the crowd are salesmen, barbers, bookmakers, bakers, butchers, and almost every other type of the young manhood of the day. Perhaps there may be a few confidence men, bunco steerers, and types of even more dangerous classes, but they are not to be feared. They are there for recreation, not for business; for they know very well that if they made the slightest effort to ply their calling in that place they would be promptly spotted and handed over to the authorities. As to the feminine portion of the assemblage, one is at a loss to convey an adequate idea of it in an off-hand description; it varies with the seasons and the weather. As a general thing, however, you will see there from fifty to two hundred girls and women, some of them the wives and sisters of the mechanics and tradesmen above mentioned, who, like their male relatives, are out for a good time, but the majority are young girls of quite independent standing — servant girls, saleswomen, and others, many of them strangers in the city, perhaps, possessed of no sterner guardians than their own consciences, and are pleased to select whatever means may suit them best to pass their spare time. They see no reason why they should not spend at least one evening in a little uproarious festivity. When the dance is at its height and the enthusiasm of the dancers roused to its highest pitch, the visitor invariably receives the worth of his money. It does him good to see so many people enjoying themselves, and there is very little doubt that if he is of fairly presentable appearance and sufficiently discreet to work the matter rightly, he may without much difficulty obtain a partner for himself and join in the general *melee* of ecstatic enjoyment. As a general thing the festivity winds up about midnight, but if a few select parties desire to remain a little longer, no very serious objection is likely to be made. A very agreeable evening may be passed in this place, and the fact that the pavilion has remained where it now stands for more years than one cares to count without any serious protest from the aristocratic residents of this neighborhood speaks well for the order with which it is conducted.

On the east side of 31st Street, between Rhodes and Vernon Avenues, there is a much more pretentious concert and dance hall than either of those previously mentioned. It, also, is the enterprise of the same Mr. Baum who runs the 22nd Street place. It is a much more imposing structure, having a stone front and a wide entrance brilliantly lighted by electricity. An admission fee of ten cents is charged, and the great hall at the rear, in which the stage performance takes place, will accommodate nearly one thousand people. Much the same class of entertainments as those to be witnessed at Engel's are presented here, with the difference, however, that there are no stage boxes, no balcony for ladies, and no means, so far as one may ascertain, of making acquaintances among the performers. Occasionally some singers of higher merit procure engagements at this place, and the quality of the music that they contribute to the entertainment is not improved upon in many of the down-town theatres. Half of the hall, the east side, is reserved for ladies escorted by gentlemen; the other half is for the exclusive use of the male patrons. Refreshments of all sorts are served all through the evening at the polished round tables, thus enabling the visitor to satisfy his hunger, as well as his thirst, with any sort of a meal during the progress of the performance.

On the second floor is a ball-room of imposing dimensions and magnificent furnishings. On off nights it is rented out to various societies for their dances, but on very frequent occasions the proprietor advertises a ball that is invariably attended by the youth and beauty of the middle classes residing in the neighborhood. As is the case at all places where liquor is indiscriminately dispensed, a pleasant feeling of informality, not to say hilarity, prevails; the chance visitor, who may nearly always procure admission for himself and his fair companion, if he has one, by the payment of the stipulated fee, may be certain of passing a pleasant time.

There is a place on the West side, near the Ashland club, 575 Washington Boulevard, which is for that reason known as the Ashland Club Annex. There is no especial reason for mentioning it save that the weary way-farer, if he happens to learn the pass-word for the night, may enter at almost any hour and secure hilarious enjoyment. The place nearly always contains a rollicking crowd of young men who are up to any and every sort of mischief and manage by their antics to create unlimited amusement for any strangers who choose to happen in. As a rule the "password," if it may be so called, consists in a series of variegated taps on the window with the end of a lead pencil, their number and regularity signifying to those inside whether the applicant is to be trusted or not. This precaution is considered necessary on account of the fondness of the West side policemen for descending upon such places entirely without notice and carting off all the inmates to the station on a wholesale charge of disorderly conduct, which disorderly conduct consists in their frequenting such a place after lawful hours. It has been a long time, however, since such a raid was made.

The Lyceum theatre, while perhaps not deserving of the title of a free and easy resort, is, nevertheless, a place where variety shows of a broad description are to be seen at any time. The Olympic, on South Clark Street, opposite the Sherman House, is another resort of the same calibre. There is an afternoon show at the Olympic every day in the week, and as a rule it attracts good audiences. The rates of admission at both of these places are very low, and, considering that fact, the entertainments offered are in every way satisfactory.

CHAPTER VI.

CHURCHES AND CHURCH SERVICES.

WITH a large portion of the people who remain in Chicago over Sunday, the desire to attend some sort of divine service, as well as to see some of the principal edifices devoted to religion, is the first thought on awakening. The finest churches are located at a business centre. Before the fire there were a number of churches in the heart of the downtown district, but when they were once destroyed they were never rebuilt, and it is along the residence streets that the handsomest structures may be seen. The transient population is cared for, however, by clergymen who hold services in certain of the theatres Sunday mornings — of whose work more anon.

The churches of Chicago represent every Christian denomination, there being nearly 500 places of worship, the total Sabbath attendance at which is estimated at 120,000. Among these are many splendid specimens of architecture, but the two great Catholic edifices — the Church of the Holy Family, corner of May and West Twelfth Streets, and the Holy Name cathedral, corner of North State and Superior Streets

— are the most imposing from an architectural standpoint. Other noteworthy churches are the Cathedral of St. Peter and St. Paul, Grace and Trinity (Episcopal), Immanuel (Baptist), Second Presbyterian, Plymouth and New England (Congregational), St. Paul's (Universalist), Centenary (Methodist), Unity and the Church of the Messiah (Unitarian).

There are some very eloquent preachers in Chicago, and a visitor who does not attend a church solely for the purpose of getting inside of it and seeking forgiveness for his sins may enjoy a very profitable hour in listening to an admirable sermon in any quarter of the city he may choose to select. There are several clergymen in Chicago who receive $6,000 to $8,000 per year, and at least three whose salaries, it is said, are $10,000.

The principal churches of the West side are located for the most part along Washington and Ashland Boulevards, and there is a cluster of them in the vicinity of Jefferson and Union Parks — small breathing-places a couple of miles from the business centre. The church district of the North side is between Clark and Dearborn Streets and north of Ontario. On the South side the principal religious edifices are east of State Street and south of Twenty-second, the buildings growing finer, as a rule, the further south one goes. There are several very fine churches in the recently-annexed suburb of Hyde Park if one cares to travel that distance.

It is a peaceful feeling, if nothing else, to find oneself within sacred walls on a bright Sabbath morning, and if it is merely for sight-seeing that you find yourself there — which it is to be hoped is not the case — you will not be disappointed. If there are ladies in your party, they will be on the look-out, as ladies always are, for fine clothes worn by other ladies, and if so, why, it is very certain they will not be disappointed.

Some of the South side congregations are very wealthy. In some of them a dozen of the male worshipers could raise between them enough ready money to buy up several adjacent blocks — say a million dollars apiece — which, considering that, according to Holy Writ, "It is easier for a camel to go through the eye of a needle than for a rich man to be saved," or words to that effect, makes the spiritual outlook for these wealthy gentlemen a poor one. However, it is always interesting to watch how rich men behave themselves in church, and one of the ushers will not be likely to refuse to point out to you a devout millionaire or two if you ask him to do so.

Speaking of high salaried preachers (though the highest-salaried are not always the most popular) suggests the mention of a few of the most celebrated divines of the city: Rev. S. J. McPherson, pastor of the Second Presbyterian church, Michigan Avenue and Twentieth Street, always preaches to a full church. Dr. McPherson is not a poor man himself, having been bequeathed a little fortune by the late John Crerar. Then, too, he has a large income for wedding fees, for he has such a charming manner in performing the ceremony that he is in great request with prospective brides. Dr. Gunsaulus, pastor of Plymouth Congregational church, is also very popular. For a time he conducted Sunday evening services at Central Music Hall, State and Randolph Streets, but abandoned that field to the Rev. Flavins J. Brobst, who in turn retired. The famous Jewish pastor of the city is Rabbi Emil G. Hirsch, of Sinai congregation, Indiana Avenue and Twenty-first Street, who is also a writer of some renown. Many Christians attend this church for the sake of the Rabbi's eloquent sermons, which are liberal and large-hearted enough to suit all denominations. A preacher of the good old, stern, denunciatory stripe is Dr. Poindexter S. Henson, of the First Baptist church, corner of South Park Avenue and Thirty-first Street. Dr. Henson's sermons are pitched very frequently in a topical key. He would just as soon discuss politics as the Bible from his pulpit, and whenever the city administration stands in need of a little "roasting" the Rev. Poindexter is tolerably certain to supply the need. By reason of these sermons the Rev. Poindexter succeeds in getting himself into the newspapers about as often as any divine in town, and it is quite safe to say that the stranger who selects his church as the one to visit will not regret the selection. For those who admire a high church service, the Episcopal cathedral, at the corner of Washington Boulevard and Peoria Street, will be found to answer all requirements; the Right Reverend Bishop McLaren is the pastor. Dr. Clinton Locke presides over Grace Episcopal church, 1445 Wabash Avenue, with dignity and grace, and Bishop Cheney fills the pulpit of Christ's Episcopal church, Michigan Avenue and Twentyfourth Street. The Rev. J. P. Brushingham, a clergyman whose record was once marked by a particularly stormy series of events, draws good congregations to the Ada Street Methodist church. Dr. William Fawcett, another eloquent Methodist divine, preaches at Park Avenue church, on Park Avenue, at the intersection of Robey Street. Rev. Frank Bristol, pastor of Trinity Methodist church, Indiana Avenue and Twenty-fourth Street, is noted for his great store of learning as well as his flood of eloquence, and so is Dr. N. T. Meloy, pastor of the First United Presbyterian church, Monroe and Paulina Streets. Rev. M. Woolsey Stryker holds forth at the Fourth Presbyterian church, corner Rush and Superior Streets, and the very aristocratic congregation of St. James', corner of Cass and Superior Streets, is presided over by Dr. Tompkins.

The clergymen above mentioned are among the most famous in the city, but there are many others almost equally prominent. The wayfarer, however, will be interested in learning of the popularity of the services at "Central" church and the People's church, conducted at Central Music Hall and McVicker's theatre, respectively, by Prof. David Swing and

PROFESSOR SWING IN THE PULPIT.

Dr. H. W. Thomas. Both these gentlemen possessed large followings when their Congregations were formed. Prof. Swing is one of the leading personalities of the religious life of the city. He is a man of exceedingly plain exterior but his sermons are sound and forcible. It would be difficult to analyze his creed or that of the people who go to hear him. Central Music Hall is filled every Sunday morning with a large gathering of well-to-do people whose religious ideas could not, perhaps, be very accurately defined, but who would not go anywhere else under any inducement. There is also a large sprinkling of outsiders. The manner in which Prof. Swing's followers appreciate his ministrations in their behalf is evidenced by their paying him a salary ample enough to enable him to build a palatial summer home at Lake Geneva, a nearby hot weather resort whose grassy banks are lined with the villas of Chicago millionaires. Dr. Thomas is a little more orthodox in his tenets, perhaps, but his services are no less popular than Prof. Swing's. At both of these temples of worship, operated, as they are, in places devoted throughout the week to public amusement, chance visitors are made heartily welcome and many strangers who would not inconvenience themselves to ride out to one of the orthodox churches take advantage of the nearness of these two to their hotels and drop in on Sunday morning for an hour or so of spiritual enlightenment.

CHAPTER VII.

PANORAMAS AND LIBBY PRISON.

THE panoramas of Chicago have become justly celebrated. They are patterned after the famous panoramas of Europe, being contained in huge circular buildings. There are at present three panoramas — the Battle of Gettysburg and the Falls of Niagara, on Panorama Place, a mile south of Madison Street on Wabash Avenue, and Chicago on Fire — the latter being a splendid representation of Chicago as it looked at the time of the awful conflagration that drew the eyes of the civilized world upon the suffering city. The Battle of Gettysburg is the oldest of the three. The portrayal of the greatest battle of the war of the rebellion is realistic beyond description. It is impossible for the spectator to detect where the canvas blends with the natural presentation beneath the feet. Hundreds of thousands of people have visited this attraction. The Wabash Avenue cable cars take the visitor direct to "Gettysburg" and to "Niagara," which is just across the street. "Niagara" is a faithful delineation of the world-famous falls, the portrayal being so realistic that the spectator, in fancy, can almost hear the roar of the water.

The panorama depicting the fire is shown in the building formerly consecrated to the Battle of Shiloh, on Michigan Avenue, near Madison Street. Here the visitor may stand for an hour lost in wonder at the realism of the scene so artfully drawn on canvas. The panic of a great city in the throes of a hopeless battle with the destroying element is admirably pictured, and from a view of that speaking and truthful canvas one may gain a slight idea of the bitter agony of those hours when the proud city was laid low in the face of as horrible a calamity as ever befell a community. The panoramas have a uniform admission fee of fifty cents.

The Libby Prison War Museum, located on Wabash Avenue, between Fourteenth and Sixteenth Streets, belongs to the same class as the panoramas in the amusement category, inasmuch as the visitor may enter and wander around for half a day or so if he chooses, taking his own time to view the attractions offered. Libby Prison is one of the

leading permanent attractions of the city. On the outside, fronting on Wabash Avenue, is a massive stone wall, and on the inside is the identical Libby Prison in which the soldiers of the north were incarcerated during the war. The building was purchased in Richmond by Chicago capitalists and has been put up, brick for brick, exactly as it stood during the time when the nation was convulsed by the horrors of civil war. Within its walls will be found portraits of all the leading soldiers and statesmen, northern and southern, of that period; all kinds of firearms and ammunition, ancient and modern; a fine collection of historical documents, including the will made by John Brown an hour before his execution; and many other war relics. It may be easily imagined how deep an interest this place possesses for old soldiers, union or confederate. Old comrades, separated since the close of hostilities, often meet there, and many are the reminiscences exchanged. The Libby Prison is open day and evening. The admission fee is fifty cents, children half-price.

Not far from Libby Prison, on Wabash Avenue, is another structure that possesses a strong historical interest. This is the fort of John Brown, transported entire to this city and enclosed in a neat iron building. Enterprise has no compunction in these days, and it is hard to tell what the visitor to Chicago will not see if he waits long enough.

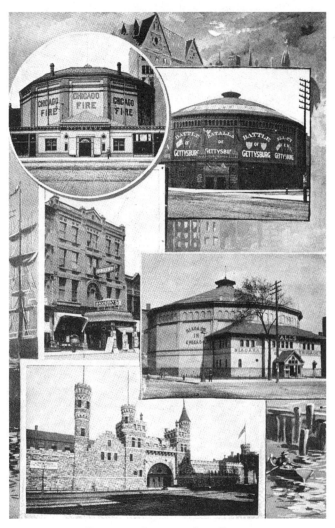

PANORAMAS, CASINO, AND LIBBY PRISON.
Clockwise from top left: Chicago Fire Panorama; Battle of Gettysburg Panorama;
Niagara in Chicago Panorama; Libby Prison; Haverly's, also called the Casino.
Background image of unidentified buildings, fishermen, and ships.

CHAPTER VIII.

PERILS AND PITFALLS.

It is not insulting the intelligence of the stranger to warn him against the unscrupulous persons who will beset his path, for they are so numerous and make their appearance at such unexpected times and places that the very smartest of us all are occasionally in danger of being victimized. There are probably more "crooked" people in Chicago at the present writing than any other city in the Union, and it is altogether probable that this number will be largely increased during the progress of the Fair.

The criminal classes who infest Chicago at all times are extremely varied. The common tough, whose exterior and manner of comporting himself proclaim his worthlessness, is not very much to be feared. Such gentry will be well cared for by the police during the great rush to the Fair. Indeed, it is quite probable that all suspicious or known disreputable characters will be spotted at once and given a chance to leave the city, a failure to avail themselves of which will result in their imprisonment until the Fair is over. But there are other gentry who are infinitely more dangerous. The term "bunco-steerer" perhaps best signifies their calling. The term bunco-steerer originally meant a decoy, or "capper," who led or "steered" the confiding stranger against a bunco "lay-out." Lately, however, its meaning has broadened. By "bunco-steerer" is now meant the oily, genial gentleman who approaches you on the street corners and politely inquires after your health, supplementing this query with another as to whether you would not like a chance to get into any sort of game whatsoever. The bunco-steerer will turn his wits to almost any scheme to make money at the expense of his more honest fellow-creatures. He belongs to the great army of confidence men who prey upon mankind in general and upon gullible strangers in large cities in particular.

The confidence man! Ah, beware of him if you value your peace. He may make his appearance at any moment and in any guise. The very suave and polished gentleman who sits opposite to you at the table in the dining car and chats so delightfully with you as you ride into the city together may be a wolf in sheep's clothing, with designs on your purse. The very clumsy confidence man who walks up and slaps you on the back with a cordial "How de do, Jones, how are all the folks?" and immediately tries to scrape up an acquaintance, is not to be dreaded except by very green people who have never been in a big city before. It is the polished villain, the polite, well-dressed person who, while preserving a dignified demeanor, nevertheless tries to scrape up an acquaintance and then proceeds to divulge — as he will sooner or later — a chance by which a little easy money can be made, who is to be feared. A very good rule to go by is to preserve a polite manner to all strangers, but not to enter into confidential relations with any man who hasn't been introduced to you by some one whom you thoroughly know. The pleasures of a chance acquaintance may be great but they are accompanied by dangers to your purse. If you go into a quiet little game of cards at a hotel, it is a "cinch" that you will lose your money, because the men who invite you into it are cheats and will not give you a fair show. They are confederates and the money they show cuts no figure, because they have entered into a combination to fleece the stranger.

BUYING BANANA STALKS.

The rhapsodical gentleman who rushes up to you and proceeds to tell you glibly of all the people who live in your town has spotted you for a victim. Look out for him. It is easy to account for the knowledge he displays. Such people make a habit of hanging about the hotel and studying the history of every guest. That is how this sleek gentleman succeeded in ascertaining so much about you, my friend. The hotel people watch very closely for such gentry, and when one of them is caught, he is never given an opportunity to repeat his offense.

There are two bits of advice which if followed closely will probably save the unwary stranger from all harm. In the first place never enter a place you would be ashamed to have your family at home know you entered; and in the second place never sign any papers or lend any money or valuables at the request of strangers.

Among the devices for snaring the wayfarer's honest dollar is the "snap" auction sale. Passing along a leading thoroughfare, one encounters a big shop flanked on the outside by two well dressed young men who are doing all they can to attract custom. Inside, a red-faced auctioneer is expatiating on the magnificence of the plate and jewelry he is offering for sale. Don't be deceived by the plate and jewelry. It would probably be expensive at $5 a ton. Nevertheless, the auctioneer is eloquent. It is possible, too, that he may exhibit for a moment a really valuable watch or ring, only to deftly conceal it and substitute a worthless one for it as soon as somebody shall have made a bid. Scattered about among the spectators are numerous "cappers" who, whenever an article is put up, bid a few dollars against each other. As soon as a stranger makes a bid of any sort the article is promptly knocked down to him and handed over. When he gets away, he discovers too late that he has been duped.

One has not space at command to cite all the methods by which the unwary are fleeced out of their wealth. Besides, new and treacherous schemes are constantly being invented. It is impossible to tell what plot the genius of the confidence man will strike next. These shrewd geniuses have even gone so far as the selling of banana stalks to farmers for seed. It must not be supposed by this that all Chicagoans are dishonest, although many foolish people who contrive to get fleeced generally go home uttering loud cries at the greed and dishonesty of the big city by the lake. But as long as there are geese to be plucked, there will be rascals looking out for the chance to do the plucking. Take reasonable precautions and you stand in no danger. But make merry with chance companions in questionable resorts, and, unless Providence has taken you under its especial charge, you will go home a sadder, wiser, and poorer man.

CHAPTER IX.

AS TO ADVENTURESSES.

This should perhaps have been included under the head of the preceding chapter, for if there are any pitfalls and perils more dangerous than those laid by fair and unscrupulous members of the fairer sex, we have yet to be made aware of them. The adventuresses of Chicago, however, deserve a brief and exclusive chapter, inasmuch as they constitute a separate class which might, with very great propriety, be asked to go about labeled with the initials D. F. (signifying "Dangerous Females"). Even then, however, it is safe to say, they would not want for victims, for there are some men who would run after a pretty woman if they were morally certain that the pastime would lead to their everlasting damnation.

The term adventuress is applied to women of careless reputation who, being much too smart to endure the ignominious career of professional demi-mondaines, resort to various shrewd schemes to fleece the unwary. Some of their class work in concert with male partners, and in such cases the selected victim generally becomes an easy prey. The confidence man may be dangerous; the confidence woman, if she be well educated and bright, as well as pretty, is irresistible except with the most hardened and unsusceptible customers. The shrewdest old granger of them all, who steers safely through the shoals and traps set for him by male sharpers, will go down like the clover before the scythe under a roguish glance, as it were, from a "white wench's black eye," as Mercutio said.

There is no mortal man in this universe of ours, be he never so homely or ill-favored, who does not cherish in his heart of hearts the impression that there is a woman or two somewhere whom he could charm if he wished to. It is the spirit of masculine vanity that forms the material upon which the adventuress may work. With the art of an expert she sizes up the dimensions of her victim's vanity the instant she has made his acquaintance and plays upon it to just the extent she deems expedient and profitable. If it were not for masculine vanity, the American adventuress could not exist.

Suppose, for instance, that Mr. John Smith, who is a merchant in comfortable circumstances at home and quite a great man in his town, is taking a stroll down State Street in the bright afternoon sunshine. He has just gotten outside after a good dinner at his hotel, prior to which he had a good shave and a cocktail — just the combination to make a well-to-do traveler with a little time on his hands feel literally "out of sight," as the slang phrase goes. Suppose then, as John passes Marshall Field's, he observes a magnificent creature, a royal blonde, mayhap, or a plump brunette (either will do for the sake of illustration) peeping shyly at him from beneath long silken lashes and smiling ever so slightly. Now John may be a deacon in the church at home; he may even be the father of a large family, but if he is human, and animated by the latent vanity that is the paramount trait of his sex, he will instantly experience a sensation of pleasure and attribute the strange beauty's attention to his own long dormant power to fascinate.

That splendid creature with her fine clothes, her exquisite complexion, and her graceful bearing, an adventuress? Impossible! At least so John Smith thinks. She may even have a carriage at the curbstone into which she steps daintily, with her eyes still slyly following the amorous John. There is a delicate invitation in the glance, and if John is courageous he will — pshaw! Let us hope he won't, for it is a dead certainty that the coy beauty is an adventuress of the deadliest and most conscienceless sort. John, who in his confiding soul has set her down as a duchess or a society queen at least, fondly imagines that it is his person of which she is enamored. We, who are better posted, know that it is his worldly wealth that she is after and that even as she gives him an attack of palpitation of the heart by her warm glance, she is figuring on how she may most easily possess herself of that wealth.

The schemes of the city's adventuresses are quite as numerous as those of the confidence man, but blackmail is their great card and the one that they play most successfully. As a rule, a prosperous citizen of good reputation and standing in his own town who misconducts himself when away from home would rather pay any sum in reason than have his friends at home know of that dereliction. That is where the skilled adventuress makes her strong play. If she has the power to lure her victim into a liaison, she has surely had the tact to draw from him in the two or three days they have spent together all the particulars she needs as to his relations in his own town. What a disheartening shock it must be, must it not, to have this splendid creature, who has vowed a thousand times to the doting John Smith that she loves him for himself alone, strike him on the morning of his projected departure for home for a cool thousand dollars in cash? Of course he demurs, but when she pleasantly hints at the trip she intends to make to his town and the exposure that must necessarily follow, what is to be done? Poor John Smith! He is not such a gay dog now. It gradually ends in a compromise of some sort, for the lady is seldom too exacting, and if John is inclined to be docile — to the extent of four or five hundred, maybe — she will probably be very good-natured and let it go at that.

CATCHING ON.

This is the highest type of adventuress — the aristocrat of her profession. From her the types descend in grades, down to the very lowest of all, the birds of the night who prowl the streets in search of victims whom they may lure to the dens of their male accomplices, there to be vulgarly drugged or "slugged" and robbed of their portable valuables.

The "indignant husband" game is a favorite one with adventuresses of the second class, by which term is signified such fair and frail creatures as occupy a somewhat lower place in the plane of rascaldom than the fairy who relies solely upon discreet blackmail without publicity for her means of support. This game is usually played upon very green persons for the reason that very few others would fall victims to it. The fair decoy makes the acquaintance of her quarry on the street, at a matinee, or elsewhere. For the first interview she is on her good behavior, and by her repression of any approach to familiarity that her newly acquired friend may make she creates the impression that she is a very nice and decorous person indeed — a little disposed to flirt, that is all. She does, however, write him to call upon her and of course he does so — perhaps to-day, perhaps tomorrow, but he calls, anyway. By letting fall certain artful hints she contrives to let her victim know that she is a married woman. This of course lends an added spice of interest to the adventure. The idea of poaching on forbidden ground is attractive to the dupe. So an hour passes in pleasant converse, and in the natural course of events the caller becomes sentimental. This much accomplished, he is hers, so to speak. At the very moment that the poor victim is congratulating himself upon his conquest there is a thundering knock at the door.

"My God!" screams the lady, with the dramatic intensity of a Bernhardt. "My husband!"

The startled fly in her net squirms in his seat. Who would not, situated as he is? "What is to be done?" he asks weakly.

"Hide! hide!" says the poor "wife" frenziedly and straightway rushes him into a convenient closet. The "husband" enters and, singularly enough, finds no difficulty in discovering the interloper's hiding-place. He is gruffly ordered to come out and as like as not finds himself looking down the barrel of a big revolver.

Of course he is willing to make any sort of settlement in order to escape with a whole skin. If he has no currency the "husband's" wounded "honor" will be healed with a check, although he would rather have his watch, seeing that the payment of checks can be easily stopped at the bank.

It must not be inferred from the foregoing that any peaceable gentleman who walks the streets is liable to be dragged by the nape of his neck into a compromising situation and compelled to disgorge all of his portable wealth at the point of a pistol. Far from it. He who walks the straight path of virtue is in no danger whatsoever. It is your frisky gentleman, who is out for a little lark and is reckless in his manner of carrying out the enterprise, who is likely to find himself in a snare. "Be good and you will be happy" is a maxim (modernized) that applies very handsomely to this sort of thing. "But you will miss lots of fun!" the frisky man may respond. Well, well, even so, but be very careful, for you know not how soon or how abruptly the languishing angel at your side may change into a fiery harridan, determined to have your money, your reputation, or your life — whichever may suit her best.

Only a shade removed from the "indignant husband" game is the old "panel" enterprise, which is so very vulgar and simple in the manner of its operation that it would not be worthy of mention were it not for the author's desire to warn strangers of every grade of intelligence against every possible danger that may lie in wait for him. Beware! O sportive young gentleman in search of a little diversion, of the young woman who on the shortest term of acquaintance invites you to accompany her to her flat or her boudoir, as the case may be. It may be that she has a pair of sharp scissors in her pocket with which she deftly snips off your money pocket; but failing this device, the "panel" is brought into play. While the interview between the more or less affectionate lovers is in progress, a panel in the wall slides back, pushed by invisible hands, and a third person, the male confederate of the damsel, slinks through it into the apartment. The amount of plunder he secures depends entirely upon the degree of absorption with which the quarry is wooing his charmer and the progress that he has made in her affections, but however that may be he is tolerably certain to emerge a heavy loser. If the presence of the third party is discovered (and it is surprising how seldom this is the case), a fight is in order and the victim is fortunate if he escapes with only the loss of his valuables to mourn and no physical injury to lament.

It is a sorry subject and one is glad to leave it. Before doing so, however, remember one thing, and remember it very distinctly: No young lady, however irreproachable her appearance, who enters into a street flirtation can safely be regarded as other than dangerous. Act on this suggestion and you will run no risks. In other words, "Be good and you will be happy." A repetition of the maxim will do no harm.

CHAPTER X.

THE TIGER AND HIS HAUNTS.

WHILE gambling of all sorts and conditions is to be strongly deprecated, it is nevertheless a fact that a large percentage of the strangers who flock to this great city of the West find themselves possessed at times with a desire to view the feverish scenes of which they have heard so much. Gambling as a confirmed vice is a terrible affliction. It frequently happens, however, that men who never dream of gambling at home, finding themselves with a little superfluous time on their hands in a strange city, actually yearn for a little of the excitement that is to be obtained by staking a small sum at a game of chance or skill. It's not the amount of money invested or the hope of gain that animates them; it is the pleasant excitement that the game affords. Such men usually regard the small sum so risked as so much money thrown away; and as a matter of fact that is the right way to regard it, for those who pit their money and skill against gamblers sufficiently educated to make a living in Chicago possess more nerve than discretion. The compiler of this little work advises everybody to forego all games of chance while resident in this city. Confident, however, that with many people old enough and wise enough to know better this advice will utterly be disregarded, a few remarks upon the present status of the gambling fraternity in Chicago may not be thrown away.

In the old days, during the administration of both parties, so far as one can remember, the gambling industry flourished like the proverbial green bay tree. The South side, in the business district, fairly swarmed with "hells" of all descriptions, while the residence portions of the city were scarcely less favored. Passing along Clark Street on sultry summer evenings, when the heat of the atmosphere necessitated the opening of doors and windows, the rattle of the chips and the monotonous voices of the *croupiers* could be distinctly heard by the wayfarer. All that, however, is now changed. Mr. Washburne's administration, when it came into power, set its face sternly upon "wide-open" gambling; from the very outset the well-known places were compelled to close their doors on pain of a raid and the destruction of their contents. It is, nevertheless, a fact that there are still a large number of professional gamblers in Chicago — presumably there always will be — and

A MINION OF THE TIGER.

while there are no notorious houses open, the stranger who is yearning for a little action for his spare cash can be readily accommodated. The notorious Hankins castle on Clark Street is tightly closed, but every night there may be found in that vicinity any number of "sporty-looking" gentry who will be only too glad to guide the inquirer to a secluded spot where he can be accommodated with as large or as small a game as his inclination may dictate or his means allow.

That the sporting fraternity live in hopes of the advent of happier times is very evident. Costly gambling furniture in large quantities is stored away in anticipation of the coming into power of a mayor who will look less rigorously on the "profession." Mr. Hankins himself is credited with having paid the rent of $8,000 per year for two years in advance for his place, which shows his faith in his ultimate ability to re-open. In the old days Hankins' place was known as the "dinner-pail" home, presumably by reason of the large *clientele* of workingmen, clerks, and other people of small means who deposited their slender earnings with great regularity in his coffers every Saturday night. To this day they tell how a wagon used to drive up to the door a few minutes before ten o'clock every Monday morning and carry away to the bank the load of silver dollars, halves, quarters, and dimes left there by the patrons of the establishment within the preceding twenty-four hours. The place in those times was a sight for gods and men. On three floors games were in progress, and the rooms thronged to the suffocating point with a variegated assortment of humanity, all bent on the one project — namely, the acquisition of riches on the hazard of the cards or dice. Should the place ever be re-opened the sight will well repay a visit, even though it be merely one of curiosity. Nobody who enters is asked to play, though those who do not are regarded with suspicion. A few minutes, however, is all that is necessary in which to see all that is to be seen.

This description of Hankins' will serve for any large gambling house. At the present time, however, the industry is carried on *sub rosa*. There are two or three places which can be readily discovered by the curious, where the "boss" gamblers are in the habit of meeting and, failing the presence of the common prey, proceed to cheerfully "wolf" each other. The game chosen is the great American game of poker, and a nervous man is liable to suffer from shortness of breath at the sight of the bets that are made. There are other places where other games are carried on, but the visitor, if he is sensible, will steer clear of any or all of them. The facilities for running such money traps are so limited and the risk of arrest and punishment so great that the chances of encountering against a "brace" game are about 100 to 1 against the patron; the only consideration with the "slick" gentry who manipulate the games being how to most expeditiously relieve the wayfarer of his wealth at the least possible risk to themselves. Take the advice of an old hand and give the polished and gentlemanly professional gambler of Chicago a very wide berth.

For people of wealth who, afflicted with the speculative mania, desire a larger field of operations than mere roulette, faro, or other trifling games, such a field is not difficult to find. On the Board of Trade, where colossal fortunes are sometimes lost and won in an hour, every facility is offered the stranger who desires to take a "flyer." Stop in any commission house and signify your desire to "play" the market. No introduction is necessary — only sufficient money to "margin" your deal. For the benefit of the uninitiated, the system of speculation in grain and provisions may be briefly explained.

If you are possessed of a notion that the market price of wheat or oats is too low to be justified by circumstances

and wish to back your expectation of a rise with money, nothing is more simple of accomplishment. In that case order your commission man to buy you 5,000 or 10,000 bushels of the commodity you desire to trade in and deposit whatever sum he demands for margin. Some houses will make trades on a basis of one cent per bushel margin; but that sort of trading is not very satisfactory inasmuch as he will sell you out at the first point or two the market goes against you. The profits or losses on such a deal are easily figured. An advance of one cent a bushel, over and above the agent's commission of 1/8 of a cent for buying and selling, means a profit of $50.00 from the transaction. A corresponding decline means a loss of the same amount. But if the speculator thinks that the article in which he is dealing is too high in price, he puts up his margin and "goes short;" that is to say, he instructs his broker to sell, instead of buying the amount. Sell what one hasn't got? Well, that would ordinarily be difficult, but the system of margins enables you to do it on the Board of Trade.

If the price advances after you have sold "short" you are so much out of pocket; if it goes down you are so much ahead, less always the commission.

This is the principle on which a "flyer" may be taken on the Board. This outside speculation is of course only a feature of the vast legitimate buying and selling that is transacted on the Board; but it is there, just the same, and it will remain just so long as it is legal to deal in "futures." There is a bill now before Congress making it unlawful to deal in "futures" when those market price of the futures affect the necessaries of life. If the bill should become a law, it would put a sudden stop to outside speculation on the Chicago Board of Trade. The proposed measure has awakened such a storm of opposition, however, that it is hardly likely to go through. Many people claim that such a law would virtually kill business on the Board and that it would result in direct disadvantage to the farmer, for whose benefit it was framed.

SATELLITES OF THE TIGER.

Quite aside from the facilities that it presents for a bit of high speculation, the Board of Trade is in itself an interesting place to visit. The great stone building at the head of La Salle Street, where so many colossal fortunes have been lost and won, is invariably one of the first places that strangers seek. It is the largest institution of its kind in the world, being constructed mainly of gray granite. The height of the tower is 322 feet above the street. Around the great hall where the daily sessions of the mammoth exchange are held are galleries to which visitors are admitted free. During periods of great excitement, caused by a rapid advance or decline in prices, these galleries are thronged with people who watch with thrilling interest the half-wild human panorama below. At such times the stranger may be excused for imagining that Bedlam had broken loose. Groups of brokers stand about shouting at each other like so many madmen. Messengers are scurrying hither and thither, and at times the scattering yells break into a chorused roar beside which the screeching of a dozen locomotives in unison would seem tame in comparison. The Board of Trade has 2,000 members. The membership fee is $10,000, but the places of members who die or resign may occasionally be purchased for about half that amount. While the claim is always made that only legitimate business is transacted on the Board of Trade, the statement cannot be disputed that it presents the greatest opportunity for high gambling in the whole world. Perhaps it is not altogether gambling, either, inasmuch as it is not so much a game of chance as a game of judgment and skill, in which the cleverest and not the luckiest players come out on top.

However that may be, there have been some mighty fortunes won and lost on the Chicago Board of Trade. There was one memorable Saturday morning, nearly ten years ago, before the Board moved into its present quarters, when a dozen houses that had hitherto been regarded as the most substantial among the substantial went down with a crash. It was the year of the famous lard corner. Peter McGeoch, the great speculator and capitalist, tried to buy all the lard in sight. He succeeded in advancing the price considerably, but the inevitable break came and lard suddenly declined $3 a tierce. All the other products declined in sympathy. McGeoch, in the parlance of the day, went broke, and he dragged a lot of other men with him. Old operators say they never saw such scenes on the Board as were witnessed that day. Strong men stood about crying like babies at the sight of their vanishing fortunes, and even those who were earning thousands of dollars with the flight of every five minutes stood transfixed with terror lest prices should suddenly bulge the other way and land them in ruin before they had time to realize their profits. There was another very similar scene in the year 1887, when E. L. Harper, President of the Fidelity Bank, of Cincinnati, tried to "corner" wheat in Chicago. He and the syndicate he represented came within an ace of success. They ran the price up nearly 15 cents a bushel and had an enormous profit on paper. But there came a call for more "margins." Hundreds of thousands of dollars in greenbacks were shipped to Chicago from Cincinnati, but the sum sent was not big enough, and before the required amount could be raised the reaction came. There were rumors one bright morning that a crash was pending. The crash came and wheat dropped 20 cents a bushel in one hour. The syndicate was ruined and the very men who had sold "short" and had risen that morning in the expectation of meeting ruin themselves found by the same freak of fortune which had overwhelmed their adversaries that they were enriched by hundreds of thousands of dollars.

The aftermath of that famous corner is history. It was found that Harper had used the Fidelity Bank's money as well as his own, and the United States authorities took charge of the institution. Harper was tried and sent to the penitentiary for ten years.

In order to realize the splendor of such a game, one must ponder on the actual facts. If Harper had been able to raise about $50,000 more (he had already put up $500,000 in margins), he and his friends would have cleared millions. As it was they just fell short of the mark and were irretrievably ruined. But would not any confirmed gamester claim that such a royal game was worth the risk?

The attempts to run a corner on the Chicago Board of Trade have not always been unsuccessful. B. P. Hutchinson, an old gentleman who afterward went to New York as offering a more profitable field for his operations, was one of the few men who have had money enough to engineer a "corner," run it to its end, and pocket the enormous profits. "Old Hutch," as he was then familiarly named, was credited with losing a half a million cold dollars in the Harper deal. The gentlemen who got this money were of course those who sold "short," and they were said to be a group of millionaires who "had it in" for "Old Hutch" and had laid a trap to catch him. Whether these rumors had any substantiation in fact the writer knows not. If so, however, it may go on record as a fact, the "Old Hutch" got right royally even with the gentlemen who "did him up" on this occasion. For a year or so after this Harper deal he ran a corner in wheat entirely on his own account. It was the option for the month of November to which he turned his attention. Be that as it may, he bought all the wheat that was offered him and paid for it at prices ranging from 90 cents to $1.10. The month drew to a close. The "bears" had one day in which to fill their contracts to "Old Hutch" at ruinous prices. They held off and on the last day of the month, at the expiration of which the men who had sold "short" to Hutch were compelled to either pay their difference or default (that is, fail), the old gentleman stepped up and bought a single car-load of wheat at $2.00 per bushel, in order to establish a price, and in slang parlance, "that was where he had 'em." He not only recovered his losses but milked the alleged clique of millionaires for at least a million dollars besides. They were able to pay the loss, and "Old Hutch" went on his way rejoicing. It was whispered about that time that "Old Hutch's" intellect went a little awry after this terrible strain. He disappeared, and the newspapers were full of dire hints as to the probability of his having wandered off and drowned himself, or else blown out his brains. He turned up all right in New York, however, carrying on his operations with the old-time skill and nerve, and is, presumably, still making more money to leave his sons. A very fat and interesting volume might be written about Mr. B. P. Hutchinson and his operations in the Chicago grain market.

The very magnitude of deals like those above described is calculated to appall the average mind. Let not the reader suppose, however, that the same opportunities of which the millionaire capitalist avails himself lie open to every one. Far from it. Unlimited resources and a life-long familiarity with the intricacies of the market are necessary adjuncts to the manipulation of a corner. If the wayfarer desires to try his luck to the extent of a $50 bill, or a $100 bill, or a $1,000 bill — all well and good. But he is not advised to do so. He would better let it alone. Only on the supposition that there are some men who cannot keep out of a glorious game like this are the foregoing hints given.

On the Board of Trade proper nothing smaller than a 5,000-bushel lot of grain or a 250-package lot of provisions can be dealt in. On the other side of the street, however, is the Open Board of Trade, to the floor of which strangers are admitted free, and where one may deal in 1,000-bushel or even 500-bushel lots. Here is a place where quick action may be had for one's money. The intending speculator may make his deal, watch the blackboard, close out, and walk away $50 richer or $50 poorer, as the case may be, inside of ten minutes. The speculator takes big chances — he must never forget that he is playing against a certainty of a loss of 1/8 of a cent a bushel (the commission), but the profits, if there are any, are handsome. So are the losses. That, however, is merely information. If you are wise stay away from it, but if you must go in take an old-timer's advice and go slow.

In addition to the two Boards of Trade there are numerous "bucket-shops" all over town where the stranger can, if he chooses, relieve himself of his wealth without the trouble of a visit to either Board. A bucket-shop is a snap commission house which claims to operate on the Board of Trade quotations. Their existence is forbidden by law, but plenty are to be found, nevertheless. The quotations come over a "ticker." The customer buys or sells grain or stocks at a certain price, reports his "margins," and awaits events. In an hour at the outside he will get "action" for his money. There are some bucket-shops that ignore the Board of Trade and carry on their operations by telegraphic quotations from the New York Stock Exchange. If the customer, therefore, would rather operate in Wall Street than on the Chicago Board, he can readily be accommodated.

The Chicago Stock Exchange, located at the corner of Dearborn and Monroe, is a comparatively new institution but one that flourishes exceedingly. It is devoted to the purchase and sale of Chicago securities of all sorts, such as bank and street railway shares, stocks, bonds, etc. Several of the banking and commission houses connected therewith have private wires to the New York Stock Exchange, and if their customers grow weary of "playing" Chicago securities, which do not often fluctuate largely or rapidly, they can be transported to Wall Street as quickly as the telegram can transmit the deal they wish to make.

And here the chapter on gambling may be brought to a close. It is only presented as showing the opportunities that the city affords for those of speculative tendencies, and once again the author, conscious of having performed his task with all the conscientiousness at his command, gratuitously advises the reader to let gambling of all sorts and conditions severely alone during such time as he may remain in Chicago. For, while a few may win, the vast majority lose. Always remember that.

As the bully of the school said when the new boy licked him within an inch of his life, "Nuff said."

CHAPTER XI.

MASQUERADES AND SIMILAR ENTERTAINMENTS.

THE more or less stereotyped forms of entertainment to be found in the various theaters do not always cater fully to the varying tastes of the transient crowds that throng the streets of Chicago at all times. That "variety is the spice of life" is endorsed by the popularity of the different festivities that are being constantly arranged and that invariably secure profitable patronage. Dancing, as a pursuit for pleasure-seekers, is always popular, and its votaries are countless. There are any number of ordinary dance-halls located in every quarter of the city, and the particular style of entertainment they offer may always be ascertained by consulting the advertising columns of the evening newspapers. There are several high-class dancing academies which, however, would hardly be classified as public dance-halls, their privileges being really confined to the pupils and classes who receive regular instructions there. They may, however, be particularized as follows: Bournique's academy, a handsome brick structure located at 51 Twenty-third Street, where the youthful scions of the "first families," so called, receive instructions in terp-sichorean art; M. De Long, 78 Monroe Street; Horace Beek, 164 Warren Avenue; and Martine's academy on Ada Street, between Madison Street and Washington Boulevard.

Conceding that these places are for "society" — for the aristocrat, so to speak — one comes to consider those that are dedicated to the people — places where a small sum of money is the passport for admission and circumspect conduct the condition of remaining. If an ordinary dance or ball is enjoyable, how much more so is a masquerade — that merry carnival in which identities are mysteriously hidden and all manner of pleasant pranks indulged in by the maskers, whose brilliant and variegated costumes transform the aspect of the thronging floor into a kaleidoscopic expanse of ever-changing beauty. The accompanying illustration depicts the sort of jolly scene to be encountered at a typical Chicago masquerade — a scene which, witnessed for the first time, is rarely forgotten until it is eclipsed perhaps, by another later and even more novel.

Some prodigious masquerades have been witnessed in Chicago, and, though the fall and winter months constitute the regular masquerade season, the mercurial spirit by which the population is animated occasionally manifests itself in a masquerade of large or small dimensions at almost any period of the year. The most extensive masquerades of all have been held in Battery D, the roomy building on the Lake Front, in which has been held every style of entertainment, from floral displays and dances to prize-fights and dog shows. While these masquerades may be attended in safety by anyone who goes in the capacity of spectator and is animated by a determination to keep quiet whatever happens, some quite stirring scenes are occasionally witnessed there. Like a

THE MASQUERADER'S DREAM.

disordered but by no means wholly unpleasant dream comes over the writer the memory of a certain masquerade at Battery D, which was a gigantic affair, given under the auspices of the Board of Trade Clerks Association, a *coterie* of youthful and devil-may-care spirits whose only object outside of business hours is to discover agreeable methods by which to slay time. The admission fee was fifty cents per head, ladies free. A commodious bar contained unlimited refreshment for the revelers, who were of all classes, from the young "chippie" of the cheap dry goods shops and her red-necktied escort to the opulent banker and his friends who viewed the fun from the galleries. The variety of costumes was simply infinite. There were clowns, knights, devils, harlequins, kings, princes, queens, shepherdesses, queens of hearts, fairymaids, witches; in fact, every sort of character it is possible to imagine. The fun commenced at eight o'clock and continued until — well, they say it was about noon the next day when the music finally stopped and the last of the revelers disappeared. Some of the scenes that were witnessed were simply too wonderful for description. After midnight, when the musicians as well as the maskers found themselves vinously fortified to sufficient extent, all formality was dispensed with and care thrown to the winds. Frolicsome gentlemen turned somersaults and handsprings, landing not infrequently with their feet in the stomachs of their friends, and equally frolicsome ladies indulged in high-kicking contests and other acrobatic feats that materially added to the spirit of the occasion. And fights? Well, fights were quite numerous but not very deadly. A soft blow or two exchanged, maybe, and then the combatants, animated by the general hilarity, kissed and made up with charming good-nature and *abandon*. Nobody bore any malice. A gentleman who punched another gentleman was promptly forgiven and the reconciliation sealed with a drink. The gentleman who got punched as a rule got even by punching somebody else. People who were knocked down and walked upon got up with a lenient smile on their faces and at the earliest opportunity walked on other people. Once only was there cause to fear a serious affray. A young man of very good family and great wealth succeeded in incurring the displeasure of a band of very tough citizens from some region near Canal Street district. His offense consisted solely in his wearing a swallow-tail coat. Be that as it may, he was backed into a corner and gruffly ordered to apologize.

"Apologize for what?" he asked. The leader of the tough gang, who was manifestly drunk, peremptorily ordered the victim to cease "monkeying" and apologize; if he did not know what to apologize for, he could apologize on general principles. The situation was desperate. The young man knew it was time to think and think quickly. It was a case of apologizing for the mere fact of his existence or suffering facial disfigurement for three months. He desired to call next day on the charming young lady to whom he was engaged and so he wisely apologized, and the menacing horde of roughs, who were preparing to tear him limb from limb, at once retired, in the best of humor, and let him escape.

This, of course, was a masquerade of the lower order. It is only described to acquaint the reader with the style of entertainment in which he may readily mingle if he cares to look for it. There are plenty of other masquerades where the company is more select. The halls along North Clark Street, notably North side Turner Hall, advertise masquerades and plain dances the year round, some of which are very select.

The finest masquerades of all, however, are given at the Germania Club, on North Clark Street, near Division. Admission is solely by invitation and one must possess an acquaintance with some member of the club in order to secure entrance, and even then it is very difficult. Such entertainments, however, are very popular and much sought after. At no time, though, is there a scarcity of public dances which will afford the visitor all the pleasure of that sort he is seeking, at a very trifling admission fee.

CHAPTER XII.

ON SHOPPING.

THE FAIR SHOPPER.

A PARTY of visitors in which there are one or more ladies will unquestionably go on a shopping excursion of greater or less extent, according to the tastes of the fair ones and the length of the purses possessed by their escorts. It is not intended to give any advice as to where to go on such occasions. To do so would be to "get oneself disliked," as the saying goes. It is not possible to mention all the great shops or stores in detail; it would be manifestly unfair to praise a few to the exclusion of the many. There are a few great houses, however, the names of which are in a sense landmarks, and have nothing to lose or gain by being either spoken of or omitted.

It has been said that one can buy absolutely anything on State Street, from a stick of candy to an elephant. Certain it is that there are some stores on that thoroughfare, notably Marshall Field's, Gossage's, the Boston Store, Mandel's, Schlesinger & Mayer's, the Fair, the Leader, J. H. Walker &

Co.'s, and Siegel & Cooper's, that contain almost everything obtainable for money. State Street is the great retail thoroughfare of the city, and in any of the stores mentioned the customer is certain of fair treatment and his money's worth. These houses are all extensive advertisers in the daily newspapers, and if extensive purchases are contemplated, it is just as well to scan these advertisements for notices of "special sales," as they are called. During "special sales" of certain articles the reduction in the prices of those articles is very low, and much is to be gained by looking out for announcements that may save the purchaser considerable money. The first five houses enumerated are located between Randolph and Madison Streets. The Fair, which is a wonder in itself, and very popular, owing to the cheapness of its goods, stands opposite to the Leader, at State and Adams Streets. James H. Walker & Co. have a large building on Wabash Avenue, at the corner of Adams. Siegel & Cooper's great place, occupying nearly a block, from Van Buren to Congress Streets, is one of the sights of the city, being, it is said, without exception the largest store in the world which is devoted to the sale of general merchandise.

All the leading stores have high-class restaurants attached to them, a feature keenly appreciated by lady shoppers, who find it very convenient to rest from their arduous labors long enough to take luncheon and then resume the happy pastime of getting rid of the dollars that their husbands and fathers have bestowed upon them for this purpose.

CHAPTER XIII.

CARROUSELS.

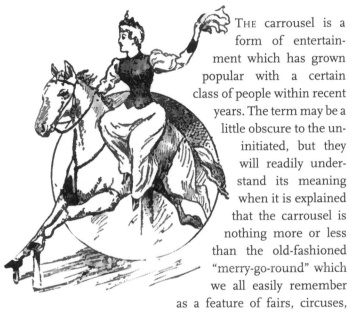

THE carrousel is a form of entertainment which has grown popular with a certain class of people within recent years. The term may be a little obscure to the uninitiated, but they will readily understand its meaning when it is explained that the carrousel is nothing more or less than the old-fashioned "merry-go-round" which we all easily remember as a feature of fairs, circuses, and other out-door entertainments. There are at the present writing several carrousels in the city, but it would be quite useless to specify their location, because they change places so frequently that to do so would only be misleading. They are here today, there tomorrow; but there never need be any difficulty in finding them. An inquiry of the hotel clerks or any other well-posted person will secure the desired information as to where the nearest carrousel is to be found.

Various newspapers have from time to time waged war

upon the caroussel on the ground that it is prejudicial to the morals of young people who patronize it. This work does not assume to criticize but to state facts. It is a fact that the carrousels are well patronized as a rule and that the young people who do the patronizing appear to extract no end of fun out of the whirligig process.

The caroussel or "merry-go-round" is generally situated in a flimsy building on some convenient vacant lot, rented for the purpose at a pinch, so to speak. The fiery wooden steeds that go whirling round and round in a circle, to the spirited music of a brass band or snorting orchestrion, bear on their backs sundry youths and maidens, with now and then an old boy or girl thrown in as a leaven to offset the general juvenility, who indulge in all manner of sportive remarks and jests as they go on their circular journey. It must not be supposed that the ride itself forms the chief part of the entertainment. By no means. A very little of that goes a long way. The principle part of the fun is derived from standing among the many rows of spectators and listening to the witticisms that are indulged in at the expense of the riders. These are often very pert, not to say cutting, and the lively repartee (not always very refined) that is exchanged between equestrians and spectators is always productive of infinite amusement to the chance visitor. A too pointed remark not infrequently leads to a spirited argument, which spirited argument not infrequently results in a row in which the friends of the participants are as likely as not to take part. In such an event that is the time when courtesy and all semblance of it abruptly ends and simple muscle then comes into play. This is good time for the outsider to withdraw to a safe distance, but though the combat is never very deadly — no shooting scrape, according to the writer's recollection, ever having taken place in a carrousel — it is just as well to avoid the risk of a black eye or a bloody nose that may result from a chance whack from a too enthusiastic pleasure-seeker who has become embroiled in the fray with or without his consent. The battle, inconsequential as it always is, invariably terminates before it is found necessary to call in the police.

The ground upon which certain of the great editors of the city have attacked the carrousel is that of the temptation to wrong-doing which it presents to the young. Certain it is that wherever a carrousel is located a large *clientele* of girls of tender age seems to follow in its wake. These girls are of the sort irreverently referred to by the very tough young men of the period as "chippie." They do not seem to be burdened with a great supply of innocence, but it is beyond question that the surroundings of the carrousel lead them to indulge in such behavior as they would not be guilty of elsewhere. In this respect the caroussel has in a measure taken the place of the skating-rink. Roller-skating some years ago was a craze, and while the carrousel craze has never assumed the dimensions of that popular "fad," its associations are very similar. There is always a liberal supply of alcoholic beverages to which the patrons of the carrousel, male and female, have easy access. Indeed, in some cases, there is a saloon directly attached. From this fact it may be easily imagined that this is not the sort of place from which a girl of fifteen or thereabout can be expected to derive any lasting benefit — and any number of such girls will be found enjoying themselves at the various carrousel enclosures.

Whatever be its merits or demerits the carrousel constitutes one of the features, good, bad or indifferent, of a great city. As such it is mentioned here, and for no other reason whatsoever. It may interest you to go and take a look at one.

CHAPTER XIV.

TURKISH BATHS — MASSAGE — MANICURES.

THE heading of this chapter may at the first glance seem peculiar. If so, you don't have to read it, do you? Nevertheless, a little space may be devoted, in a haphazard sort of way, to a feature of Chicago life that is not without its charms for those who are initiated.

Chicago is nothing if not metropolitan. The Turkish bath is a feature of metropolitan life which should not be deprived of its proper share of attention.

Ever taken a Turkish bath? No? Then remedy the deficiency in your education at once and at the same time taste one of the sublimest sensations that falls to the lot of man in this prosaic world of ours!

To particularize all the Turkish baths of the city would consume too much space. They can be found in connection with most of the leading hotels. The Palmer House baths, located beneath the barber shop, the floor of which is studded with silver dollars, is perhaps the most celebrated. They are open day and night — as all Turkish baths naturally are — and enjoy a large patronage. There are other places, quite independent of the hotels, notably Franks', on Wabash Avenue. The visitor is well cared for and given a taste of Oriental cleanliness and luxury at any hour of the day or night.

The Turkish bath owes a good deal of its popularity, I fear, to its revivifying effect on the toper. A man may enter a Turkish bath with the most aggravated case of "jag" on record and emerge in a few hours fresh, cleansed, and glorified — "clothed and in his right mind," as Holy Writ has it. Not to say that only tipplers patronize the baths! Far from it. People of unimpeachable sobriety indulge regularly in them for their health-giving qualities alone. In hot weather, when the clothing sticks with disagreeable closeness to the body, there is no easier method of "cooling off" than a passage through this fiery, or rather steaming, ordeal. Listen a moment and learn how it is done.

You descend a flight of stairs into a basement and enter the mystic portals. A colored servitor, almost nude, escorts you politely to a dressing-room. The torrid atmosphere has already produced a feeling of enervation, and you doff your clothes with alacrity. You then wind about you the sheet with which you have been provided and emerge, giving all your valuables to a clerk, who deposits them in the safe. You are then led to the "hot-room," as it called, in which you remain as long as you like.

Hot? Well, rather. The senses become numbed and dulled under the great heat, but the sensation is delicious beyond description. Lying full length on the couch, fairy visions float before the mind. Try to think connectedly and the effort will be a failure. The mind becomes a strange jumble, in which people and events, real and imaginary, mix themselves without volition of yours in a kaleidoscopic mass of pleasant pictures. A copious and wholesome perspiration breaks out at every pore. After awhile even the strongest of us has had enough of it, and another stage of the process is reached.

The bather is now laid full length on a marble slab, with a blown-out rubber pillow under his head. A stalwart negro takes him in hand. He is rubbed, pinched and pounded and kneaded with a vigor that at any other time might be unpleasant. In the drowsy languor of the moment, however, it is all right, and when the servitor presently smears him all over with sweet smelling suds only to rinse him copiously a minute afterward with a bucket of tepid water, the subject of the operation would not change places with the king of Siam or any other potentate of whom he has heard great things. This done, he is led to the shower bath, where the gentle stream falls over him for a few minutes, at first warm, then colder, until he rushes out from under a veritable stream of ice-water. Acting under instructions he plunges without hesitation head-foremost into the big swimming bath that stands ready to receive him. In this he may sport and gambol at will until he is tired, and in the cool embrace of the spacious tank the fever of the hot-room is forgotten and his body brought back to a normal temperature. Emerging from the swimming bath he is rubbed perfectly dry by an attendant and escorted to a couch in a large, cool room, where, wrapped in a sheet, he may lie as long as he likes in the sweet, dreamless sleep of the happy and the just. If it is his first experience he will vow on leaving the place that, as well as being refreshed and revivified, he feels cleaner than he ever felt in all his life, and, as cleanliness is said to be next to godliness, this is something by no means to be despised. A Turkish bath in a first-class place costs $1, though there are plenty of places where the charge is lower. Most Turkish bath establishments have an apartment especially provided for ladies.

Massage — a good deal is contained in the word. There are massage parlors in Chicago and again there are — massage parlors, or at least those called such by their proprietors. There are legitimate massage parlors conducted by competent physicians, employing skilled male operators who treat the applicant with every consideration. Massage — which consists of rubbing weak or otherwise affected parts of the body with the hands — is recommended by many physicians as a cure for rheumatism and kindred ailments. The applicant seeking such treatment, however, should assure himself that he is going to a place where he will receive such treatment as he needs and nothing else.

For there are so-called massage parlors — extensively advertised in some of the daily papers as employing lady operators — that are nothing more or less than improper resorts in disguise. There have been times when the "massage" question has received critical and analytical attention from one or more sensational papers, and the disclosures that have been made from time to time have been anything but edifying. The visitor will receive a sort of a Turkish bath at the hands of a

THE PRETTY MANICURE.

"lady" operator, but other entertainment will not be difficult to procure if he should express a word or two to that effect. From a standpoint of morality as well as prudence it is a good plan to let such "massage" (?) establishments as brazenly advertise their employment of "lady operators" severely alone.

"Manicuring," by which term is signified the treatment of the hands, is an industry that is only mentioned in this chapter by reason of its bearing on the care of the person or the toilet. The manicuring establishments are in every way respectable. For the sum of one dollar a pleasant-faced young woman washes one's hands in a preparation of her own manufacture and so trims, polishes, and fixes up one's fingernails that the average customer does not recognize them as his own after she has finished the delicate task. Aside from the neatness imparted by the operation, few men object to the sensation produced by having a pretty woman manipulate scientifically and dally with his clumsy hands for half an hour or more.

CHAPTER XV.

HACKMEN AND THEIR WAYS.

THE GUILELESS HACKMAN.

THERE is a well-grounded suspicion in some quarters that only the hackmen of Niagara can compete with the hackmen of Chicago in their fondness for extortion and their success in practicing it. Yet, while it is very true that most Chicago hackmen are imbued with a praiseworthy desire to earn all they can, and are none too conscientious in their ambitions to acquire riches rapidly, there is a very easy manner in which to avoid disputes, namely: make your bargain with your Jehu before you enter his vehicle. If, after such an arrangement, he endeavors to impose upon you at the end of the ride, you may be sure he is trying to give you the worst of it. In such a contingency, which may arise in very rare cases, pay him nothing whatever until you have called a policeman. It is part of every policeman's duty to familiarize himself with the schedule of legal cab fares, and he will settle the dispute in very short order. It will be found, however, that most of the public hackmen are pretty square fellows, a little bit prone to try for the best, it may be, but always amenable to reason — particularly if it be a uniformed officer who talks the "reason" to them.

As a general thing it will be found that the street-cars provide ample facilities for transportation to any given point in any direction. There is a uniform fare of five cents on all the lines, and for this trifling sum one may ride many miles on any of the cable lines. These lines run direct to all the parks, and most people choose this inexpensive mode of traveling. Occasionally, however, parties desire a more luxurious mode of transit, preferring to visit the parks in a carriage and drive about in the pleasant intricacies of the leafy aisles instead of traveling afoot; in which case an understanding with the driver before the start is made becomes an imperative necessity. But in order that there may be no mistake it is just as well to set forth briefly the legal rate for cab-hire established by the city ordinance.

The charge of conveying one or two passengers from one railroad depot to another in a hack — by which term is signified a vehicle drawn by two horses — is one dollar; for conveying one or two passengers any distance over one mile and less than two miles, $1.50; for each additional two persons of the same party, fifty cents. For conveying one or two passengers any distance exceeding two miles the charge is $2.00 — fifty cents more for each additional passenger of the same party. Children between the ages of five and fourteen years call for half rates, but there is no charge for youngsters under five — providing that the distance they are carried does not exceed one mile. In case it is desired to charter a hack for the day, the charge is $8. Four persons may ride in this way, from point to point, stopping as often as they may wish. Or the hack may be chartered by the hour, the charge for which system is as follows: Two dollars for the first hour and one dollar for each additional hour or part of an hour. As to baggage, each passenger is allowed to carry without charge one trunk and twenty-five pounds of other baggage. For each additional package so carried the driver may charge fifteen cents. Baggage of course is only carried on short trips, between railroad depots and hotels, it being presumable that no traveler wishes to take his trunk with him out to the park or to the World's Fair grounds.

The rates for hansom cabs, or other one-horse vehicles, is much lower, being twenty-five cents per mile or fraction of a mile for each passenger. By the hour, seventy-five cents for the first hour and twenty cents for each quarter of an hour thereafter. For service outside the city limits and in the parks: for the first hour, one dollar, and twenty-five cents additional for each quarter of an hour thereafter. It should be remembered that no time engagements will be made by any driver for less than an hour.

It is the duty of every hackman and cabman to have posted conspicuously in his vehicle the rates of fare as quoted above. The law requires him to do so. But even if he has complied with the legal requirements, it is just as well to make the bargain with him before starting, particularly if the journey be a long one. Disputes can be most easily avoided in that way.

Many people prefer to secure their carriages from the hotel livery stables. The charge in that case will be somewhat higher, with a corresponding advantage, of course, in the point of style.

When a party of twenty to thirty people wish to take an outing in the parks, the best plan is to charter a coach, or "tally-ho," as it is generally called, and the charge for which is $25 to $30 for the afternoon or evening. When divided up equally between the gentlemen of the party, the cost is by no means ruinous. These coaches are drawn by four or six horses, and the ride is always an enjoyable, not to say exhilarating, one. It is considered *de riguer* on such occasions for the two handsomest men in the party to station themselves at the foot of the ladder and help the ladies up to the best seats on the roof of the coach.

For the journey to Jackson Park and the World's Fair grounds hacks and cabs are little in demand for the reason that, if the cable cars are not considered quick or commodious enough, the Illinois Central trains, which run every few minutes, stop at the South Park station, at the very gates of Jackson Park.

CHAPTER XVI.

THE CITY'S MORAL SIDE.

CHICAGO has been called, in its time, the wickedest city in the world, and somehow or other (in exactly what manner it matters not) the impression has gone abroad that it is really a very wicked place indeed. It is with the idea of counteracting this impression in some degree that reference is about to be made to some institutions, the very existence of which denotes a desire on the part of the respectable majority to do all they can for the benefit and improvement of the minority, given over to evil ways.

Every great city in the world has its wicked side. Chicago is not an exception to the rule, but it may be maintained, with earnest emphasis, that it is at least no worse in this respect than its contemporary cities. It contains, moreover, some institutions that should atone, in the eyes of its critics, for some of the evils that are undoubtedly to be found within its borders.

THE WOMAN'S TEMPLE.

It is possible for a perfectly moral person, one used to all the refinement and peace of the most law-abiding and self-respecting of communities, to spend any length of time in Chicago without being contaminated by the evil that may be found easily enough if sought. This statement is made with due consideration and careful thought. It may seem a bold one, but it is true, nevertheless.

In a previous chapter, on the churches of Chicago, the author has given the reader some idea of the strictly religious institutions of the city. But there are other institutions, semi-secular in their nature and tone, but wholesome in their effect upon the moral welfare of stranger and native alike, that deserve especial mention.

This allusion does not apply to the inebriate asylums, the hospitals, or charitable institutions. They are too numerous to particularize, but they all exert a wholesome effect upon the moral welfare of the city. But the Young Men's Christian Association, or, rather, the Chicago branch of it, deserves some special attention. The present home of the Association, on the south side of Madison Street, between Clark and La Salle, was for a long time able to provide for the wants of members and strangers. A new building, however, is in course of preparation. The site of the new building adjoins the present property. The lot has a 52-foot front on La Salle Street and 185 feet on Arcade Court. One-third of the space in the new building will be utilized for Association purposes and the remainder for offices, the ground floor being rented for stores. The Y. M. C. A. proper will have two stories fronting on La Salle Street and seven on Arcade Court. The estimated cost of the new building, which will contain libraries, reading-rooms, gymnasium, etc., of the most approved description, will be $1,400,000.

The Young Men's Christian Association is an organization whose influence is felt around the world. Its branches extend to every inhabited portion of the globe, and it goes without saying, perhaps, that a member of the Y. M. C. A. from another city is always sure of a welcome at the home of the Association in this city or elsewhere. In addition to the members, strangers are always welcome at the Association rooms and every consideration shown for their benefit and comfort.

The Chicago membership is over 5,000. There are five branches in different parts of the city.

The Public Library is an institution the good influence of which can hardly be over-estimated. It is at present located on the fourth floor of the City Hall building, though in future years it will occupy a splendid home of its own now in progress of erection on the vacant lot known as Dearborn Park, Michigan Avenue, between Randolph and Washington Streets. It is one of the largest free public libraries in the world, and its reading and reference rooms are at all times open to strangers. A card signed by some respectable citizen is the only passport needed to its circulating shelves.

The new Women's building, at the corner of La Salle and Monroe Streets, must remain an everlasting monument to the influence of good women upon the existence of mankind, at least so far as Chicago is concerned. It was erected under the supervision of the Woman's Christian Temperance Union, of which Miss Frances Willard is President, and is devoted to all the purposes in which female organizations are interested. The building is fifteen stories in height and the architecture is superb. Lady visitors will find it more than worth their while to inspect it.

The Permanent Art building, now in course of erection on the Lake Front, on the site of the old Exposition building, is to take the place of the old Art Institute, corner of Michigan Avenue and Van Buren Street, recently purchased by the Chicago club. The structure has a frontage of 320 feet on Michigan Avenue, a length of 178 feet and a depth of 208, with a main entrance facing Adams Street. In it, when complete, will be found as fine an art collection as any on the American continent, upon which the visitor or student may spend hours in meditative gazing. The World's Fair directory contributed $200,000 toward the erection of the building, $275,000 more was raised by the sale of the old building, and $125,000 by private subscription. The structure, when completed and filled to the satisfaction of its projectors, will be one of the sights of Chicago.

There are many other features that might be mentioned as embracing the workings of Christian influence upon the mighty and ever-increasing population of the city, but those mentioned will suffice. There are a hundred avenues open to peaceful enjoyment for old and young, rich and poor.

It is possible to spend any length of time in this city and enjoy yourself in a quiet, unostentatious and perfectly moral way without being contaminated by the evil that confessedly exists in certain spots.

CHAPTER XVII.

THE PARKS AND BOULEVARDS.

THE PRETTY WHEELWOMAN.

So much space having been devoted, not without reason, to the attractions of Chicago after the evening shadows have fallen, it is with a feeling of pleasure that one turns to the charms of the city by day. If there is a city in the world calculated to offer the tourists opportunities for pleasure in the daytime, it is Chicago. It is natural, perhaps, in considering these opportunities, to refer to the parks and boulevards of Chicago, which, as good judges of such matters have said, constitute a whole host of attractions in themselves.

The park system of Chicago is something upon which the city prides itself perhaps more highly than on anything else. There is no city in the world that contains such a complete system of breathing-places for the people as is to be found in this one. The parks of Chicago embrace a total area of 2,074 acres, which is exclusive of grounds covered by park boulevards. The park system makes the circuit of the city, being connected by boulevards and embracing a total length of perhaps 40 miles. The system is divided into three divisions, each one of which is under the control of park commissioners, which commissioners are elected by the courts. There are therefore three separate or distinct government bodies: the South park commissioners, the North park commissioners, and the West park commissioners, who care for the territories under their control, which are maintained by a tax upon the three divisions of the city above signified. The city government maintains the control over numerous small parks or squares, which are maintained by the city treasury. All of the great parks are easy of access, being easily reached by any of the cable lines at the rate of five cents per passenger. South Park, Jackson Park, and Washington Park may be speedily reached by the Illinois Central at the rate of 25 cents for the round trip.

Chicago's boast that it possesses the finest parks of any city in the world will be found on investigation to be borne out by the facts. The area of territory under care and cultivation, the artistic manner in which the grounds are laid out and the general excellence of the *tout ensemble* so provided cannot be rivaled by any of the cities in the Old World. It is not proposed in this modest work to give a technical description of the various parks of the city but rather to convey a general idea of the natural and artificial beauties to be found within their limits. On summer nights, when the hot air of the streets drives the crowds from the business district to seek a refuge or breathing-place, the cars that lead to the various parks are thronged to the guards with people whose only universal desire is to get away to some cool spot where they may enjoy a gentler atmosphere, with perhaps a cool breeze thrown in.

Of the many parks of which the city boasts, Lincoln Park is perhaps the most popular. This, perhaps, is because it is nearest to the business centre and is also one of the largest, situated, as it is, on the very shore of Lake Michigan and stretching from Diversey Street on the north to North Avenue on the south, being bounded on the west by Clark Street.

Lincoln Park is reached from the south by the Lake Shore Drive, which is already the finest boulevard drive in Chicago, and which, when it extends, as is promised, to the military post at Ft. Sheridan, will be unequaled in all the world. The drive proper commences at North side water works on Pine Street and skims along the lake to the northern extremities of the park itself, connecting at the park's northern most end with the Sheridan Drive, which, when complete, will extend a distance of 25 miles along the lake. Along this drive are grouped some of the finest private mansions of which the city can boast. Noticeable among these is the home of Potter Palmer, the proprietor of the Palmer House, whose wife occupies the proud position of president of the Board of Lady Managers of the World's Fair. The Palmer castle, as it is called, is a giant structure of dark-gray stone, and its towers and turrets present an appearance very little less imposing than the ancient castles of the Old World. The Palmer castle is pointed out to the visitors as one of the sights of the city. On the right side of the drive is a strong embankment surmounted by a wall of solid stone, against which the waves beat ceaselessly. On bright days the drive is fairly thronged with brilliant equipages, and the sight is a very gay one. A boat racing course, especially designed for regattas, commences just beyond the entrance to the park, being protected from the fury of the sea by an outer pier.

Lincoln Park itself is about 250 acres in area. In old days it was a cemetery, and the tomb of the Couch family is one of its land-marks. It has been under state supervision since the year 1869, when the first board of commissioners was appointed. All that art can contribute to nature has been directed upon the project of beautifying this lovely place, and the winding avenues, the glassy lakes, the rich foliage, the gorgeous beds of flowers, and masses of shrubs combine to produce as attractive a picture as mortal mind could conceive or human eyes delight in. Aside from the natural beauties of the place, Lincoln Park possesses other attractions in the way of statuary and a zoological collection, which exercise a peculiar charm for visitors. Notable among the former is the Grant monument, facing Lake Michigan on the Lake Shore Drive, the cost of which was $1,000,000, the same being defrayed by popular subscription. There is also the Lincoln statue, by St. Gaudens, which faces the main entrance and was presented, together with a drinking fountain, by the late Eli Bates, statue and fountain costing $150,000. Other monumental works, notably the Indian Group in bronze, presented by the late Martin Ryerson; the La Salle monument, presented by Lambert Tree; the Schiller monument, erected by German residents of Chicago; and the Linne monument, erected by the Swedish residents of Chicago, are to be found at various points of the park. There are also magnificent conservatories, in the flowery mazes of which the visitor may wander at will, feasting his senses on beauties there to be found. A feature of Lincoln Park is the new palm house just erected, the dimensions of which are 168 by 70 feet, with a rear extension, and in which every variety of tropical palm will be exhibited. The cost of this structure was $60,000, and it will well repay a visit.

From Lincoln Park to Douglas Park is a long jump, but for the sake of continuity that jump may be appropriately taken, for the West side parks come next in importance to Lincoln

Park when one is considering the entire system. The area of Douglas Park is 180 acres. It is situated in a northwesterly direction four miles from the Court House, being bounded on the north by 12th Street, on the west by Albany Avenue, and on the south by W. 19th Street. The 12th Street cars take the passenger to the very gates of the park. Douglas Park is located in a neighborhood which some years ago was almost entirely destitute of residences, but within the last few years it has been built up to such an extent that those who saw the neighborhood in the days of its primitiveness would scarcely recognize it now. The people who live in that neighborhood have great affection for Douglas Park, which is artistically laid out and very skillfully cultivated. There is a large lake with a boat-house and refectory. It has also an artesian well whose waters are said to contain fine medicinal properties.

The chief park of the West side, however, is Garfield Park, which is reached by the W. Madison street cable cars, being situated four miles directly west of the court house. It is bounded by Lake Street on the north, Madison Street on the south, extending a mile and a half west from Washington Boulevard. In order to drive to Garfield Park one may traverse Washington Boulevard, which, lined as it is with fine residences, is one of the prettiest and most attractive to be found in the whole city. It is an exceedingly well paved boulevard, and on certain occasions, when the police are not too vigilant, some smart brushes between the rival owners of fast horses are occasionally to be seen on its broad stretch of smooth road-way. This park was not always known as Garfield; its first name was Central Park, but this was changed in honor to the memory of the martyred president. The park itself is picturesque beyond measure, its drives and promenades being laid out in such a manner as to cater to the most exacting of tastes. Among its features may be mentioned a handsome fountain, the gift of Mrs. Mancel Talcott, and an artesian well 200 feet deep, which discharges mineral water at the rate of 150 gallons per hour. Beautiful as Garfield Park is at the present writing, it bids fair within the next few years to be advanced to an even more perfect state. The people of the West side are determined that it shall be one of the handsomest parks in the city and are sparing no efforts to make it so. The West side cable cars reach a terminus at this point, but connecting with them is an electric line which carries passengers out to the town of Cicero, through the suburbs of Austin and Oak Park, at the uniform fare of 5 cents.

Humboldt Park is another West side breathing-place in which the residents of the locality in which it is situated take especial pride. Its area is 200 acres and it lies four miles northwest from the court house, being bounded on the south by Augusta Street, on the east by N. California Avenue, on the west by N. Kedzie Avenue, and on the north by W. North Avenue. Humboldt Park is beautifully laid out, and its trees, shrubs, and flowers are of superb beauty. It has a fine conservatory and an artesian well 1,155 feet deep.

The South side park system is the most complete of any in the city, and it monopolizes the favor of visitors who desire to make a speedy circuit of the three handsomest parks in the town within the short space of half a day. The system of boulevards leading to these parks cannot be equaled in the whole world. Michigan Avenue Boulevard, which commences at Jackson Street and the Lake Front, is the open sesame to a drive as delicious as the most exacting soul can desire. This street is one hundred feet wide from curb to curb and skirts the Lake Front park at its commencement. Speeding up Michigan Avenue, in whatever sort of conveyance the taste of the tourist may select, a fine view is obtained of some of the finest residences to be found in the whole city, many of whose millionaires have built palatial homes at distances greater or less from the business district. Michigan Avenue proper extends south to 35th Street. At 35th Street commence two boulevards, Drexel Boulevard and Grand Boulevard. Drexel Boulevard commences at Oakwood and the junction of Cottage Grove Avenue and 39th Street and has a double drive-way 200 feet wide, having in its centre a wide strip of turf dotted with shrubs and flowering plants and at its western side a soft track for equestrians. It was named after the Messrs. Drexel, the famous bankers of Philadelphia, who, in appreciation of the compliment thus bestowed, have erected a fine bronze fountain at the intersection of Drexel Avenue. Grand Boulevard is a very similar stretch of road-way in all respects. It runs south from 35th Street, where South Park Avenue joins that thoroughfare, and forms the northwestern entrance to Washington Park. It also presents a beautiful road-way for driving and has a side strip for equestrians, with flower beds, shrubs, and green turf on either side. Both of these boulevards are dotted by magnificent private residences, the chosen homes of the wealthiest class in the city. They form dual entrances to the circuit of boulevards leading to the famous Washington Park race-track, of which mention will be found in another chapter.

Washington Park, then, is entered from the beautiful drive-way on Drexel Boulevard, is most delightfully situated a little over a mile from Lake Michigan and nearly seven miles southeast from the court house, being bounded on the west and north by Cottage Grove Avenue and 51st Street, on the south by 60th Street. In the opinion of many people it is the finest of all of Chicago's parks, being 371 acres in area, its floral beauties and its charms of hillocks, shrubbery, woods, and water being almost beyond description. There is a great play-ground 100 acres in extent, upon which any one is free to indulge in any sort of athletic game that fancy may dictate, also a large lake upon which boating may be indulged. There is also a splendid conservatory, in which many rare flowers of all lands may be viewed at any time. The floral display is in charge of a great army of skilled gardeners, who change the designs from season to season and always manage to turn out something new.

Jackson Park proper, the extreme southern part of which has been selected as the site for the World's Fair, lies about eight miles southeast of the court house, being bounded as follows: on the west by Stony Island Avenue, on the north by 56th Street, on the south by 67th Street, and on the west by the blue waters of Lake Michigan. The works incident to the preparation for the World's Fair include the excavating and dredging of the little lakes connected with Lake Michigan. The preparations for the Fair have not materially interfered with the northern portion of the park, the major portion of which is devoted to a huge play-ground which is utilized all through the summer by the devotees of tennis, base-ball, and cricket, or by the militia as a parade ground. Surrounding this open expanse of turf are beautiful wooded avenues, while on the east side is a sea wall and promenade from which a superb view may be had of the lake. Midway north and south in the park, on the very edge of the water, is a large stone pavilion, in which thousands of people may find shelter in rainy weather, and which is sometimes used for dances and other festivities during the summer months.

Visitors who desire to make a circuit of the South park system cannot do better than patronize the phaetons which start every few minutes from the northern terminus of Drexel Boulevard and make the circuit in about one hour, the charge for which is 25 cents.

It should be remembered that in case the visitor desires to make the circuit of all the parks in a day, the chain of boulevards extends completely around the city. It is impossible to lose one's way, and the merest hint at a desire for information at any point of the journey will meet with the readiest response. In addition to the parks herein described there are a number of smaller pretensions, mere breathing-places, scattered about the city, that, while not affording much opportunity for study, will, nevertheless, be found to greatly enhance the attractions of the journey. The scene in any of the great parks, particularly at night, when they are filled with pleasure-seekers, will be found to be well worth investigation. At that time there are all sorts and conditions of people to be found, all bent upon the enjoyment of the hour and determined to console themselves so far as they may for the trials and vexations of the day. The moon is shedding an indulgent light down upon the merry-makers as they stroll to and fro in laughing groups beneath the whispering trees. There is light, mirth, laughter everywhere, and the merriment of the idling wanderers is echoed from time to time by the rippling of the water as it laps upon the sandy shore. It is indeed a pleasant picture. Far away in the distance, separated by only a few miles of dusty roads, is the great city, teeming with life, turmoil, and wickedness. Here all is peace. The air is soft and balmy, the spirits of the merry-makers are at their highest without being vexed either by the recollection of the tumult of the day or care for the morrow. The benison of night, assisted by the art of mankind, is perhaps responsible for the beauty of the scene and the spirit of happiness and content that prevails. Visit any of the parks on a hot summer night for an hour or two, when all the world is devoted to calm relaxation, and see if you do not subscribe to the sentiment.

CHAPTER XVIII.

RACING.

THE national love of horseracing, which is growing in intensity year by year, finds nowhere a better ground for development than in Chicago. There are in active operation in this city during the months of summer and autumn three admirably equipped race tracks, where the fleetest horses in the world are entered in daily contests for fat purses. Attached to each are commodious betting-rings, where the spectator may indulge in any size of wager he desires, from a dollar upward. On any fine day during the summer the roads leading to the tracks are thronged with gay equipages, which add spirit to a scene always varied and beautiful. Two of these tracks are located on the West side, one at Hawthorne (Corrigan's) and the other at the western extremity of Garfield Park (the Garfield Racing Association). The other, and by far the most famous of the three, is the Washington Park Club, at the southern end of Washington Park. The Washington Park Club, under whose auspices the races there are given each year, is a somewhat aristocratic organization, composed of a number of the well-to-do citizens of Chicago. The commodious club-house occupies a commanding position to the west of the grand stand, and admission thereto is confined to members and their friends. To the grand stand and enclosure adjoining, the public is admitted at a charge of one dollar per head. The betting-ring is under the grand stand, and, from the fact that one hundred book-makers are sometimes doing business there at the same time and paying the club $100 per day apiece for the privilege, it may be inferred that the industry is highly profitable.

The races given every year at this beautiful track are famous the country over. They commence early in the month of June with the American Derby, a race for three-year-olds, for which a stake of over $20,000 in value is annually hung up. Derby day is one of the events of the year in Chicago. Every vehicle capable of transporting two or more people to the pleasure ground is bespoken for weeks beforehand. Along Michigan Avenue the gay cavalcade goes — tally-hos with their freight of gallant knights and ladies fair; wagonettes, dog-carts, man phaetons, with their clanking chains and glossy steeds; tandems, cocking-carts — the new fashionable vehicle drawn by three horses abreast — down to the simplest and most democratic of conveyances. Away they go, and every window along the route contains its group of people who, while not going to the Derby themselves, intend to see the best part of the show. For hours the procession continues, the vehicles turning from Michigan Avenue into the boulevards and then winding into the parks, to emerge presently at the great gateway of the tracks and unload their pleasure-seeking occupants.

The scene when the bell is rung for the great race is one which impresses itself on the mind beyond all possibility of effacement. Spectators are packed in the paddock like sardines in a box. The grand stand is a solid mass of men and women, the toilets of the latter presenting a brilliant picture in the gorgeous sunlight. In the centre of the great in-field, as it is called, jockeys and stable boys are walking about, and scattered here and there are some of the noble brutes that are to take part in the day's contest. The horses convene on the track and a buzz sweeps over the vast assemblage as they go cantering to the post. A few minutes of suspense and then — "They're off!" cries the crowd, and past the grand stand they sweep like a splendid troop of cavalry, the jockeys sitting like statues on the struggling beasts, each one of which is animated by an almost human determination to conquer in the struggle. A moment more and it is over, and a roar goes up as the winner sweeps past the judge's stand. The great Derby has been lost for some and won by others. After the subsequent and lesser races are over the cavalcade sweeps back to the city again, the winners shouting and singing for joy and the losers solemn in their silence.

The Washington Park meeting lasts till the latter part of July. The present officers of the club are as follows: President, George Henry Wheeler; vice-presidents, Samuel W. Allerton, Albert S. Gage, H. I. McFarland, Charles Schwartz; treasurer, John R. Walsh; secretary, John E. Brewster; assistant secretary, James Howard; directors, N. K. Fairbank, Norman B. Ream, Samuel W. Allerton, James W. Oakley, Columbus R. Cummings, Charles I. Barnes, John R. Walsh, Henry Norton, A. S. Gage, S. H. Sweet, G. H. Wheeler, Thomas Murdock, H. J. McFarland, C. J. Singer, and others.

The Garfield Park and Corrigan tracks commence operation at the close of the Washington Park meeting. The gatherings at these tracks are by no means so aristocratic, but the purses offered are rich and the racing is of the first quality.

The betting facilities are ample. For a while the admission to the Corrigan track was free, but it is a question whether the practice will be followed in future.

At present Chicago is one of the liveliest racing centers in the country during the season, and the visitor who desires to see a little of this exciting sport will find the amplest facilities at his command for so doing.

CHAPTER XIX.

OPEN-AIR ENTERTAINMENTS.

THE HUCKSTER.

UNDER this head come the open-air shows of different dimensions, one or more of which are always running in Chicago during the summer months. Last year Thearle & Cooper gave the public a treat with an entertainment that they styled "A Night in Pekin." The location was the great vacant lot at the southern limit of Washington Park, across the street from the race-track of that name. Tiers upon tiers of seats accommodated thousands of spectators, who watched the drama, enacted in pantomime, of the destruction of the city of Pekin by the British naval forces. The work of desolation was preceded by games, slack-wire walking, and other interesting feats. The bombardment itself was a magnificent spectacle. As the big buildings came toppling down in ruins and the inhabitants rushed screaming about, showers upon showers of fire-works were discharged and the roaring of the great guns kept up until the work of demolition was over. It was conceded at the time that the spectacle, from a pyrotechnical standpoint, was the finest ever seen in Chicago, but from all accounts the shows to be given this year and next will eclipse it. For the World's Fair year the Kiralfys, those consummate masters of the spectacular, have promised a production on the same order as the "Night in Pekin" that shall totally eclipse anything in the line of an open-air show ever before seen or heard of. Its exact nature has not yet been outlined, but if all the promises are kept, it will be something very wonderful.

The attractions of this sort of an entertainment are manifold. Aside from the show itself, which is always interesting, there is the pleasant, happy-go-lucky spirit that always pervades great crowds bent on an evening's fun. The peanut and lemonade venders ply their calling briskly and come in for the usual share of "guying" that such merchants always excite. In hot weather the outdoor spectacles detract from the attendance at the theatres, people preferring to secure their entertainment in the open air if possible. Spectacles like "Pekin," it is perhaps unnecessary to say, cost many thousands of dollars to produce.

THE CIRCUS SPRITE.

Speaking of the peanut and lemonade men reminds one that the two great circuses, Barnum & Bailey's and Forepaugh's, exhibit in Chicago every summer. They generally appear for two weeks each, and of course parade in due form, according to custom, through the streets of the city on the opening day. Who shall picture the delights of the circus? Are they not as old as the memory of man? Strange but true it is, that the older we get, the circus that we remember as the circus of our youth strengthens its charm upon our memory, and we would not miss a sight of it if we could. We have the added pleasure of taking our little ones to see the sights that so delighted us in our own childhood, and that should be the keenest pleasure of all.

A summer rarely passes without a succession of smaller shows in the open air, such as balloon ascensions, bicycle races, cricket and base-ball matches, and so on. There is a resort known as Cheltenham Beach, a strip of sand twelve miles from the City Hall, reached by the Illinois Central railway and known as "The Coney Island of the West," although it has never touched the real Coney Island in point of prosperity. At Cheltenham Beach there is always a show of some sort going on. It may be athletics. It may be a broad-sword combat between mounted gladiators. It may be an ascent by a parachute artist, a nervy gentleman who soars a thousand feet in the air in a balloon and then descends gracefully to the earth (at the imminent and exhilarating risk of his neck) under a parachute to which he clings by a thin trapeze bar. This is a hair-raising exhibition frequently seen and quite often ending in the maiming for life of the hardy serial navigator. At Cheltenham Beach, however, everything "goes," as it were, and nobody ever complains unless it is on account of the small amount of beer doled out for the conventional nickel. Occasionally they have barbecues and clam-bakes at Cheltenham Beach, which, though at times enjoyable, are not exactly the class of entertainment to which one would invite the ladies of his family.

There are always vast crowds of people in Chicago athirst for amusement. That is why amusement caterers grow so rich when they give good shows. It has been the purpose of the present chapter to show that there is plenty of amusement to be found out-of-doors.

CHAPTER XX.

AN IDEAL AFTERNOON.

THE charms of Chicago as a summer resort have been sung ever since one can remember. No matter how sultry the atmosphere in the down-town district, there is generally a cool breeze from the lake to temper the fierceness of the sun if one can only get where it is blowing. It is the purpose of the present chapter to describe how a simply ideal afternoon may be spent, provided the weather is suitable, by a drive along the north shore, taking in two well-known summer resorts in the journey.

About three in the afternoon is a good time to start. By that time the sun has moved well around toward the western heavens and the extremity of its fierceness has departed. Let it be understood for the sake of illustration that the traveler has secured a companion for the journey — for who likes to go driving alone, I should like to know? — and this makes him seem so much the better natured when he asks the hotel clerk to procure him from some first-class livery stable the particular sort of a rig he may fancy. It may be either a modest one-horse buggy, a high-wheeled cart (if it is desired to make an attempt at style), a mail-phaeton with a spanking team, or any one of half a dozen other styles of conveyance to be had at short notice. It may even happen that he has secured a lady companion for the trip, and if so, the lucky dog is to be envied, eh? Who does not know how much more pleasure is attached to the task of holding the ribbons when one's left elbow is continually jolting against the shoulder of a pretty woman at one's side.

The start is made in due season. The pace is necessarily careful up Michigan Avenue and on to the big Rush Street bridge (we are to have a mammoth viaduct hereabouts some day, so "they say") but once on the North side the gait may be accelerated to a slashing trot, the smart pace of which will lend an added color to the cheek of the charmer at your elbow — always supposing the companion to be feminine. Turning into Dearborn Avenue at Ohio Street the smooth asphalt pave is encountered on which the hoofs of the spirited animals sound smartly. It is only a few minutes until North Avenue is passed and Lincoln Park reached, upon which we swerve gently to the right, pass around the curves by Mr. Yerkes' great electric fountain, and the Lake Shore Drive (referred to in a previous chapter) is reached. Hence and away there stretches a wide and smooth expanse of roadway two full miles straight to the northward. The blue waters of the lake are dancing and sparkling in the sunlight. The refreshing breeze is coming straight from the east and rustling the green foliage of the trees on the left. Is it any wonder that the blood flows quicker through the veins and that the tug of the horses at the bits produces an exhilaration that leads to a desire for increased speed? Even the beasts feel the spirit of the thing and dash ahead buoyantly over the broad roadway.

A Summer Concert Garden.

Other vehicles swarm over the pleasure course — heavy family carriages, in which fat dowagers are taking an airing; dog carts driven tandem by smart young men whose fathers have big bank accounts, and here and there an actual exercising cart with a blooded trotter between the shafts — it all makes up a gay panorama, and the probabilities are that if you are human, you will let out a link in the lines and indulge in a wee bit of a race just to see if the horseflesh you are in charge of is not just a little better than the next man's. This will go all right until the mounted park policeman motions you to moderate your pace. His mandate must be obeyed or an arrest and fine will be the result. The policemen are sometimes conveniently blind, however, and sometimes enjoy a bit of a brush as much as anybody, but really furious driving is against the law and will not be tolerated.

But the two miles have been passed by this time, and Diversey Street and the northern limit of the park is reached. A few yards further and it is time to stop, for we have reached the great gateway of the famous summer garden, formerly known as "Fischer's," but which is now conducted by a gentleman of another name. No matter what the name is; it is still Fischer's just the same. Driving through the gates into the grounds a servant takes charge of the team, leaving you at liberty to stroll down to the covered pavilion which abuts on the very edge of the lake and sit and drink in the cooling breeze to your heart's content. There are other refreshments that you may indulge in if you choose, but it is generally conceded that the breeze alone is worth the price of admission.

Fischer's is an established North side resort. Besides being a favorite objective point for a drive it is also pleasantly accessible by water. There is a landing for boats, many of which arrive there during the afternoon and evening hours, freighted with many young folks who laugh and sing gaily as they come skimming over the water to the common haven. On certain evenings during the summer, generally three in each week, Professor Rosenbecker's orchestra (see Sunday concerts) gives a concert at the garden, and then is the time to see whole bevies of pretty girls and women, decked out in all the attractive bravery of summer attire, sipping sherbet or lemonade in the moonlight and contributing their quota of charm to a scene as picturesque and brilliant as any to be found in the West.

The stop at Fischer's, however, is merely for a brief rest and change of scene; with the team freshly rubbed down we may start on the drive to Sunnyside. A quarter of a mile north of Fischer's we turn west to Evanston Avenue and speed through the pretty suburb of Lake View. The branches of the trees at the side of the road will brush our hats off as we go by if we don't look out. But the horses spin onward, past neat villas, with their snow-white barns in the rear — pictures of comfort; past smoothly shaven lawns, upon which young people of both sexes are engaged in rattling games of tennis; past lissome beauties who look coyly up from the hammocks in which they are indolently reclining; past all manner of interesting objects, each of which lend their separate and special charm to the journey. We are skimming through Edgewater presently — nicknamed by the irreverent "the dude town," by reason of its being so very spick and span. Then a sharp turn to the left and a long stretch of highway, lined on one side by pretty trees. It begins to look like the country at last, for here are some fields in which thrifty husbandmen and their wives are at work. A rattle and a thud as we cross the railroad tracks, the dust flying from the hoofs of our nimble steeds.

One more sharp turn, a start into a private driveway, and here we are at our destination — Sunnyside.

One reason, perhaps, why the summer hotel — roadhouse, some people call it — named Sunnyside is so popular is that it is just within comfortable driving distance of the city. An hour and a half, or two hours (counting for the customary stop at Fischer's) is the time allowed for the journey. The hotel itself, kept by the Dowling family for years, is a great rambling old wooden building standing in the midst of spacious grounds. A peculiarity of the place is the beautiful independence of the proprietors, an independence that manifests itself in their refusal to cater to the whims of guests. A supper bill of fare is arranged by them. Supper costs one dollar per person served. No orders for special dishes are taken. You can take what is there or go without it. But no one was ever heard to complain of the fare. There is beef-steak, from the loins of fat cattle slaughtered by old man Dowling himself. In addition, maybe, there is a plump chicken raised in old lady Dowling's own poultry yard and whose neck was blithely wrung by her own fair hand that very morning. There is green corn and ripe tomatoes and young onions and other delicacies all raised on the Dowling demesne, and all included in the dollar. If there has been no joke about it and you really are accompanied by the charming damsel I have hinted at, the meal is doubtless all the more enjoyable. Having youth and good appetite, sharpened by the ride, you can do justice to the homely and honest fare. You may have a little private dining-room all to your two selves, bless your dear hearts, and every two minutes or so Mother Dowling will come bustling into the room, eager to see if you are satisfied with the service and anxious to supply any deficiencies. She is a sweet old dame, and if by the merest chance she should catch you in the very act of conveying to your inamorata an idea of the high estimation in which you hold her — if, indeed, she should detect your face in too close proximity to your inamorata's face, her joyous laugh, strident and cracked though it may be under the stress of the many years that have rolled over her head, will echo uncannily through the corridors, awakening all the echoes and making you wonder if your fair companion will look as well as she does when she is as old.

Dear old Lady Dowling! Venerable high priestess of the quaint old sanctuary of Sunnyside! Many a time and oft, as the writer has heard some merry party of noisy but honest fellows, of whom, alas! he was one, roll out the rare old drinking chorus:

"Then here's to Mrs. Dowling,
Drink her down! Drink her down!"

has he marvelled at the fewness of the wrinkles upon thy brow — considering all that thou hast passed through in thy progress through this earthly vale of tears.

The repast concluded, an adjournment to the wide verandah is in order, there to enjoy a peaceful smoke and ruminate upon the experiences of the hour. There may be at the other end of the verandah a party of frolicsome youths who have driven out on a six-horse tally-ho and who have brought their mandolins and guitars along. Their songs and laughter fall pleasantly upon the balmy air. If the songs and laughter grow wearisome, you may wander among the trees and shrubbery — and, always supposing that fair feminine companion a pleasant possibility — who may picture the enjoyment of such a stroll? The sly old moon, always indulgent enough toward lovers to shrink gracefully behind a cloud at the critical moment, smiles down a jocund benediction upon the scene, and it is all too soon that one is reminded of the flight of time and that the proprieties demand a return to town.

Within three minutes of signifying a wish to that effect, the conveyance is brought to the front door by a cheery hostler, who gracefully accepts from you the small douceur that you may give him, and which is the only charge — even that being voluntary — that is made for the entertainment of your team. A chirrup to the horses and off you go, the frolicsome youths upon the verandah lifting their hats and gratuitously wishing you a pleasant voyage home as you speed away.

The drive back? Well, the pleasure thereof always depends upon circumstances. If that pleasant possibility before hinted at is an actuality — why, what is the use of picturing it? Have we not all, as it were, been there before? But the whispering breeze, the ceaseless murmur of the wavelets on the shore, and the same old moon smiling so persistently and blandly form delicious adjuncts to an experience that once enjoyed will not soon be forgotten. The spirited horses still tug lustily at the lines, but they are homeward bound and you can afford them a little latitude if the supposititious companion seems to demand a little more of your attention than she did on the outward journey.

Pshaw! What does it all matter? It is only a few hours of pleasure, after all; yet I think you will confess to me, as your horses trot back over the Rush Street bridge, that it has been an ideal afternoon.

CHAPTER XXI.

ON THE WATER.

THE part Lake Michigan will play in the transportation of people to and from the World's Fair Grounds has not at this writing (May, 1892) been definitely determined upon. It is beyond question, however, that some proper arrangement in this direction will have been made long before the Fair opens, for it would seem highly impossible that the great facilities for water transportation should not be properly utilized.

For some reason or other aquatic sports and pleasures have not flourished in Chicago as they should, considering the immense advantages in that direction that are lying, as it were, at our very doors. Some people attribute the small interest of the average Chicagoan in aquatics to the unstable character of the great sheet of water known as Lake Michigan — an unstability which is shown sometimes in the quick gathering of storms. The lake may be shining like a sheet of glass one hour and in the next heaving tumultuously under the influence of a squall. This sort of thing puts a check on

the ambition for boating to some extent but is hardly a sufficient reason why the sport of yachting — one of the grandest
of all sports — should not flourish. The yachtsmen of New
York, Chicago amateur mariners are fond of arguing, have
infinitely greater risks to run in New York bay than we have
in our harbor and lake, but yacht clubs flourish there, and in
fact in all the cities on the Atlantic coast, while in Chicago the
enjoyment of this royal sport is confined to a few enthusiasts
who vainly endeavor to enlist the sympathies of the multi-
tude in the pastime they find so delightful.

There are few sailing yachts in commission nowaday, but
there are several yacht clubs, and the time may come when
the sport will be properly revived and encouraged. The Chicago Yacht Club, whose office is at 655 Rookery building, has
many members. Its officers are A. T. Fisher, commodore;
Harry Duvall, secretary; J. W. S. Brawley, treasurer. The President of the Countess Yacht Club is Mr. Sidney W. Wood-
bury, and the treasurer, E. W. Herrick. The Countess Yacht
Club derives its title from the somewhat celebrated craft of
that name. The *Countess* is a magnificent sloop, and the club
is composed of the gentlemen who own her and take their
enjoyment on board of her. The *Countess* was built in Canada
and named originally the *Countess of Dufferin*, in honor of the
wife of the then Governor-General of the Dominion, the Earl
of Dufferin. She was built to contest for the American cup
but did not succeed. The name was changed to the *Countess*
when she was brought to Chicago. The *Countess* may be seen
any bright summer day gallantly riding the waters of the bay
opposite Lake Front Park. It is an enthusing sight to see her
starting bravely out into the lake with all her canvas set, heel-
ing gracefully on in deference to the breeze. Dozens of smaller but none the less ambitious craft swarm about her and

endeavor to keep the pace, their snow-white sails showing prettily against the blue sky. But the *Countess* is too speedy for them and out-fools them all.

Perhaps the most active yachting organization in Chicago is the Lincoln Park Yacht Club, organized two years ago. Its list of officers is as follows: Commodore, James J. Wilson; vice commodore, S. S. Johnson; rear-commodore, A. E. Back; treasurer, H. A. Paus; secretary, C. O. Andrews. This club possesses an advantage inasmuch as the vessels of its members find a safe haven and anchorage in the new slip, protected by a break-water, at Lincoln Park, which has been constructed especially for regattas. From ten to fifteen yachts find shelter here, and some splendid yacht races may be witnessed during the summer over what is termed the Lincoln Park course, extending some five miles out into the lake. The race is always made outward and return, and the spectacle is beautiful to witness when half a dozen of the fleet craft are speeding over the waves in the contest for supremacy. The yacht races during the summer naturally heighten the attraction of this most popular of all the parks.

There are many boat clubs. The Catlin Boat Club has a clubhouse at the foot of Pearson Street, on the North Side. The Ogden Boat Club's house is at the foot of Superior Street, half a mile further south. The Farragut Boat Club is the most pretentious of all, however, possessing as it does, in addition to its boathouse at the foot of Thirty-third Street, a handsome clubhouse on Lake Avenue, just below Thirty-first Street, which is the scene of many noteworthy social events. The clubhouse contains, in addition to its comfortable parlors and reception rooms, a bowling alley, poolroom and lavatories, while the upper story is devoted to a dancing hall and theatre with a seating capacity of 400.

So much for the private aquatic organizations. While a visitor with influential friends finds no difficulty in securing an introduction to any of them, and a consequent temporary share in their privileges, they are, of course, more or less exclusive, and the reader's interest will naturally go to such provisions as are made for the enjoyment and entertainment of the stranger and the unknown.

Down on the Lake Front, just across the Illinois Central tracks, will be found from ten to fifteen pretty yachts, owned by their captains, who will take a party out for an hour's sail at the rate of 25 cents per hour. In case there are only two of you the charge will be a dollar, the owners never moving out for less than that sum. These crafts are sound and seaworthy and in the charge of old sailors whose skill and nerve are to be trusted and relied upon in any sort of weather. It is a most delightful manner of spending an hour. When the heat in the city is stifling and not a breath of air is stirring, try the experiment of a spin over the blue waters and see how refreshing is the breeze that is invariably blowing briskly over on the Michigan shore. There is not even time to get sea-sick, no matter how violent the motion of the staunch little vessel, yet if any of the passengers should feel squeamish, the captain is only too ready to put about and return home.

If the pleasure-seeker prefers steam to canvas as a motive power, he can take his choice between a trip to the government pier or waterworks crib, and a longer sail to Jackson or Lincoln Park. The fare to the pier and back is ten cents; the round trip to and from the crib or either of the parks is 25 cents. There are several more pretentious vessels that go out at night for moonlight excursions on the lake. They start both from the Lake Front and from the river, in the latter case generally at the Clark Street bridge. They always secure a large patronage, and there is generally a good time enjoyed by those who make up such excursions. The decks are crowded with pretty girls and their escorts, it somehow generally happening that the girls outnumber the boys, and, as a dance is always begun the minute the vessel is well out in the lake, the pair of strangers who have resolved to try this manner of spending the evening are apt to find their company very much in request. The advent of another year will probably see a large increase in the number of excursion steamers, and during the Fair the lake will doubtless

MUSIC HATH CHARMS.

be drawn upon to its fullest extent as a source of pleasure for the visiting throng.

All the foregoing applies to short trips. There are steamship lines whose vessels make very extended journeys.

It not infrequently happens that visitors take advantage of the excellent opportunities afforded and make one or two voyages that they remember with pleasure long after their return to their homes in the country. The Graham & Morton Transportation Company's steamers leave from the dock at the foot of Wabash Avenue for St. Joseph and Benton Harbor daily, at 9:30 in the morning and 11 o'clock at night, arriving at St. Joseph 1:30 P.M. and 3 in the morning. On Sunday one trip is made, leaving at 10 A.M. and arriving at 2 o'clock. The fare for a single trip is $1 but the round trip can be made for that price if the passengers return the same day. The fine side-wheel steamer *City of Chicago,* one of the handsomest on the lakes, is the star of this line. The Sunday excursion on this ship costs $1.50. The voyage is directly across the lake, about 40 miles, and is made on schedule time in good weather; adverse winds and waves are apt to cause a little delay.

The Goodrich line, however, is the leading line of lake steamers as well as the oldest. The company's dock is at the foot of Michigan Avenue. The steamers ply between Chicago and all ports on Lake Michigan, such as Racine, Milwaukee, Sturgeon Bay, Menominee, Grand Haven, Muskegon, Green Bay, and Manistique. The trip to Muskegon, which takes one night, is especially enjoyable, and many people indulge in it for the purpose of seeing the greatest lumber town in the world, which distinction Muskegon enjoys; the night trip to Milwaukee is also a favorite, especially in hot weather. Milwaukee, as is ever known, is a sort of Gretna Green for youthful and impressionable Chicago couples, who are in the habit of eloping to that happy haven, getting safely married, and then returning on the next boat to seek the parental forgiveness which is almost invariably bestowed if they wait long enough. The Saturday night boat rarely starts in the summer months without at least one such eloping couple on board.

Some of the Goodrich line vessels will bear comparison with the finest ocean steamers. The dimensions of the *Virginia,* for instance, are as follows: 278 feet over all, 260 feet keel, 38 feet beam, and 25 feet deep. The hull is divided into six water-tight compartments, so constructed that if the vessel were cut squarely in two halves, it would float. The interior decorations and equipments are of the most magnificent description. No one should fail to at least inspect this, by all odds the finest vessel that floats the lakes. Other fine vessels of this line are the *Indiana, City of Racine,* and *Menominee.*

The steamers of the Lake Michigan & Lake Superior Transportation Company, which are all elegantly appointed, carry passengers between Chicago and Duluth, at the head of Lake Superior. These staunch steamers leave Chicago Wednesday and Saturday evenings, leaving the dock at Rush Street bridge at 8:30, and call at Mackinac, Sault Ste. Marie, Marquette, and all Lake Superior ports. The passenger traffic on this line during the summer is enormous and increases constantly with the fame of the northern summer resorts, which are yearly growing more popular.

The pleasure-seeker is hardly likely to be interested in the commercial side of the Chicago lake marine. The story of its magnitude, however, may be told in one brief paragraph:

The daily arrivals and clearances at Chicago exceed those of New York by fifty per cent, being nearly as numerous as those of Baltimore, Boston, and New York combined. Figures talk, and these are the figures that Chicago modestly presents to the observation of the wondering stranger.

CHAPTER XXII.

THE RESTAURANTS OF CHICAGO.

THE WAITER.

In response to the question, "Where shall we eat?" one might say: "You pay your money and you take your choice." There are more than six hundred restaurants in Chicago, and you will admit that the declaration is not imperfect. That is to say, there are over six hundred now, but at the present ratio of increase there will doubtless be a thousand or more a year hence. It eventually follows that these restaurants are of all grades. There are places where you can get a meal for ten cents; others where no single dish costs less than 50 cents to $1.00. All the leading hotels — the Richelieu, Auditorium, Victoria, Wellington, and Palmer, as well as the family hotels, like the Metropole and Virginia, have restaurants or *cafes* (that is the fashionable term) attached, where the service is very elegant and the price pitched in a corresponding altitude. Cheap restaurants are to be found in every quarter of the city. There is scarcely a block without one, but the downtown trade is monopolized by a few large and well established institutions that serve all sorts of meals at moderate prices.

Kinsley's, No. 105 Adams Street, is a place which caters to all classes. On the ground floor is a lunch-room or restaurant in which a good meal may be purchased for twenty-five to fifty cents. On the next story are two fine *cafes*, one for the exclusive use of gentlemen and the other for ladies, or ladies with escorts, in which the service and prices are on the same grade as the hotel *cafes*. Other floors are devoted to private dining-rooms of all sizes. There is also a banquet and ball-room, which is at the service of large parties.

Other large restaurants, where good, plain food only is served at moderate prices, are Thomson's, 143 and 145 Dearborn Street; Saratoga, 155 and 157 the same street; Central, on Randolph Street near State; and Tacoma, northwest corner Madison and La Salle Streets.

The oyster houses of Chicago form a special feature in themselves. There are four of this class. The Boston Oyster House, Clark and Madison Streets; Chicago Oyster House, Madison Street between Clark and La Salle; the Lakeside, Clark and Adams; Rector's, Clark and Monroe. Three of these serve all kinds of meats when desired, as well as fish of every variety, but Rector's is an oyster house pure and simple, where only fish and game are served. Rector's is a favorite resort after the theatre. From eleven o'clock to midnight it is crowded with people of all classes, with a very strong sprinkling of the sporting and professional element. There are pretty actresses galore, some of whom are attended by their hard-working husbands who have places in the same company with them; others by young men of means who enjoy the prestige of having been acquainted in that particular sort of social worldliness. It is a gay scene in any event, and the fun is often kept up until long after midnight.

There are at least three places that make a specialty of catering to patrons who desire the seclusion of private dining-rooms. These are Lassagne's, on South Clark Street, opposite the court house; Weber's; and the Vendome, State Street, between Madison and Monroe. Lassagne's, as the name would indicate, is kept by a Frenchman, and the cooking and service are essentially French. The service at Weber's

A PETIT SOUPER.

and the Vendome is similar in almost every respect.

The prices charged at these places are not at all exorbitant, and a private dining room is always in great demand with affectionate couples who desire a tempting tete-a-tete meal that would not be nearly so enjoyable if it lacked the charm of privacy and the opportunities for the display of sentiment which such privacy permits. These dining-rooms are small apartments, neatly partitioned off and graded in sizes to suit parties of from two to twenty. That these are liberally patronized may be inferred from the merry bursts of laughter that are occasionally heard pealing through the carpeted halls as the busy waiters go scurrying to and fro with their piles of well filled dishes. It has been said that it is from the sale of wines that the proprietors are enabled to maintain these private-dining-rooms, consequently it is the proper caper to wash down the very reasonably priced dinner with a bottle or so of one's favorite style of grape juice if the person can afford it, and if you can't, why, you have no business there.

The *table d'hote* has become quite an institution in Chicago within the past two or three years. It is presumed that every reader of this book knows what the term signifies, but it will do no harm to explain it. The term is a French one, signifying "the hotel table." The *table d'hote*, then, is a course dinner, given at a fixed price, upon payment of which the patron is entitled, if he wishes for it, to a taste of every dish mentioned on the printed bill of fare. To so grade the courses of a big dinner as to pamper the appetite and leave, with the consumption of each course, a desire for the appearance of the next, is a splendid art, second to none in the opinion of some people, and at least one *table d'hote* in Chicago comes very close to perfection. This is the *table d'hote* inaugurated by Mr. Leland and since maintained by the purchasers of the hotel of that name. The price of this dinner is $1.00, and in addition to the twelve courses of eatables each person is entitled to a bottle of excellent red or white wine. An orchestra stationed somewhere discourses sweet music during the meal, which is served from 5:30 to 8:00 P.M. A very similar *table d'hote*, but without wine, is served at the Palmer House at the same price. A most excellent dinner may be had at a little French restaurant on Monroe Street, one door west of the Columbia theatre, for seventy-five cents.

In one respect the *table d'hote* is a most excellent arrangement. Considering the lavishness of the spread, a dollar is a very reasonable price; the same dinner could not be purchased in a first-class restaurant *a la carte* for less than five or six dollars, if not more. If a party of four or six people want to enjoy a jolly dinner at a reasonable price, amid pleasant surroundings, they should patronize the *table d'hote*, always supposing they have plenty of time. The dinner takes an hour to serve comfortably. Those who are rushed for time should go elsewhere.

A chapter on restaurants would be incomplete without a reference to the innumerable boarding-houses of Chicago. For a person who contemplates a more or less extended stay, a boarding-house is perhaps the best place to go. It is certainly much more economical than living at a first-class hotel. Excellent accommodations in boarding-houses in the best parts of the residence districts may be secured at rates varying from $4 to $10 per week, room and board. No need to describe the location of boarding houses. A glance at the advertising columns of the daily newspapers will show you a quick route to hundreds of such. If it is not desired to go to the trouble of selecting a boarding place for yourself, call at any of the many agencies — all of which print cards in the "Board Wanted" columns of the Sunday papers — and tell the people there exactly what you want. In nine cases out of ten they will send you to a place which will be found suitable. There is no charge for this service. The usual way is to charge the applicant a dollar, which sum is deducted from the bill at the establishment he may select from the list furnished by the agency.

CHAPTER XXIII.

THE HAYMARKET MONUMENT.

THE statue which stands in the Haymarket, the broad square on Randolph Street extending from Desplaines to Halsted, commemorates an event only second in importance in Chicago's history to the great fire of 1871. It stands as a mark of that awful night, May 4, 1886, when the mouthings of the anarchists culminated in the hurling of a bomb — the only bomb ever thrown in America — into a squad of police, of whom seven were killed and sixty-six laid low with awful wounds.

While looking at this monument, the figure of a policeman in heroic size, the visitor may, if he chooses, try to imagine that scene, when Desplaines Street bore the appearance of a battlefield, and the station house nearby, whither the dead and wounded were carried, that of a hospital. Think over it all, as you gaze at the monument, and try to realize the importance of the bloody epoch which it typifies.

May day of that year had been fixed upon as the proper time to inaugurate the eight hour movement. Prior to that date the anarchists had become thoroughly organized. They held meetings every Sunday afternoon on the Lake Front, when their leaders made fiery speeches, advocating the murder of capitalists and the destruction of property. On the first of May, strike after strike occurred in quick succession. Within two days there were thousands of unemployed workmen in the streets; the anarchist leaders did all they could to foster a spirit of mischief and incite the strikers to deeds of violence. The Haymarket riot itself originated in the great strike at the McCormick Reaper works, which transpired February 11, the strikers' places being filled by non-union men. Police were put on guard at the works, and such anarchist leaders as August Spies, Albert Parsons, Henry Fielden, and Michael Schwab improved the opportunity to further excite disturbance and disorder and to increase the hatred of the mob for the police. On the evening of April 28, 1885, the new Board of Trade building was opened and a swarm of anarchists, both men and women, marched to the building, waving red flags and breathing death and destruction to the "aristocrats," as they called them. It was a strange scene. Inside the glittering building there were fair women, in dazzling toilets and decked with gems, who shuddered as they gazed through the windows at the menacing populace without — the same class of misguided beings who turned Paris into a Hell during the revolution. The police drove the mob away. The raving hordes dispersed, uttering curses and threats as they went. This incident is related merely to show the spirit which prevailed among the anarchists prior to the deadly deed of the following year.

It was Monday, May 3, when the riot at McCormick's occurred. As the workmen left the building they were attacked by a great army of men and women. The police were called and a battle, or rather a series of battles, resulted, in which knives, sticks, stones, and pistols were used. The police were fired upon repeatedly by the mob and promptly returned the fusillade. In all, six rioters were killed or injured, and several police officers were wounded. One officer narrowly escaped being lynched and succeeded in breaking away from his captors as they were about to string him up to a lamp-post, to which a rope had already been attached. Immediately after this bloody affair the famous "Revenge" circular was distributed — an incendiary document written by August Spies and supposed to have been the principal cause of the bomb-throwing. As a historical document it is worth quoting:

Revenge! Workingmen, to arms! Your masters sent out their blood-hounds, the police. They killed six of your brothers at McCormick's this afternoon; they killed the poor wretches because they had the courage to disobey the supreme will of your bosses; they killed them because they dared to ask for the shortening of the hours of toil; they killed them to show you, free American citizens, that you must be satisfied and contented with whatever your bosses condescend to allow you or you will get killed. You have for years suffered unmeasurable iniquities; you have worked yourselves to death; you have endured the pangs of want and hunger; your children have been sacrificed to the factory lords — in short, you have been miserable and obedient slaves all these years. Why? To satisfy the insatiable greed, to fill the coffers of your lazy, thieving masters. When you ask them now to lessen the burden they send their bloodhounds out to shoot you — kill you. If you are men, if you are the sons of your grandsires, who have shed their blood to free you, then you will rise in your might, Herculean, and destroy the hideous monster that seeks to destroy you! To arms! We call you to arms!

YOUR BROTHERS.

Events followed fast upon the issue of this circular. A number of minor conflicts occurred, and then the *Arbeiter Zeitung,* of which Spies was editor, called the Haymarket meeting in the following notice:

ATTENTION, WORKINGMEN! Great mass meeting tonight, at 7:30 o'clock, at the Haymarket, Randolph Street, between Desplaines and Halsted. Good speakers will be present to denounce the latest atrocious acts of the police — the shooting of your fellow workmen yesterday afternoon.

THE EXECUTIVE COMMITTEE.

The hour came. The Haymarket Square and Desplaines Street were crowded. From the top of a wagon, Parsons, Schwab, and Spies made inflammatory speeches. Fielden was in the midst of his when a platoon of police, over a hundred in number, appeared, headed by Captain Ward and Inspector Bonfield. Ward commanded the people to disperse, and at that instant the bomb was thrown. It sputtered through the air like a comet and fell with an awful roar in the ranks of the police, exploding with deadly effect. Without wavering an instant,

THE HAYMARKET MONUMENT.

the surviving officers poured a volley of pistol shots into the mob. For several minutes the battle raged. When it was over, the ground was littered with the dead and dying. The wounded were taken to the Desplaines Street station.

The ringleaders were arrested the following day. Schnaubelt, the man who threw the bomb, was arrested but released by some mistake and disappeared as completely as if the earth had swallowed him.

Spies, Engel, Parson, Fielden, Fischer, Schwab, Lingg, and Neebe were tried for conspiracy to murder. The trial was the most sensational in Chicago's history and lasted thirty-six days. Neebe was sent to the penitentiary; all the others were sentenced to death. All the men made long speeches in court, protesting against the sentence, but its justice was affirmed by the Supreme Courts of Illinois and of the United States. The execution was fixed for November 11, 1887. A petition asking for clemency was sent to Richard J. Oglesby, then Governor of the State. The sentences of Fielden and Schwab were commuted to life-imprisonment. The day before that set for the execution, Lingg, who was the most ferocious anarchist of all, committed suicide in a horrible manner. He placed a fulminating cartridge in his mouth, cigar-fashion, lighted the fuse, and calmly waited until the thing exploded and blew off his head. The four others, Spies, Parson, Engel, and Fischer, was executed a few minutes before noon the following day.

The writer of these lines saw these men die, being seated just below the scaffold, with a complete view of the proceeding. The assertion may be ventured, that every witness of that awful event was impressed by the bravery with which the doomed four met their fate. They had lived misguided lives and died ignominious deaths, but there was not a coward among them. When they perished, the anarchists of Chicago ceased to exist as a political power. Their party, which suffered a staggering blow by reason of the event of the preceding year, was obliterated, effaced by the tragedy on the scaffold which vindicated the righteous power of law and order. The anarchists of Europe no longer look to this country as a pleasant or profitable ground for the dissemination of their doctrines.

When you gaze upon the Haymarket monument you may ponder on these things. That simple figure typifies the rise and fall of anarchism in Chicago — one of the most thrilling periods in all its history.

CHAPTER XXIV.

"CHEYENNE."

A CHEYENNE FAIRY.

THIS is an excellent neighborhood to let alone, however curious you may be. The small section of city to which the nickname of "Cheyenne" has been given comprises the district bounded by Harrison Street on the north, Twelfth Street on the south, Dearborn Street on the east, and Fifth Avenue on the west. In this district reside more dangerous characters than there are in any other portion of the city. It might almost be called a negro colony, so many colored people reside in it; but there are also large numbers of foreigners — the scum of the large cities of Europe — who are fruit-peddlers and organ-grinders by day and by night — heaven only knows what! They herd together like animals, twenty families sometimes finding lodging in one tenement. It is a historical fact that the police once literally "cleaned out" a house in which sixty-one Italians were living. The sixty-one comprised several families, as many as a score of persons sleeping in one room.

So desperate are many of "Cheyenne's" known characters that no policeman who patrols a beat in that locality is permitted to do so alone. The officers move about in squads, armed to the teeth, for they never know when a gang of habitual criminals, out on a drunken frolic, may not swoop down upon them and evidence their traditional hatred for law and order by inaugurating an attack upon the officers with clubs, pistols, and knives. When an arrest is contemplated in "Cheyenne," a dozen armed officers go to the objective point in a patrol-wagon, prepared for any sort of an encounter; for it is a well-known fact that every prominent Cheyenneite has an army of followers who regard it as a point of honor to resist his arrest as bitterly as possible. The degree of importance enjoyed by the gentleman whose arrest is contemplated serves as a guide to the police authorities; if he is in any sense a leader, twenty stalwart men are none too few to be entrusted with the mission.

It is with no idea of speaking disparagingly of the fair sex that one remarks on the presence in "Cheyenne" of several dusky female characters of whom the police have a wholesome dread. Most officers would rather engage in a grapple with half a dozen male desperados than with one of those formidable negresses. They are Amazonian in physique and, being thoroughly abandoned, are ready for any hideous devilment which may or may not turn up. "Big Mag," the wickedest and most notorious character in "Cheyenne," was recently sentenced to five years at Joliet and will therefore be safely caged during the Fair. She has raised riots without number in "Cheyenne" in her time. She is nearly six feet in height, as straight as an arrow and of such marvelous strength that no officer on the force would undertake to arrest her singlehanded. She had a record with the pistol, too, and there was easier breathing at the Harrison Street Station when she went "over the road" for a comfortable five years.

As a general thing, there is not much noise or tumult in "Cheyenne" after nightfall. But its very quietude is its most deceptive feature. Woe to the guileless countryman who, having been celebrating his visit to the city not wisely but too well, ignorantly strolls into the dangerous canton. There are dark forms lurking in the alley-ways and doors, eager for prey. They carry razors as well as pistols and will stop at nothing when booty looms in sight. But there are other times, generally on holidays when some electrical spark touches "Cheyenne," and then the whole settlement goes, as it were, on a roaring tear. At such times the police are kept busy. There was one occasion — 'twas last Thanksgiving Day, if one remembers aright, when the inhabitants of "Cheyenne," male and female, turned out for a series of athletic contests. The open streets served as a race-course, and the dusky Amazons were the candidates for honors; the men preferring to stand and lay wagers on their prowess. A herculean negro lined the "mares" up for the start and sent them away to the crack of a pistol — no matter where the bullets went; such trifles are not considered in "Cheyenne" — the Amazons picking up

CHEYENNE TYPES.

their skirts and tearing down the "track" to the cheers of their applauding friends who lined the sidewalks. Between races the saloons were patronized and the termination of the sport may be imagined. So long as the Cheyenneites confined themselves to mere racing, the police did not interfere, but when the bad whisky got in its work to such an extent that fights occurred at the conclusion of every race, an army of blue-coats swooped down and made wholesale arrests. The scene which followed will never be forgotten. It is a wonder that any policeman who figured in the raid escaped alive. The mob of desperate blacks surged round the officers trying to rescue the prisoners who had been gathered in at the first rush. Pistols were drawn and many shots fired. Nobody was killed, but many heads were cracked. The affair is talked of to this day in Cheyenne, and no police officer who figured in it has any desire for a repetition of the experience.

It is just as well perhaps that so much of the dangerous element of the city should be grouped or colonized in this one spot; as the authorities know exactly where to look for it and can always be prepared to check any lawless demonstration that may emanate from it. If this locality is visited at all, it should be in broad daylight and in good company. "Cheyenne" might fitly be termed the Whitechapel of Chicago.

CHAPTER XXV.

CANDIES AND FLOWERS.

COMMUNITY's prosperity is always to be gauged by the amount of money it is able to spend on luxuries. And if candies and flowers are to be classed as luxuries, Chicago must be very prosperous indeed, for the city supports a large number of large stores that are devoted to the sale of one or both of these articles.

A high-class florist in these days simply coins money. He ought to do so with Jacquiminot and La France roses often at $12 a dozen. There are several Chicago florists who are in a fair way to become millionaires. The immediate profits of the candy business are not quite so large, perhaps, but there is less risk. Roses fade in a day and if they are not bought are a dead loss. The sweet stuff on which the young ladies of the period dote lasts a little longer and is disposed of more readily. Perhaps the best customer of the florist and the candy man alike is the susceptible youth who wishes to make the fair object of his adoration think her best of him and for that reason bestows gifts of flowers and candy upon her as long as he seems to entertain the ghost of a chance of getting any sort of return for his money. It is the proper caper, if you are an engaged man, to send your *fiancee* flowers and candy every day. This is where the profits of the purveyor of these luxuries come in, for, when a marriageable young man gets what is known as "the mitten," it stands to reason that he is very soon going to find somebody else upon whom to lavish the same gifts so fruitlessly bestowed upon the cruel one. Of course when he actually does marry, the florists and candy men may mark him off their books, for who is so foolish as to suppose a man is going to buy flowers and candy for his own wife? But, while the flower and candy men are apt to deplore marriage on this account, they find comfort in knowing that for every marriage that is taking place there are twenty young men arriving at a marriageable age and thereby taking the place of the rescued victim.

To mention all the florists of Chicago would take up too much space. There are over two hundred of them. It is the fashionable thing nowadays to join the two businesses, having flowers for sale on one side of the shop and candy on the other. This is the case with the Spencer store in the new Masonic Temple building, on State Street, at the corner of Randolph. The windows of this store are adorned with rare palms and other handsome plants that prepare one for the beauties to be found within. It is a splendid stand for a store of this character and commands a large patronage. An establishment of a very similar character, and quite as imposing, is the store of P. J. Houswirth (successor to Charles Reissig) in the Auditorium building. It is a convenient place to rush into during an operatic performance in the Auditorium and purchase a $1,000 bouquet to fling to a favorite singer. Perhaps the best-known florist in Chicago is Michael H. Gallagher, whose store is located in the Palmer House block, 163 Wabash, and whose greenhouses are at 5649 Washington Avenue. Mr Gallagher's trade is very large. "The superb floral decorations were by Gallagher," is a familiar phrase in the newspaper reports of weddings, receptions, and kindred gala events. Mr. Gallagher is said to have made a large fortune at the business. Among the other prominent down-town florists may be mentioned the following:

Joseph Craig, 84 State Street; Charles Fisk, 149 State; Joseph Curran, 242 Wabash Avenue; Walter Krintberg, 231 Wabash Avenue; J. C. Vaughan, 88 State Street (with a branch at 148 West Washington).

Coming to the consideration of candy, confectionery, and fine fruits, the name of Charles Gunther first challenges attention. The Gunther store, 212 State Street, is without doubt one of the sights of the city, containing, as it does, in addition to the regular stock-in-trade, the Gunther museum, which the proprietor has spent the best years of his life in collecting. The museum embraces curios of all sorts, and some of them are of great value. The entire collection is worth a fabulous amount, and there is a well-defined impression abroad that the owner intends to give it to the city some day.

The furnishings of the Gunther store are magnificent. Tall mirrors reflect the customer's shape at every step. The rear part of two floors is dotted with tables, at which iced drinks, ice cream, and light luncheons are served. Whether with a view of purchase or not, the store will well repay a visit. Gunther's candy is advertised the country over, and the concern enjoys an enormous out-of-town trade.

The new Berry candy store, at the north-east corner of State and Adams Streets, challenges Gunther's for brilliancy. The walls and ceilings are lined throughout with mirrors, set at all angles, and the effect at night when all the electric lamps are in full blaze is one of dazzling brillancy. The usual soda water fountain and ice cream branch is also to be found here. The store is the head-quarters of John Berry, the proprietor, who, however, has branches at 155 East Madison, and 167, 241, 581 West Madison Streets. The factory is on Washington Boulevard, corner of Sangamon Street.

Huyler's, 161 State Street, is a branch of the famous New York house of that name and enjoys a large patronage. It is a favorite resort for ladies who, tired out with shopping journeys, stand in need of a little refreshment. Plow's, in the new McVicker's theatre building, is another popular store. On matinee days especially it is crowded with purchasers. Boles & Kehoe, in Central Music Hall, claim that their candy is equal to the best, and to judge by the size of their trade the claim is well founded. The Kranz store, on the opposite side of the street, is particularly gorgeous in its furnishings, and its refreshment tables, as well as its counters, are always crowded.

There are many others that might be mentioned. The candy purveyors of Chicago number over a thousand, and no one who is in need of a package of the toothsome stuff need go away disappointed.

CHAPTER XXVI.

SUMMER NIGHT CONCERTS.

USIC hath charms to soothe the savage breast," said Shakespeare, and whether it does so or not, it soothes the ruffled feelings of the thousands who attend the summer night concerts at the new First regiment armory on Michigan Avenue near Sixteenth Street. For the last ten years the summer night concerts in this city have been given under the direction of Theodore Thomas in the old exposition building, but with the demolition of that time-honored structure Thomas has retired from the summer musical arena, leaving his baton to be wielded by Max Bendix, who for several seasons played the first violin in the Thomas orchestra. The great exposition building, dirty and weather-beaten as it was, had charms for the thousands who congregated there. It is true that the occasional weird and unearthly shriek of a locomotive on the Lake Front interfered sadly with the witching harmonies of Schumann or Gounod and even drowned, at times, the ponderous volume of Wagnerian outbursts. But it was delightfully cool and refreshing to sit among the potted shrubs with which the great hall was dotted and drink in the seductive strains simultaneously with one's Seipp or Bass and watch the never-ceasing procession of comely youths and airily clad maidens who passed to and fro.

The atmosphere surrounding the armory concerts this year is perhaps rather less democratic than that of the vanished exposition building, but the general effect is the same. The massiveness of the structure as viewed without heightens the pleasant impression received on stepping within. The polished floor is covered for the most part with long rows of neat chairs, but at each side of the big hall is a row of boxed fir-trees behind which are scattered the miniature tables at which light refreshments are served. Overhead are flags and bunting, while light is supplied by rows of big electric lamps depending from slender wires. Placed in niches at intervals along the walls are electric fans, the incessant whirling of which supplies a pleasant draught, almost a breeze, in fact, in the sultriest of weather.

As the hour arrives for the commencement of the concert, the hall fills up. The stream of amusement-seekers contains all qualities of people, from the society belles of the adjacent avenues and their escorts to the musically-inclined shop-girl from the West Side, and the plump capitalist to the thrifty book-keeper or ribbon salesman. Music is the ostensible attraction for all, but it is quite as much to chat with their friends in quiet nooks and to see what the other girls are wearing that the prettily attired belles have made their appearance. And some of the costumes are veritable dreams. The warmth of the summer season affords every opportunity for the display of fetching feminine apparel, and Solomon in all his glory was never arrayed like some of the dames who patronize the summer night concerts.

The music itself is of the very best quality. Certain nights are devoted to certain music. There are two "request" nights, when the programs are made up from the numbers patrons have asked Director Bendix to play. There are "popular" nights, when the classical idea is pushed into the background for the nonce and the simplest of compositions, the comprehension of which does not involve the knitting of one's brows and the tearing out of one's hair by the roots, played. There are two "ball-room" nights, when the best style of dance music is played. Thus all tastes are catered to and all desires satisfied. He who hankers for classical music may attend on such nights as classical music is given and stay away on others. Others may consult their tastes in the same way.

The general idea, that of supplying two hours of light entertainment each night through the hot weather season, is a most excellent one. The delicious strains discoursed by the fifty skilled musicians float through the air, sending the listener into dreamland, their soothing effect enhanced, possibly, by the magic effect of a mug of golden Bass and the clouds blown from a fragrant weed. And ever and always there is the procession of beauty, daintily clad, that pampers the eye and gives rein to pleasant imaginations. A garden of pretty girls in a setting of sweet sound — that is a good definition of the summer night concerts in Chicago.

The concerts at the armory are given under the direction of Mr. Anson Temple, the same active gentleman who manages the Schiller theatre on Randolph Street.

CHAPTER XXVII

SPECIAL FEATURES OF CHICAGO.

HERE are not a few sights worth seeing in Chicago a detailed description of which has been overlooked in the compilation of the preceding chapters. It may not be amiss to set down a few of them as briefly as may be and permit the reader to suit himself in the matter of paying them a visit of inspection or not.

First in importance of these, perhaps, is the elevated railroad, running from Congress Street to Thirty-ninth through the alley between State Street and Wabash Avenue. This is the South Side Line. The West Side, or Lake Street "L" road, is in rapid course of construction but will not be finished for some time yet. Another road, along Ogden Avenue, is also projected, and though it is reasonably certain to be built some day, its completion is too far distant to merit extended notice.

The South side "L" road commenced operations about the first of June of the present year. Its cars are well built, roomy, and well ventilated, and the run over the route to Thirty-ninth Street is made in about fourteen minutes. The road is to be extended south to the world's fair grounds in time for the opening of that great enterprise. Accustomed as Chicagoans have always been to the introduction of novelties, the sight of the elevated railroad cars skimming along on a level with the second-story windows of the houses along the route excited curiosity and interest for several weeks, and it stands to reason that strangers, while taking their first ride in the elevated cars, will experience the same pleasant emotion. On the day that the road was formally opened to travel a number of prominent citizens were invited to take the trip, and from the accounts published at the time it is to be surmised that many interesting sights were seen along the journey. The families living in the rooms facing the alley were wholly unprepared for the passage of the train, and the clear and unobstructed view that could be had into their windows was productive of no end of merriment. Gentlemen whose pleasures of the night before had caused them to sleep late were surprised at their shaving mirrors, and ladies in every variety of demi-toilette were fain to dodge behind closet doors or hastily draw the curtains as the train loads of voyagers swept by. This sort of thing was encountered all along the line, and, while the occupants of dwellings whose rear windows face the alley have learned to look for the trains by this time and guard against surprise, one is still occasionally caught napping. The elevated railway affords a rapid and pleasant mode of transit. Its trains run at all hours of the day and night. The fair is five cents for the entire journey.

Although it is not altogether a pleasant place to visit, the county jail is inspected by parties of strangers who have a desire to glance at a dark side of life in a big city. There may or may not be a number of interesting prisoners in the jail at the time of your visit, but if not there are spots that will be shown you by the affable clerk, Ben Price, that are full of historical interest. "Murderer's Row," the line of dingy cells in which candidates for the gallows are confined, generally has at least one occupant, and let us hope it will be empty when the reader sees it. The petty criminals, or those awaiting trial, are allowed to roam during the day in the cage and converse at stated intervals with their relatives or friends through the wire grating. In this place Louis Lingg, the anarchist, whose dreadful suicide is referred to in another chapter, used to enjoy weekly interviews with his sweetheart, the young girl who is said to have given him the bomb with which he cheated the gallows by blowing off his head. In interviews of this sort the prisoner stands on one side of the wire grating, the visitor on the other. "Lingg's girl," as the jail habitues used to call her, is said to have given her sweetheart the bomb by means of a kiss between the bars, passing the deadly little instrument from her mouth to his at the moment their lips met. This is of course only a jail story, but as there is no other known manner in which the doomed man could have secured the bomb, it must be accepted in lieu of a better explanation.

There is a "visiting" day at the jail each week, on which the friends of the prisoners are permitted to bring them delicacies. Old women with baskets in their arms trudge in and stand with tearful eyes as their hopeful sons or grandsons greedily devour the contents. Many a pitiful sight is to be witnessed, and the visitor may, perhaps, come away with a strengthened determination never to get into jail himself if he can help it. A call at the sheriff's office is all that is necessary to secure a pass to the jail. It is situated on the north side on Michigan Street, close to Clark.

Some of the great buildings of Chicago, recently finished, are well worth inspection. One of the newest of these, the Temple, on La Salle Street, is one of the sights of the city. Its cost was $1,100,000, and the estimated income from its rents is $250,000 a year. Just across the street, in the Home Insurance Building, is the office of Armour & Co. There are three hundred well disciplined employees here, and they move about their business like clock-work. Mr. P. D. Armour, who is, perhaps, the richest man in the west, sits at an unpretentious desk among his "boys," as he calls them, and spends as many hours here daily as any of them. Other great buildings within fifteen minutes walk of this one are the Rookery, Royal Insurance building, Republic Life building, Tacoma building, Phoenix building, Monadnock and Kearsage building, Manhattan building, Insurance Exchange building, Pontiac building.

The gigantic Masonic Temple, at the northeast corner of State and Randolph Street, deserves special mention. It towers skyward until its roof is almost lost in the clouds. The idea of a grand Masonic temple in Chicago is twenty years old, and western Masons are responsible for the erection of the superb structure, which is an everlasting honor to themselves and a credit to the city. The building, which is without doubt one of the finest in the world, was completed this spring. The company erecting it is capitalized at $2,000,000, the price per share being $100. It has an interior court measuring ninety feet north and south by forty five east and west, the walls of which are faced with marble of variegated colors, with a bronze staircase winding its devious way from the ground floor to the roof. There are fourteen passenger and two freight elevators, each of which makes a round trip every three minutes. An entire morning may be profitably passed in inspecting this mighty structure, the magnificence of which, perhaps, cannot be duplicated on the continent, if indeed, in the entire universe.

A GROUP OF FOOTLIGHT FAVORITES.
Clockwise from top left: Maurice Barrymore, Georgia Cayvan, Richard Mansfield, Hattie Harvey, Margaret Mather, and Jessie Bartlett Davis. *Center:* Isabella Irving.

CHAPTER XXVIII.

A FEW FINAL WORDS.

THE AUTHOR MORALIZES.

In view of the fact that the remainder of this little work will be devoted to the World's Fair — that mighty gathering of all nations in myriads of manifold variety, which will concentrate the attention of the civilized earth upon Chicago — a few farewell hints to the stranger may not be out of place.

An effort has been made to carefully describe the places of public entertainment, of all sorts and conditions, within the city's confines — in short, to furnish the visitor with a faithful and accurate "pleasure-seeker's guide" in fact as well as in name. How well that task has been accomplished is a matter resting with the opinion of the investigating reader.

In treating of resorts in attractions that are not of a kind to excite the admiration of people of tender sensibilities or strongly pronounced views, no effort has been made to descant on any impropriety or undesirability that may exist. The author, throughout this work, has been actuated by one motive — to tell facts and to tell them briefly.

The multitudes from all nations who will make the great city by the lake their Mecca during the Fair will find here a hearty welcome and innumerable ways of spending their time pleasantly. They will also find, probably, the same crowds of rascals, in all guises, that kept the police so busy during the Philadelphia and Paris exhibitions. Every man's good common sense must be his own guide, both in looking out for crooks and in seeking channels of legitimate diversion for his unoccupied hours.

That is all — and it is enough. We pass on now to a consideration of the colossal project which is to make Chicago's name a household word on the tongue of the world's enlightened nations.

THE GREAT WORLD'S FAIR.

PART I.

THE PROJECT OF THE WORLD'S COLUMBIAN EXPOSITION.

ADMINISTRATION BUILDING.

EVEN at the present time, nearly a year before the date set for the opening of the World's Columbian Exposition, the site upon which it is to be given forms the main object of interest to Chicagoans as well as visitors. This interest will, of course, be heightened as time passes on until it culminates in the attendance of visiting millions at the exhibit, which will stand unrivaled in the history of the nations.

The World's Fair grounds are in Jackson Park, seven miles from the business center of the city, and any one who has noticed within the last year or so the great expanse of swampy, uneven ground would not recognize it to-day, so stupendous has been the transformation. The great expanse, half wilderness, half prairie, which stretches away southward from the Park on the shores of the Lake, has been transformed into a miniature city, and the great buildings, several of them in a state bordering on completion, tower high toward the skies, giving promise of the magnificent effect they will create when finished. If the millions of people whose eyes are directed in fancy upon this scene could view it in reality, they would feel satisfied that the promises made as to their entertainment will be much more than fulfilled.

The shore line of the Lake approaching the World's Fair grounds is graced by a sweeping promenade of flag-stones. Entering the grounds one is greeted by a splendid vision of graceful lagoons, wooded islands, and colossal buildings, gracefully ornamented and striking the beholder dumb with admiration.

The history of this World's Fair project reads like a romance. All the great cities of the country contested for the honor of holding the Fair within their gates. By dint of splendid work, admirably strengthened of course by the natural advantages it possessed, Chicago won the prize, and the manner in which the city's pledges have been carried out fully justifies the selection. The citizens of Chicago raised over five million dollars for a guaranty fund and pledged themselves to have a like amount in addition ready in case it should be needed. That is one of the reasons why Chicago secured the Fair; it was a case where "money talked." This Fair, which marks the four hundredth birthday of this great and mighty Nation, will be thrown open next year to the delight of the civilized world. The following is the proclamation by which President Harrison invited the Nations to participate:

Whereas, satisfactory proof has been presented to me that provision has been made for adequate grounds and building for the uses of the World's Columbian Exposition, and that a sum not less than $10,000,000, to be used and expended for the purpose of said Exposition, has been provided in accordance with the conditions and requirements of Section 10 of an Act entitled "An Act to provide for celebrating the four hundredth anniversary of the discovery of America by Christopher Columbus, by holding an International Exhibition of arts, industries, manufactures and products of the soil, mine and sea, in the city of Chicago, in the State of Illinois," approved April 25, 1890.

Now, therefore, I, Benjamin Harrison, President of the United States, by virtue of the authority vested in me by said Act, do hereby declare and proclaim that such International Exhibition will be opened on the first day of May, in the year 1893, in the city of Chicago, in the State of Illinois, and will not be closed before the last Thursday in October of the same year.

And in the name of the Government, and of the people of the United States, I do hereby invite all the Nations of the earth to take part in the commemoration of an event that is preeminent in human history and of lasting interest to mankind by appointing representatives thereto, and sending such exhibits to the World's Columbian Exposition as will most fitly and fully illustrate their resources, their industries and their progress in civilization.

In testimony whereof I have hereunto set my hand and caused the seal of the United States to be affixed.

Done at the city of Washington, this twenty-fourth day of December, in the year of our Lord One Thousand Eight Hundred and Ninety, and the independence of the United States the One Hundred and Fifteenth.

By the President.   [Signed] Benj. Harrison.
[Signed] James G. Blaine, Secretary of State.

The World's Fair grounds embrace a total of 1,037 acres, and the two adjoining parks, Jackson and Washington, form a part of the magnificent park system of Chicago, which has been fully described in a previous chapter. It stands to reason that a project of this scope can only be undertaken under the supervision of a great host of officers. The principal officers of the World's Columbian Exposition are:

President, William T. Baker; Vice Presidents, Thomas B. Bryan, Potter Palmer; Secretary and Solicitor General, Benj. Butterworth; Assistant Secretary, J. H. Kingwill; Treasurer, Anthony F. Seeberger; Auditor, William K. Ackerman; Traffic Manager, E. E. Jaycox.

BOARD OF REFERENCE AND CONTROL.

William T. Baker, Potter Palmer, Ferd W. Peck, Fred S. Winston, Thomas B. Bryan, Lyman J. Gage, Edwin Walker, H. N. Higinbotham.

EXECUTIVE COMMITTEE.

William T. Baker, President; Thomas B. Bryan, Vice President; Potter Palmer, Second Vice President; Ferd W. Peck, Robert A. Waller, William D. Kerfoot, Robert C. Clowry, Edwin Walker, H. N. Higinbotham, A. H. Revell, Lyman J. Gage, Charles H. Schwab, Martin A. Ryerson, Charles L. Hutchinson, John J. P. Odell, Marshall M. Kirkman.

The officers of the National Commission are:

President, Thomas W. Palmer, Michigan; Director-General, George R. Davis, Illinois; First Vice President, Thomas W. Waller, Connecticut;

Second Vice President, M. H. De Young, California; Third Vice President, Davidson B. Penn, Louisiana; Fourth Vice President, Gorton W. Allen, New York; Fifth Vice President, Alexander P. Andrews, North Carolina; Secretary, John T. Dickinson, Texas.

The National Commission is composed of eight commissioners at large and two for every State and Territory in the Union, with two alternates. There are standing committees as follows: Executive, Judicial, Tariffs and Transportation, Foreign Affairs, Fine Arts, Science, History, Literature and Education, Agriculture, Live Stock, Horticulture and Floriculture, Finance, Auditing, Ceremonies, Classification, Manufacture, Commerce, Mines and Mining, Fisheries and Fish Culture, Electrical and Pneumatical Appliances, Forestry and Lumber, Machinery, World's Congresses, Printing, Grounds and Buildings, Federal Legislation, Awards, Reference, and Control.

There is also a Board of Lady Managers composed of two members for every State and Territory of the Union, with alternates, under whose supervision woman's share in the exhibit is being prepared. The following are the officers in the Board of Lady Managers:

President, Mrs. Potter Palmer; First Vice President, Mrs. Ralph Trautmann; Second Vice President, Mrs. E. C. Burleigh; Third Vice President, Mrs. Charles Price; Fourth Vice President, Miss K. L. Minor; Fifth Vice President, Mrs. Beriah Wilkins; Sixth Vice President. Mrs. S. R. Ashley; Seventh Vice President, Mrs. F. B Ginty; Eighth Vice President, Mrs. M. B. Salisbury; Vice President at Large, Mrs. R. D. Harrison; Secretary, Mrs. Susan G Cooke.

There is also a body known as The World's Congress Auxiliary, which is an organization authorized and supported by the Exposition corporation for the purpose of bringing to Chicago a series of world's conventions of leaders in the various departments of human progress during the Exposition season of 1893. The auxiliary has also been recognized by the Government of the United States as the appropriate agency to conduct this important work. Its general announcement has been sent to foreign governments by the department of State, and an appropriation for its expenses has been made by act of Congress.

The Auxiliary consist of an active membership of persons residing in Chicago or sufficiently near to attend committee meetings without inconvenience and a nonresident membership divided into advisory councils of the different departments of progress and honorary and corresponding members. Each committee has its own advisory council, composed of eminent leaders of the world in the department to which it relates. Honorary and corresponding members are persons not assigned to a particular department, but whose prominence and influence make their aid and co-operation desirable.

The officers of the Auxiliary are:

President, Hon. Charles C. Bonney; Vice President, Hon. Thos. B. Bryan; Treasurer, Hon. Lyman J. Gage; Secretary, Hon. Benjamin Butterworth. There is also a President of the Woman's Branch of the Auxiliary, Mrs. Potter Palmer, and a Vice President, Mrs. Charles Henrotin.

The dimensions and costs of the various buildings are shown complete in the following table:

BUILDINGS.	Dimensions in feet	Area acres.	Cost.
Mines and Mining..	350 x 700	5.6	$ 260.000
Manufactures and Liberal Arts....	787 x 1687	30.5	1.100.000
Horticulture.....	250 x 1000	5.8	300.000
Electricity	345 x 700	5.5	375.000
Woman's..... .. ..:	200 x 400	1.8	120.000
Transportation....	250 x 960	5 5	280.000
Administration.....................	260 x 260	1.6	450.000
Fish and Fisheries................	163 x 363	1.4 ⎱	200.000
Annexes (2).....................	135 diam.	.8 ⎰	
Agriculture......................	500 x 800	9.2	540.000
Annex......................	328 x 500	3.8 ⎱	200.000
Assembly hall, etc	450 x 500	5.2 ⎰	
Machinery......	500 x 850	9.8 ⎱	1.200.000
Annex....... ....·	490 x 551	6.2 ⎰	
Power House................	80 x 600	1.1	
Fine Arts	320 x 500	3 7 ⎱	500.000
Annexes (2).....................	120 x 200	1 1 ⎰	
Forestry........................	200 x 500	2 3	100 000
Saw-Mill.....	125 x 300	9	35 ·000
Dairy..	95 x 200	.5	·30.000
Live Stock (3)............... ...	65 x 200	.9 ⎱	150.000
Live Stock Sheds.................	.. ..	40.0 ⎰	
Casino........................	175 x 300	1.2	150.000
Total	....	144.4	$5.990.000
United States Government.........	350 x 420	3.4	400.000
Battle Ship.............	348 x 69.25	.3	100.000
Illinois State..................	160 x 450	1.7	250.000
State Annexes (2)...............	....	.3	....
Grand Total	....	150.1	$6.740.000

The first two of these are erected by the United States Government, and the third by the State of Illinois. They will form
a striking portion of the group of buildings surrounding the
lagoons. In addition to these buildings at the north end of the
Park, buildings will be erected that are to be devoted to individual States and the foreign Governments structures, probably one hundred in all. The latter will surround the gallery of
fine arts at the north end of the lagoon. On the Midway Plaisance the visitor will find special features, such as the bazaar

of all Nations, the street of Cairo, the Constantinople Street, the Japanese village, the German village, etc.

Among the various buildings in a more or less advanced state of construction, the ADMINISTRATION BUILDING at once challenges attention, being regarded as the finest. It stands at the west end of the great court in the southern part of the site, facing eastward, the transportation facilities and depots being immediately in its rear. The Administration Building cost $450,000, and its lofty dome is observable from all parts of the grounds. It consists of four pavilions, each eighty-four feet square, one at each of the four angles of the square and connected by the central dome, which is 120 feet in diameter and 220 feet in height. The design of this building is after the French *renaissance,* the first story being on the Doric order of architecture of heroical proportions, the tiers of each pavilion being ornamented with fine sculptures. On the second story the Ionic style prevails. There are four great entrances fifty feet wide and fifty feet high, covered with huge arched vaults. Above the entrance doors are enormous screens of glass, through which light is given to the central rotunda. Galleries connect between the different pavilions. The internal features of the building are even more magnificent. Between every two of the grand entrances is a hall thirty feet square, giving access to the offices. The rotunda is octagonally formed, the first story consisting of eight great arched openings, corresponding in size to the arches at the entrance. The second story, fifty feet in height, rises above the balcony, and from this rises the interior dome, 200 feet from the floor, in the center of which is an opening fifty feet in diameter and through which light falls from the exterior dome overhead. The interior of the dome is richly paneled and moulded, the panels being ornamented with sculpture and paintings of numerous size and splendid design. The corner pavilions are divided into offices for the administration, lobbies, and toilet rooms. The fire and police departments are located on the ground floor. In the second pavilion are the ambulance offices and other departments; in the third, a bank and post office; in the fourth, a restaurant.

Next in magnitude to the Administration Building, perhaps, is the TRANSPORTATION BUILDING, which is one of a group of edifices forming the northern architectural court of the Exposition. It is situated between the horticultural and mines buildings, facing eastward and commanding a view of the floral island and part of the lagoon. The building is simple in its outlines but rich and elaborate in detail. The cupola of the Transportation Building, reached by eight elevators, commands a most beautiful view of the entire exterior Exposition. The main entrance is in the form of a single arch, richly carved and decorated with *bas reliefs* and mural paintings. The main part of the building is composed of a continuous arcade in which numerous minor entrances are pierced, while almost at every place are grouped terraces, drinking fountains, statues, etc. The main part of the building is 960 feet front by 250 feet deep, from which extend a huge annex one story in height, covering about nine acres. In the annex, the more bulky exhibits are to be found. Along the central avenues scores of locomotive engines will be found, highly polished and greatly adding to the grandeur of the effect. In this building will be found exhibits of everything connected with transportation, from a carrier pigeon to a traction engine.

Passing from the Transportation Building one comes to MACHINERY HALL, which is said to be second only in magnificence to the Administration Building. Machinery Hall is located at the extreme south of the Park, between the west Park line and Lake Michigan, standing south of the Administration Building across the lagoon from the Agricultural Building. This building is spanned by three great arch-ways, and the interior looks not unlike three railroad train houses grouped side by side. The arches or trusses are built separately and will be sold after the Exposition is over to the railroads for use as train houses. The building has numer-ous platforms upon which visitors may stand and view all that is transpir-ing. A power-house adjoining will supply all the power needed. The entire group of buildings in this vicinity is designed so as to conform with the idea of a Spanish town, the same being considered appropriate in a Columbian celebration.

Between the Machinery and Agricultural Halls is a space covered by a colonnade and *cafe*; in the center is an archway which, if followed to the end, will lead the visitor to the cattle exhibit. There is also a portico which affords a view of nearly a mile down the lagoon. Machinery Hall has an annex covering between four and five acres, thus increasing the length of the actual building to about 1,400 feet. It ranks second of the larger structures of the Exposition.

The WOMAN'S BUILDING, it is safe to say, will be the main object of interest to a large number of visitors at the Fair. It is situated in the northwest part of the Park, facing the great lagoon with the beauty island of flowers at its front. In this building will be grouped exhibits showing woman's work in every conceivable form, and judging by the progress made at this writing, the building itself will be no less splendid than the array of marvels it will contain. In front of the Woman's Building the lagoon stretches out to a bay 400 feet in width, from the center of which a landing and staircase leads to a wide terrace. Above the terrace are other staircases giving access to the ground floor of the building itself. On the first terrace are artistically designed flower beds and shrubs, and the building itself, in the style of the Italian *renaissance* will be considered one of the most attractive points for the visitor. The main grouping of the building consists in a center pavilion with a corner pavilion at each end, connected at the first pavilion with open arcades. There is a shady promenade the whole length of the structure. The first floor is ten feet above the ground line. The pavilion is reached by a wide staircase which forms the main triple-arched entrance. The corner pavilions are two stories high, where are located the hanging gardens and the committee rooms of the Board of Lady Managers. There is a lobby forty feet wide leading into the rotunda, the latter being surrounded by an open arcade of beautiful design. On the first floor of the building will be found a model hospital and a kindergarten. As to exhibits, the whole floor of the south pavilion will be devoted to the delineation of woman's work in the past; the one on the north to reform work and charity organization. Above this are located ladies' parlors, committee rooms, and dressing rooms, all of which lead to the open balcony on the front. The balcony commands a superb view of almost the entire grounds. In the south pavilion will be found the kitchen and refreshment rooms, etc.

The MANUFACTURES AND LIBERAL ARTS BUILDING stands alone as the largest Exposition building ever designed, being 1,687 feet long and 787 feet wide and covering an area of thirty and one-half acres. The building is rectangular in form, its great central hall being its feature. The height of the roof is 245 feet at the apex, and the 380 feet space is covered by a single arch without so much as a supporting column. The height from the floor to the center of the arch is 201 feet, the roof being supported by twenty-two steel arches, each arch weighing 125 tons. An idea of the magnitude of this building may be conceived from the fact that over 5,000 tons of steel were used in the construction of the main hall. Extending around this hall is a gallery twenty feet from the floor, sixty-seven feet wide, twenty-one feet of which space overhangs the floor of the hall. Beyond the gallery is a nave 108 feet wide and 114 feet to the roof. Extending around the nave into the outside limit of the building is a gallery twenty feet from the floor and forty-nine and one-half feet wide, the two galleries being connected by twenty-eight bridges fifty feet in width and 108 feet in length. Forty-one carloads of glass were used in the construction of the roof. The immensity of the building may be still further conjectured by the fact that it is three times as large as St. Peter's Cathedral in Rome; twenty buildings the size of the Auditorium could be placed side by side on its floor, and its central floor is big enough to seat 50,000 people. The building, which is in the Corinthian style of architecture, will contain, besides pavilions and promenades, about sixteen large *cafes* and seventy-five private dining rooms. The building faces the lake and fronts upon smooth lawns and wide promenades. Its estimated cost is $1,500,000.

But the building that will challenge the attention of everybody, rich and poor, young and old alike, will be the ART

Palace, which is Grecian-Ionican style and a pure type of the most beautiful architecture. The Art Palace is 500 feet long by 320 wide. Collections of sculpture will be displayed on the main floor of the nave and transit, and on the walls of both the ground floor and balcony will be ample space for paintings. Small picture galleries will occupy the corners. All around the building are spacious galleries forming a continuous promenade. In small spaces between the promenade and the naves are small rooms to be devoted to private collections and the collections of the various art schools. There are also large annexes to the main building, which will be used for various art exhibits. There are four entrances to the main building approached by broad flights of stairs. The entire construction of the Art Palace is of the most classic order and will compare favorably with any Exposition building ever constructed. The location of the palace is the northern portion of the Park, the south front facing the lagoon, from which it is separated by beautiful terraces, and immense flight of steps lead from its main portal to the lagoon, where there is a landing for gondolas. From the north front are to be seen the wide expanse of lawn and the group of State buildings.

The Horticultural Building stands just south of the entrance to Jackson Park from the Midway Plaisance, facing east on the lagoon. The front of the terrace borders the water, its center forming a boat landing. The length of the building is 1,000 feet and its width 250. Its plan is a central pavilion with two end pavilions connected by front and rear corridors, forming two interior courts, each 270 feet by eighty-eight feet. A colossal dome 288 feet in diameter crowns the central part of the pavilion, under which are to be shown the tallest palms, bamboos, and tropical tree plants to be found anywhere on the face of the earth. The galleries in each of the pavilions have been designed particularly for *cafes*, the surroundings being considered inducive to the enjoyment of refreshments. On three sides of these *cafes* stretches an arcade commanding a fine view of the grounds. In this building will be found arrayed every variety of flower, plant, vine, and sod, together with a complete array of every implement used in horticulture. Such parts of the building as require it will, of course, be warmed to a tropical temperature.

The DAIRY BUILDING will be of special interest to the agriculturist for whose special favor and edification it was designed. Besides the exhibits of dairy products it will contain a dairy school, in connection with which will be carried on a series of tests to determine the various merits of different breeds of dairy cattle and milk and butter producers. The Dairy Building stands close to the lake shore in the southeastern part of the Park and covers one-half acre. It measures 200 feet by ninety-five and is two stories in height. It is simple in design. On the first floor appears a large open space to be devoted to the butter exhibits, while further back will be the large operating room to be devoted to the dairy. This room will contain an amphitheater capable of accommodating four hundred spectators, under whose seats will be stored refrigerators for the care of the products turned out. The cheese exhibits will be placed in the gallery, the rest of the second story being devoted to a *cafe* which overlooks the lake. The dairy school, which is regarded as of special interest, this being a great agricultural country, will continue in operation throughout the entire Fair, and will, no doubt, prove of surpassing interest to visitors.

The FISHERIES BUILDING is regarded as one of the most artistic of all, embracing, as it does, a large central structure with two smaller buildings connected with it by arcades at either end. The extreme length of the building is 1,100 feet and its width 200 feet. It stands to the north of the United States Government Building. In one of the similar buildings or annexes will be found the angling exhibit and in the other the aquaria. The architecture of the building is exceedingly quaint, the designer having arranged the ornamentation in such a way as to employ only fish and sea forms for his designs. The display of live fish will be something wonderful. In the middle of the rotunda will be found a basin or pool twenty-six feet wide, in the center of which will be a mass of moss-covered rocks. From crevices in this mass will flow streams of water to the basin below, and in this great basin all sorts of live fish will disport themselves. Outside the rotunda is a great corridor or arcade, on opposite sides of which are tanks, great and small, to accommodate members of the finny tribes. This arcade is fifteen feet wide. The glass fronts of the aquaria will have 3,000 square feet of surface.

PART II.

LOOKING AROUND.

FIGURE FROM THE LIBERAL ARTS BUILDING.

A TRIP to the World's Fair grounds even now will convince the visitor of two things, namely: the magnitude of the undertaking and the steady approach of the whole enterprise to completion. The arrangement of roadways whereby one may make the circuit of the grounds in carriage or afoot, stopping at every point desired to examine the details of the work, is excellent. An admission fee of twenty-five cents is now charged, and the readiness with which thousands of persons pay it every day for the privilege of taking a look around is some index to the probabilities with regard to the attendance a year hence.

Besides the buildings mentioned in a preceding chapter there are the following: The Forestry building, Electrical building. Agricultural building, Mines and Mining, Government building, Illinois State building, the casino and pier, the United States naval exhibit. Before proceeding further these may be briefly sketched.

The dimensions of the FORESTRY BUILDING are 500 by 200 feet. The architecture is rustic in style and is surrounded by a veranda and colonnade, the latter consisting of a series of columns composed of three tree trunks 25 feet long, one of which is 16 to 20 inches in diameter and the others of smaller girth. The tree trunks have been permitted to retain their bark, thereby creating a unique effect. They come from all states and countries, each of which has contributed a specimen of the best known tree. The building itself is constructed of slabs and thatched with various barks, the interior being finished in woods in such a manner as to show the graining and polishing susceptibilities of each. Tablets on the tree trunks forming the colonnades will inform the visitor as to where each came from, with other interesting information. Flags will float above this building, denoting the different nations whose products are on exhibition within. The forestry exhibit may be considered as one of the most interesting to be found at the Fair, comprising, as it will, logs and sections of trees and "worked" lumber in every form, such as shingles, flooring, casing, etc. Look also for dye woods, barks, mosses, lichens, gums, rosins, cocoanut shells, gourds, rattan, willow-ware and wooden-ware, tubs, brooms, etc. More than one saw mill will be seen in active operation and will be quite distinct from the exhibits of saw-mill and wood-working machinery on view in MACHINERY HALL. The Forestry Building is one of the cheapest at the Fair, costing only $35,000, but its projectors expect it to be by no means the least entertaining or instructive.

The ELECTRICAL BUILDING will be one of the most important, the exhibit of electrical appliances and devices being expected to enchain the attention of scientists and experts as well as the uninitiated millions. The building is 700 feet in width by 345 feet in length and has been constructed on magnificent plans at a cost of $345,000. It is two stories in height and contains spacious galleries from which crowds may view all that is going on below. In the north end of the building is a great semi-circle window, above which, 102 feet from the ground, is a spacious gallery, affording the visitor a wide view of the lagoon and that part of the grounds stretching to the north. In a niche at the south part of the Electrical Building is a heroic statue of Benjamin Franklin, whose name connects American history with one of the most important discoveries of modern times. The building has four pavilions, with towers 169 feet high. There are domes, spires, and columns adorning the building with an architectural and imposing magnificence that rivets the attention at first sight and makes it one of the most striking attractions in the grounds. It is needless to say that the exhibit will show everything in connection with the marvelous power, electricity, discoveries in which, some people claim, are yet in their infancy and the rapid advancements in which are destined ultimately to revolutionize the world.

BENJAMIN FRANKLIN.

The AGRICULTURAL BUILDING, 800 feet in length by 500 feet in width, stands close to the shore of the lake, its east side fronting upon a harbor of refuge for pleasure craft. The design of the building, which is but one story in height, is bold and impressive. On either side of the main entrance are Corinthian pillars, fifty feet high. The main entrance is 60 feet wide and leads into a vestibule, thence into a rotunda 100 feet in diameter. Above the rotunda is a large glass dome, 130 feet in height. To the south of the Agricultural Building proper is the vast structure to be devoted to the live stock exhibit and agricultural assembly hall. The elevated railway station affords every access to the building. In it will be held the meetings of all persons interested in live stock. There will also be a bureau of information, spacious waiting and toilet rooms; also an assembly room with a seating capacity of 1,500, and complete facilities for lectures, etc. More than twelve acres of ground are covered by the Agricultural Building and its annex.

The MINES AND MINING BUILDING is one of the most imposing on the grounds and stands at the south end of the western lagoon, between the Transportation and Electricity buildings, being 700 feet in length by 750 feet in width. From its balconies and porticos splendid views may be had of a vast portion of the grounds, and in its front are spacious lawns dotted with flowers. The wonders to be found in this building cannot be adequately described in advance. Mines of all sorts, in every stage of operation, are to be shown. The visitor may feast his eyes on piles of silver and gold in every stage, from the ore freshly taken from the earth to the gleaming double-eagles, most royal of all the coins! And silver dollars fresh from the mint. And precious stones! They will be there in every variety and all stages of preparation. A promise has been made that an African diamond mine will be shown in active operation. At one point will be seen the dusky native delving for the rarest of gems; at another a skilled workman cutting and setting brilliants of "purest ray serene." All this and much more will this wonderful building contain; and it is a question whether any other will possess so great a charm for the crowds who will be apt to stand there and let their mouths water in awesome hunger at the sight of so vast an aggregation of wealth.

The GOVERNMENT BUILDING is situated on the lake shore, south of the main lagoon, near to the buildings of England, Germany, and Mexico. It is built of iron, brick, and glass at a cost of $400,000. All the departments of the Government, such as the post-office, war office, etc., will make special exhibits. Ample space has been allotted for the exhibits of the Smithsonian Institute and interior department. The government exhibits include the mint, the coast and the geodetic survey, the bureau of engraving and printing, the bureau of statistics, the life-saving board, the light house board, and the marine hospital. The life-saving exhibit shows a life-saving station built and equipped with every appliance and a regular crew which will go through all the life-saving maneuvers in practice on the coasts. The coast survey exhibit includes a mammoth map of the United States, 400 feet square, constructed of plaster of paris, and placed horizontally on the ground beneath a covering erected over it. By a system of galleries and pathways on the inside the visitor may "walk over the whole United States" without touching it, as one recent writer has expressed himself. The scale of the map accurately shows the exact height of all the mountains and the depth of all the rivers in the United States. Here is a fine chance for a lesson in geography. The war department exhibit shows all the uniforms ever worn by United States soldiers, a telephone as it would be used on the battle-field, besides all means of army telegraphing and signaling.

The naval exhibit will without doubt attract a great share of attention. It consists of a structure, erected in the lake, typifying with marvelous accuracy one of the new coast-line battleships recently constructed for the American navy. The structure stands on piling at the edge of the lake at the north-east side of Jackson Park. Being quite surrounded by water, the structure has the exact appearance of a vessel moored to the wharf. It is fitted with all the appliances of an actual ship, such as guns, turrets, torpedo tubes, anchors, etc. The navy department will send on a special crew to serve during the exposition, and the visitors will have an opportunity to witness all the workings of an American man-of-war.

A delightful feature of the Fair will be the mammoth casino and pier. The pier runs out 1,000 feet into Lake Michigan and at its extremity is the casino, which is so constructed as to give, on the waters of Lake Michigan, a miniature representation of beautiful Venice. The casino is built on piles and embraces nine pavilions, eight of which are two stories in height, the center one rearing 180 feet. Bridges and gondolas afford communication between the pavilions. In part of the casino is a harbor for pleasure craft. At night the harbor will be lighted by incandescent lamps sunk beneath the surface of the water, and the brilliancy of the scene may be imagined.

The ILLINOIS STATE BUILDING occupies a fine site in the prettiest spot in Jackson Park. The state appropriated $800,000 for this building, and the money has been well expended. The building is 450 feet in length by 160 feet in width and is constructed of wood, stone, brick, and steel, nearly all the material having been procured in Illinois. A feature of the building is Memorial Hall, which contains a superb collection of relics of the war and other periods. An admirable view of the main exhibit hall may be had from the spacious galleries. The exhibit will include five model school-rooms, equipped and furnished under the direction of the state superintendent of public instruction. Here will be illustrated the methods of education pursued in the state, from the common school to the university. The exhibit also includes collections illustrating the natural history and archaeology of the state; an exhibition by the State Fish Commission of native and cultivated live fish, with hatchery, appliances, and equipments for transportation. Also maps, charts, etc., illustrative of all the resources of the state. The women of Illinois were promised, or presented with, $80,000 and space in this building for a special exhibit illustrating women's work in the state.

PART III.

THE DEDICATORY CEREMONIES.

Though the great exposition will not be formally opened until May 1st, 1893, the fall season of the present year will witness the dedicatory ceremonies, which will be conducted on a scale of magnificence unequaled in the history of such enterprises. The dedication of the buildings will in reality be a sort of informal opening of the Fair itself, inasmuch as the publication of accounts of the ceremonies will start the stream of visitors Chicago-ward, and all through the succeeding year, up to the time of the opening, people will journey hither to see how the colossal enterprise is progressing. If crowds are willing even now to pay an admission fee of 25 cents (which is at present charged) to see the buildings in their embryotic state, how much more willing will they be to do so after the dedication of the buildings has set the stamp of actuality on the stupendous display.

The dedication ceremonies are to take place in October of the present year, and the programme has been fully arranged. The celebration will last four days, during which one of the features will be a military encampment. The troops will be under command of an officer of the United States Army, to be designated hereafter by the Secretary of War. The ceremonies will open with a mammoth civic parade which will, doubtless, be appreciated by the thousands of visitors who will by that time have assembled. The parade will be allegorical in character and typical of the world's "march of progress." This will transpire during the morning hours. In the evening there will be an even grander display, in the form of the "Procession of Centuries," a historical representation of American progress, including scenes in the life of Columbus, and showing the gigantic strides accomplished in science and art, the discovery and development of steam, electricity, etc. This procession will be repeated each evening during the four days' celebration. The regular evening features will also include magnificent displays of fireworks at Jackson Park and along the Lake Front.

The feature of the second day's celebration will be a magnificent military parade and review, in which all the visiting troops will take part. The display of the following day will be for dedication day proper, and the main building in Jackson Park will be the scene of the memorial services. An idea of the grandeur of these services may be gained from a glance at the programme as already mapped out. Promptly at 10 o'clock in the morning the troops will parade in readiness to receive Benjamin Harrison, president of the United States, with proper military honors. After being saluted by the troops, the president will lead the way into the building, accompanied by his cabinet, the diplomatic corps (which will come on in a body from Washington for the occasion), and other distinguished foreigners. Inside the building the president will receive the representatives of the thirteen original states with proper ceremonies. After this the remaining states will be received in the order of their admission to the union. The various states will be represented by their governors and their staffs, whose brilliant uniforms, together with the banners and other insignia that they will bear, will contribute to a scene the gorgeousness of which can scarcely be imagined.

When the formal receptions are over and the great throng of people comfortably arranged, the following programme will be observed:

1. Overture — (Original music by an American composer.)
2. Prayer.
3. Address and report from Director-General George R. Davis.
4. Presentation of buildings by the president of the World's Columbian Exposition to the president of the World's Columbian Commission.
5. Commemoration Ode — (Miss Harriet Monroe) — with original music.
6. Address by the president of the United States.
7. "Star-Spangled Banner."
8. Dedication oration.
9. Hallelujah chorus.
10. National salute of forty-eight battery volleys.

On the evening of the second day the president will hold a reception in honor of the diplomatic corps, distinguished foreigners, and invited guests. On the evening of the third day there will be a grand dedication ball at the Auditorium, a ball which for magnificence and brilliancy will probably supersede anything ever seen in this country. Even now, several months before the date set, people are figuring on how to secure invitations, but as 5,000 people at the most can enter the ball-room, many of course will have to be disappointed. Participation in this gorgeous *fete* will be confined to very prominent citizens and distinguished visitors from other cities and across the ocean. Every day there will be military drills and parades, closing on the last day with a grand sham battle.

The foregoing is merely an outline of the entertaining and elaborate ceremonies. It is only reasonable to expect that the programme will be enlarged in its attractiveness as the time approaches for carrying out the carefully studied plans and features. It is to be presumed that every one knows these ceremonies will be commemorative of the completion of the world's fair buildings. The day after the ceremonies are concluded, the work of arranging the exhibits in the buildings will begin, and this will be carried on with all due expedition until the great opening day, 1st of May, 1893. The ceremonies, it should be stated, are at present under the charge of the following gentlemen, composing the committee on ceremonies of the World's Columbian Commission: Hon. P. A. B. Widener, Philadelphia, Pa.; Hon. John D. Adams, Little Rock, Ark.; Hon. Wm. Lindsay, Frankfort, Ky.; Gen. V. D. Groner, Norfolk, Va.; Hon. C. H. Richmond, Ann Arbor, Mich.; Hon. G. W. Allen, Auburn, N. Y.; Hon. M. B. Harrison, Duluth, Minn.; Gov. R. B. Furnas, Brownsville, Neb. And of the following who compose the committee on ceremonies of the World's Columbian Exposition: Messrs. Edward F. Lawrence, Chas. T. Yerkes, James W. Ellsworth, Charles L. Hutchinson, W. D. Kerfoot, Ferd. W. Peck, Charles H. Schwab, Chas. H. Wacker — all of Chicago.

Acting for the best interests of everybody concerned, these two committees, acting as the joint committee, have selected the following sub-committee to assist them with the details in connection with the preparation for the ceremonies:

On behalf of the World's Columbian Commission — Director-General George R. Davis and Secretary John T. Dickinson. On behalf of the World's Columbian Exposition Association — Chas. T. Yerkes, E. F. Lawrence and C. H. Wacker.

PART IV.

THE CHICAGO HUSSARS.

THERE is every reason to suppose that considerable interest will attach to the Chicago Hussars, a regiment of volunteer cavalry which has already secured the honor of acting as special escort to the officers of the exposition on all occasions of state. The Chicago Hussars are comprised of gentlemen who own their horses and are rich enough to afford the luxury of costly uniforms, expensive banquets, and other delights dear to the military heart. Mr. E. L. Brand, a prominent citizen, is the commanding officer of the Hussars, and the rank and file numbers over a hundred gentlemen, who, when mounted on their dashing steeds and clad in their gorgeous trappings, present a most dazzling appearance. Chicago at present enjoys the distinction of being the only city of the United States possessing a volunteer cavalry regiment. The Hussars are shortly to erect, at some advantageous point on the South Side convenient to the boulevard, the finest club-house and armory in America. This will include a riding ring, perfect in appointments and over 500 feet in circumference. The appointments include one hundred box stalls and a balcony seating fifteen hundred spectators, commanding a perfect view of the ring. The prosperity of the Hussars and their appointment by the director-general of the exposition as a special guard of honor, for properly escorting distinguished visitors and officials about the city during the continuance of the Fair, makes a membership in their ranks a prize much to be desired. The volunteer cavalrymen on the march will be one of the sights of the city. The regiment's list of officers is as follows: Captain, E. L. Brand; First Lieutenant, M. L. C. Funkhouser; Second Lieutenant, Joseph B. Keene. The staff officers are: Inspector, P. R. McLeod; Judge Advocate, A. Fouguer; Quarter-Master, Charles Kern; Surgeon, Stewart Johnstone, M.D.

PART V.

WORLD'S CONGRESS.

THE imposing structure known as the Permanent Memorial Art Palace, about to be erected on the site of the old exposition building and mentioned in a previous chapter, is to be the scene of some notable gatherings during the continuance of the Fair. The building is to be devoted to the exclusive use of the world's congresses. It will contain two large audience halls, having a seating capacity of 3,500 each, with twenty smaller halls, which may be utilized by committees and other bodies into which congresses are usually divided. These world's congresses will be interesting from every standpoint. There will be special congresses of lasting organizations, under the supervision of the auxiliary, to which will be delegated the consideration of all live questions, such congresses being conducted by their own special officers. There will also be popular congresses, open to all who may desire to attend, and at which will be presented for discussion all questions governing the results of human progress in all the channels of civilized life. The discussion will be carried on under the direction of the ablest exponent of that particular branch of knowledge whose services can be procured for the occasion. These congresses, besides providing the various organizations with the opportunity to discuss their interests, will secure to the people the opportunity to hear words of wisdom from the wisest of mankind. Suppose Mr. Gladstone, the most eminent Englishman of his time, should visit the Fair,

as is not improbable? Should he do so he will unquestionably be invited to deliver an oration. Mr. Gladstone is only
one of many European notables who are expected to attend,
and they will of course be conspicuous at these world's congresses in the Permanent Art building.

Bird's Eye View of the World's Fair.

PART VI.

THE FAIR ITSELF.

GROUP FROM THE WOMAN'S BUILDING.

WHEN Mr. Edwin Lee Brown, a pioneer, citizen of Chicago, died in the summer of 1891, there passed away the man who is said to have been the first to suggest the idea of holding a world's fair in commemoration of the 400th anniversary of the discovery of America. The mind, therefore, which conceived this mighty project, over which all the nations are agog, is now stilled in everlasting sleep, but to those of us who have memories the Fair will remain a lasting monument to the greatness of that master mind.

Mr. Brown first proposed his scheme to a meeting of citizens in 1885. His words took root immediately. Like a flash the idea rushed through the land and met with such a unanimous response that long before the plan had the sanction of Congress, the holding of the Fair was a certainty. From the time it so became a settled fact in prospect a number of cities waged a strong and at times bitter fight for the honor of having the Fair held within their favorite environ. New York was Chicago's most formidable rival, though various other cities contested determinedly for the honor. Chicago's campaign was carried on with energy. A stock company was formed and $5,000,000 subscribed — $5,000,000 more being pledged long before it was needed. Headquarters were established and agents sent all over the United States to enlist the national sympathies in behalf of Chicago. When the question of location finally came up before Congress, the struggle was sharp, short, and decisive. But a few ballots were taken when the decision was made. That night was a happy one in Chicago. Some people celebrated a little uproariously, it is true, but "everything went," so to speak, on an occasion like that, and nobody complained of the widespread enthusiasm.

ANOTHER GROUP FROM THE WOMAN'S BUILDING.

Not a day was lost. It seems a long stretch of time since then, but everything considered, the progress made has been simply phenomenal. All judges agree on this point. The great nations of the earth, in response to the president's proclamation, have signified their intention to be fully represented. The following is a list of the countries that will participate, showing the amounts appropriated by their respective governments:

Argentine Republic, $100,000; Austria-Hungary, $47,000; Bolivia, $150,000; Brazil, $550,000; Chile, $100,000; Colombia, $100,000; Costa Rica, $100,000; Danish West Indies, $10,000; Ecuador, $125,000; France, $400,000; Germany, $20,000; Great Britain, $125,000; British Guiana, British Honduras, $7,000; Cape Colony, $25,000; Ceylon, $40,000; Jamaica, $10,000; New Zealand, $27,500; Trinidad, $15,000; Guatemala, $120,000; Honduras, $20,000; Japan, $700,000; Mexico, $750,000; Dutch Guiana, $6,000; Dutch West Indies, $10,000; Nicaragua, $30,000; Peru, $140,000; Salvador, $30,000; Cuba, $25,000.

It is hardly possible, in mere words, to convey an idea of what the Fair will be like, but from previous chapters the reader will have formed his own opinion, and his imagination must supply the rest. To say that it will be the most wonderful exhibition in all history is to employ very mild language indeed. The grounds will present a sight that will never be forgotten. At night, when all the buildings are glittering with their myriads of electric lights and great showers of fireworks soaring heavenward; when the great lake itself fairly blazes under the glare of illuminated craft and the stupendous carnival is at its height, the visitor may be pardoned, if, in the excitement of the moment, he fancies that he has fallen off the earth and stepped into another world, peopled by fairies and decked with palaces reared by the magicians' wand.

PART VII.

SPECIAL FEATURES OF THE FAIR.

ASIDE from the great buildings that will of course be the main points of interest, there are numerous special features promised—features that will be unique in their way and reflecting in a great degree the manners and customs of the people who inhabit the countries of which they will be typical. It has been decided that a single entrance fee, probably fifty cents, shall entitle the visitors to see the entire exposition proper. For the special attractions on Midway Plaisance a moderate additional charge will be made. In the course of time these attractions will doubtless be added to, but even the present plans are liberal enough to give satisfaction. The Plaisance, which is a strip of land connecting Jackson Park with Washington Park, will be occupied throughout its entire length by special exposition features, largely of a foreign character, such as the "Bazaar of All Nations," "Street in Cairo," "Street in Constantinople," "Moorish Palace," "Maori Village," etc. Concessions have been granted to all these enterprises, and their production will represent the expenditure of hundreds of thousands of dollars. Panoramas, cycloramas, the sliding railway, etc., will also be located in this part of the exhibition grounds.

A person of imaginative temperament can easily picture to himself the attractions that may be found in this locality. The "Bazaar of All Nations" is a mammoth structure in which will be representatives of almost every clime under the sun, grouped in their native habitations and presenting to the visitor exactly the same appearance as that which characterizes their home routine of life. Their manufactures, occupations, and pleasures will be graphically pictured. The "Street in Cairo" is to be exactly what its name implies. A street in that sleepy and quaint old Egyptian city will be deftly reproduced, in passing down which the visitor may see sights exactly similar to those that would greet his vision if he were touring in far-off Cairo itself instead of in Chicago — the famous city that finds everything possible, even to the reproduction of an entire Egyptian city, to say nothing of a single street from such. The Moorish Palace will be a splendid structure, and within its gorgeous recesses one may wander and try to imagine how Othello felt when he paced his vaulted halls a prey to the demon jealousy.

According to recent plans fully 150 restaurants and *cafes* will be in operation in the various buildings and about the grounds. These will be conveniently distributed and will have an estimated aggregate seating capacity of 6,000 to 8,000. It is intended to have in the Fisheries Building a restaurant devoted as far as possible to the exclusive serving of fish. Fish dinners and fish, fresh and salt, served in every edible style, it is believed, will be a popular feature. In view of the present outlook it doesn't seem as though any visitor need go hungry at the Fair.

In line with the special features, perhaps, is the announcement that a silversmith in Monterey, Mexico, is engaged on a work in silver which when completed will be an exact reproduction of the Agricultural Building now in process of completion at the exposition grounds. It will be eight feet wide, will contain a quality of silver valued as bullion at $10,000, and when finished will be valued at $20,000. The Connecticut members of the Board of Lady Managers have undertaken to raise by contribution a fund with which to pay for a fine bust of Harriet Beecher Stowe. This will be their contribution toward the adornment of the walls of the Woman's Building. Copies of Mrs. Stowe's literary works will also be contributed.

The President of Ecuador has decreed that the governors of each state of the Republic shall collect and forward to Quito, the capital, exhibits of all kinds illustrating the riches and productions of their several states. The Archbishop of Ecuador has issued an order to the bishops and priests throughout the Republic directing them to do the same and also collect and forward everything which may be in their keeping illustrative of the history of the country suitable to exhibit at Chicago. The Consul General of the United States at Quito has directed the consuls and vice-consuls and consular agents at different points in Ecuador to assist the governors of states in every way possible in the matter of collection of articles relating to commerce with exterior countries. The entire exhibit so collected will be forwarded intact to Chicago.

Lieut. Baker, head of the marine section of the department of transportation, has secured a promise from the Detroit Dry-dock Company for an exhibit of a perfect model in stucco of the entire ship-building plant of that company, both at its Detroit and Wyandotte yards.

A bill has recently been introduced in Congress carrying an appropriation of $18,000 "to procure, prepare, compile for publication and publish statistics of the moral, intellectual and industrial progress of the colored people of the United States from January 1, 1863, the date of the emancipation proclamation, to January 1, 1893, as a part of the government exhibit, the same to illustrate the growth of liberty, morality and humanity of the United States."

The women of England, it is understood, are actively preparing for their participation in the exposition. At a meeting of the Woman's Committee in London, March 3, of the present year, it was announced that Queen Victoria had promised specimens of her own work in spinning and knitting, done when she was a girl; also some of her embroidering, fine drawing, and water-color painting. Princess Louise will contribute some clay modeling, Princess Beatrice several paintings, and Princess Christian some embroidery.

It is probable that the visitors to the exposition will have an opportunity to see a more extensive and finer exhibition of ancient Greek art than it has heretofore been possible to contemplate outside of Greece. Mr. P. Canreading, director-general of Grecian antiquities, has accepted the invitation to participate in the exposition, with the understanding that it will be represented only by memorials of its antiquities. Charles Walstein, director of the American school of classic studies at Athens, states that the Grecian government has agreed to make and send to the exposition casts of the principal works of ancient art now in Greece, together with maps, diagrams, and photographs. To these will probably be added casts and perhaps some of the original specimens of classic Greek art which are now distributed throughout Europe.

A wheelman's parade, participated in by 24,000 bicyclists, may be one of the sights at the exposition. Efforts are being made to bring about that result.

The Pennsylvania coal operators want to construct a building entirely of anthracite coal at the exposition and to have 50,000 tons of best anthracite on exhibition.

A continuous clam-bake will be one of the attractions which epicurean visitors will find at the exposition.

The South African diamond mine exhibit will doubtless prove an eye-opener, to use a slang expression. The exhibit will come from Cape Colony and will include 10,000 carats of uncut stones, a very large quantity of stones fine cut and polished, together with all that is necessary to show the process of mining and washing. For this it will be necessary to transport to Chicago 100 tons of pulverized blue earth, 50 tons of unpulverized earth, and a complete washing machine, which will be operated by natives. The exhibit will also include a unique collection of crocidolite, special diamond-iferous products, ostrich feathers, fleeces, etc. It is reported that a Bushman and Hottentot in native dress will accompany the exhibit.

A communication has been received by the fair officials from the British Commission asking for space to exhibit the rifle-calibre guns manufactured by the Maxim-Nordenfeldt Gun Company. The company wants to erect a building in which to exhibit its guns in practice. One end of the building will be filled with sandbags into which the projectiles of the guns will be fired. It is claimed that the arrangements are such as will insure perfect safety and will be reproductions of a similar exhibit recently given at the Royal Naval Exposition in London.

The wooded island in the exposition grounds has already begun to assume the character which in great part it will have during the Fair — that of a gigantic flower garden. The horticultural department has recently received 27,000 rose bushes and other plants, several thousand of which came from abroad. These are being transplanted on the island.

It may be said to be assured that the exhibits at the Fair

will cover a wider range and be far more numerous than any array ever before gathered together. They will present a picture of the condition and industrial progress of mankind in every quarter of the world and of its achievements in every branch of the sciences and arts. The exposition classification embraces 12 departments, 176 groups, and 967 classes. The applications for space by intending exhibitors in the United States alone numbered 2,082 in January last. The number at the Philadelphia Centennial in corresponding space was 864. Applications from foreign visitors are rapidly increasing in numbers. It seems assured that the visitors will outnumber those at any previous world's fair.

In April, 1893, grand international naval review, preliminary to the opening of the exposition, as provided for by an act of Congress, will be held in New York harbor, arrangements for which are already in progress. All the great navies of the world will participate in this vast aquatic pageant.

PART VIII.

ABOUT THE CITY DURING FAIR TIME.

AN OPIUM FIEND.

WITH the exception of the Auditorium and the Chicago Opera House, the plans of which have been heretofore outlined, the theatres, so far as at present known, have not arranged for any special attractions during the Fair. All of the down-town houses have booked more or less to the time from May to October, and the attractions for the most part are such standard renditions as have been proved popular with playgoers for the last two or three years. The patron of the regular playhouses will be able to take his choice between grand or light opera, local drama, tragedy, comedy or burlesque, and the most exacting taste will doubtless be amply satisfied. The contract between managers Abbey and Adams for the production at the Auditorium has already been signed, and the spectacle to be presented there will, it is expected, eclipse anything that these two managers have ever before attempted. At the Chicago Opera House the first great successes in the way of burlesque that Mr. Hendersen scored, "Arabian Nights," "Crystal Slipper," and "Sinbad," are to be repeated in rotation, and people will have an opportunity to witness the perfection of the class of entertainment termed by the irreverent "leg-shows" but known to the world at large by the more dignified title of burlesque.

Pain & Sons, the great firm whose pyrotechnical productions have made them famous wherever fireworks are known, are to produce their famous spectacle, "The Fall of Pompeii," at the Cottage Grove amphitheatre, near South Park, this summer. They are also, it is understood, arranging for a production on a much more wonderful scale for the Fair season in the same locality. One of the beauties of the Pain projections is their shortness. Their glare and brilliancy is generally crowded into an hour or at most an hour and a half, thus enabling the spectator to secure a surfeit of pleasure, as it were, in a short space of time, without forcing him to spend an unnecessary season in waiting, Micawber-like, for something to turn up.

The racing, the boating, the riding, and the hundred other attractions of the city have already been described in detail. None are likely to get away between the present time and the day set for the opening of the Fair. On the contrary, they are likely to be added to and enhanced, for human ingenuity is being taxed to its utmost to invent new charms for the pleasure-seeker and, incidentally, of course, to catch the nimble dollar that he is willing to disburse for the procurement of such pleasures, elevating or otherwise.

Of course no well regulated person ever enters a saloon except for purposes of investigation, but there are a few saloons and *cafes* in Chicago that are visited as much for sightseeing as for liquid refreshment. In some there hang pictures worth small fortunes. The objects represented are generally a little bit *outre* — *"saloonish,"* as I have heard it called. Hannah & Hogg's saloons, of which there are several, located in the business district at various points, are celebrated for the works of art that adorn their walls. The one on Madison Street, under the Madison Street Opera House, contains a valuable gallery of paintings, the cash estimate of which runs into thousands of dollars. This is the largest place owned by the firm; some of their branch establishments contain rare pictures that are almost as valuable.

"Handsome Harry Varnell's" place on South Clark Street, near Madison, is perhaps the most gorgeous saloon in Chicago. It was only recently completed at a cost said to exceed $40,000. All the walls and wainscoting are finished in Mexican onyx, and the outer part is designed in iron and bronze. Some oil paintings, the subjects of which are very interesting, adorn the walls. Varnell, the proprietor, is a "character." He enjoys a large popularity with the sporting classes. He is said to be interested in the Garfield Park race track and is quite a "plunger" at other games as well. He was one of the principals in the old-time "boodle" sensation, which resulted in several of the county officials of that period going to the penitentiary under sentence for bribery and corruption.

Just across the way from Varnell's is Lansing & McGarigle's saloon and restaurant, a place made famous both by the personality of its chief proprietor and by a historical tragedy that occurred there some few years ago. William J. McGarigle has held various offices. He was once superintendent of police and later warden of the county hospital. When the boodle trials were held he was tried and sentenced to two years imprisonment, but, while awaiting in the county jail the result of his appeal for a new trial, he secured permission from Canute R. Matson, the sheriff of the county, to visit his home. He drove there with Matson, and, on the pretext of taking a bath, he slipped away from the house, boarded a schooner, and got over into Canada. His flight formed one of the newspaper sensations of the hour. Matson never quite recovered from the shock. In the language of the song, McGarigle "never came back," that is to say, not until his friends had so arranged things that when he did come back he was permitted to pay his debt to the law by the payment of a fine of $1,000. McGarigle's place now is a famous rendezvous for "sports" of both sexes. The fare served is of a high quality, and the visitor may find all the enjoyment he desires in studying the people who sit at the tables near him. There are ladies of great beauty and of all ages but all of whom manifestly belong to the class whose existence reputable people endeavor to forget; there are gamblers, touts, and so on, in loud clothes and wearing much loud jewelry, both genuine and bogus. The best of order and good conduct prevail for the reason that no boisterous actions are tolerated. But sometimes all the rules and regulations in the world are not proof against the angry passions of men, a fact that was conclusively proved by the tragedy already mentioned.

The principals were "Doc" Haggerty, a well known and very muscular person, who bore the reputation of being something of a bully, and "Jimmy" Connorton, a gambler. There was a feud between the two, and when Connorton went into McGarigle's place one Saturday evening and met his foe face to face, high words and blows were instantly interchanged. Accounts vary as to who first drew the deadly pistol, but Connorton got in the first shot. He shot Haggerty through the stomach and then fled through the restaurant, pursued by the wounded man, who at every step snapped his revolver in the effort to slay his adversary. But the weapon would not explode, and it was not until the two reached the sidewalk and Connorton had almost succeeded in escaping through a line of cabs that it did respond to the fall of the hammer. Connorton sunk to the sidewalk desperately wounded. The excitement over the tragedy was only equalled by that occasioned by the Dunn-Elliott encounter in the old Tivoli. Haggerty died, but Connorton recovered and was acquitted on the ground of self-defense. At present Lansing & McGarigle's is a model resort of its kind. It caters to the sporting element almost exclusively, and happily such tragedies like the one here told do not occur often.

Hogan and Batchelder's, two well-known and popular resorts on State Street, also cater to the sporting element. They have private supper-rooms in which hilarious parties are wont to hold high revel, especially after a return from a successful day at the races.

The places mentioned are of course of a certain variety, but the reader has been told in preceding chapters of the many more quiet and more decorous places that he may visit. It is a "great big" city, full of all sorts of attractions, godly and ungodly. If the world's fair should be closed on Sundays, something that the religious element is sedulously endeavoring to bring about, the army of pleasure-seekers will be driven to the city itself for recreation.

FINIS—THE AUTHOR AT REST.

Notes

PAUL DURICA *and* BILL SAVAGE

FRONTISPIECE

Lillian Russell

The appearance on the frontispiece of singer and actress Lillian Russell (1860–1922) no doubt reflects the publisher's desire to profit on a local girl done good. Russell's biography in some respects resembles that of Carrie Meeber, the protagonist of Theodore Dreiser's *Sister Carrie* (1900). Like Meeber, Russell came from a modest background and achieved her initial theatrical success in Chicago before moving on to greater fame in New York. She was particularly famed for her performances in various Gilbert and Sullivan comic operas. At the time of *Chicago by Day and Night*'s publication, she was involved in a very public divorce from her first husband, the composer Edward Solomon, who had been accused of bigamy. Russell sustained her notoriety through a subsequent and lengthy affair with James Buchanan "Diamond Jim" Brady, legendary Gilded Age robber baron. Her famous visage would have sold books as well.

THE GIST OF IT

The organization of *Chicago by Day and Night* was a little fly-by-night; the first edition, for instance, began with Part I, which was then divided into numbered chapters. Then it had Part II, which was divided into numbered parts, rather than chapters. We've made this a bit more regular to minimize potential confusion.

3 **the Paris of America** The editors have been unable to identify the "bright-minded and discerning person" who allegedly
proclaimed Chicago the "Paris of America," and the quotation
may have been a fabrication on the part of the author(s) or a
commonplace Chicago boast. Such a comment does jibe with
the general spirit of extreme boosterism that surrounded the
World's Columbian Exposition in 1893. In 1891, John J. Flinn
wrote in *Chicago: The Marvelous City of the West* that "Not in
the Arabian Nights' Entertainments, though bathed in all the
glorious colorings of Oriental fancy, is there a tale which surpasses in wonder the plain, unvarnished history of Chicago . . .
Chicago is one of the wonders of modern times. Her progress amazes mankind. There is not on record an achievement
of human intellect, skill, and industry that will bear comparison with the transformation of a dismal swamp, in the
midst of a trackless desert, within the span of a human life,
into one of the mightiest and grandest cities on the globe."
A History of the World's Columbian Exposition (1897), edited
by Rossiter Johnson with the approval of the exposition's directors, can't help but proclaim the city a "golden circle . . .
whose radius is at least five hundred miles and whose golden
products are those most necessary to the welfare and enjoyment of the human race." According to Johnson, Chicago,
"for the present epoch at least, is the seat of empire." British
reformer William T. Stead reached a slightly different conclusion while visiting the city in 1893. Rather than perceiving the
"seat of empire," Stead encountered "barbarous gridironed
streets" populated by "many mutilated fragments of human-
ity," which led him to write the highly critical *If Christ Came to
Chicago* (1894). Stead could have found directions to many of
the targets of his critique in *Chicago by Day and Night.*

4 **swell until the two million mark is passed** Chicago would
reach a population of two million during the first decade of the
twentieth century. By 1950, the population was at a little over

3.6 million, despite the predictions by Daniel Burnham and Edward Bennett in their 1909 *Plan of Chicago* that 13.5 million Chicagoans would populate the city by then. Since the mid-twentieth century, the population has dropped to its current level of roughly 2.7 million. Fantasies of limitless expansion endured well into the twentieth century. The decidedly boosterish *Chicago: The City Beautiful* proclaimed, as late as 1943, that Chicago was "one of the first four cities of the World in population and destined to become 'The World's Largest City by 1968.'"

4   **The Author**   The writer or writers of *Chicago by Day and Night* remain unidentified, but we can deduce some things about them based on the cultural framework in which they operated. The publisher, Thomson and Zimmerman of La Salle Street, would have been under pressure to produce the book almost as quickly as the Fair Committee itself had to choose sites and architects. Chicago was a major center for the printing industry, and nineteenth-century publishers were capable of such feats. The first books about the Great Chicago Fire of 1871 (E. J. Goodspeed's *History of the Great Fires in Chicago and the West* and Colbert and Chamberlin's *Chicago and the Great Conflagration*) appeared within mere months of the calamity, albeit in New York.

The wide range of specific knowledge displayed in *Chicago by Day and Night* suggests the book was written either by a glib and loquacious Chicago Renaissance Man-about-town utterly immune to writer's cramp or by multiple authors working in parallel, each according to his or her own area of expertise. Perhaps one person could be as familiar with the preaching styles of famed Chicago churchmen; the vast variety of theatrical and other entertainments; the reputations of dozens of hotels, bars, and restaurants; the architectural details of famous buildings; notorious crimes and the strategies of various criminals; and neighborhoods as diverse as Little Cheyenne and Lake View. It seems unlikely, albeit not impossible.

Stylistic variations among the prose of the chapters also suggest more than one writer. Some chapters address the assumed reader directly, others do not; some call visitors to the city "wayfarers," while others never use that term; in some chapters French terms are italicized, and in others they are not. The mocking tone in chapter 9, "As to Adventuresses," which warns the presumably male reader against the ploys of female con artists, suggests a woman writer with firsthand knowledge of "the spirit of masculine vanity that forms the material on which the adventuress may work"(58). On the other hand, the brief and condescending chapter 12, "On Shopping," shows more than a touch of knee-jerk misogyny as it condescends to give scanty advice, since shopping merely lets women enjoy "the happy pastime of getting rid of the dollars that their husbands and fathers have bestowed upon them for that purpose"(83). The vociferously conservative political stance of the chapter on Haymarket, whose author claims to have been present at the hanging of the Haymarket martyrs, seems at odds with the usually laissez-faire attitude of most of the book.

Along with our author or authors, the book also has multiple illustrators. The various photo montages and full-page illustrations are not credited, although the engraving featuring the Proscenium Arch of the Auditorium (page 27, rather crudely broken up to fit on one page) has the annotation "J. Manz & Co. Eng. Chi." Jacob Manz emigrated from Switzerland to Chicago in 1855, and found work at a print shop. A little more than a decade later, he became the firm's owner; the J. Manz Engraving Company survived the Great Fire of 1871 to gain national prominence (and exhibited a sense of humor: one of their slogans, preserved in a plaque on the site of their former factory: "Any size job is a Manz size job"). Manz matched his business success with civic activism, serving as president of the United German Singers and as one of the planners of Switzerland's presence at the 1893 World's Fair. In 1916, at the age of 78, he suffered a tragic accident—in the early morning hours, he mistook the sill of an open window for the edge of his bed and, leaning backward, fell twenty feet to his death. The J. Manz Engraving Company continued to operate until 1962, and its massive plant at 4001 N. Ravenswood (now the Ravenswood Event Center) still bears the firm's name in its brickwork. The Auditorium proscenium arch itself was by Charles Halloway, whose neoclassical allegory of the stages of human life as represented in song won a commission competition over hundreds of other artists, including Louis Tiffany.

The drawings that appear throughout the book are sometimes signed "H. Mayer." We have been unable to identify this artist. While these illustrations might seem incidental, they contribute to themes (and humor) of the book. For instance, the first image, "The Compiler at Work," shows our writer, conservatively dressed, on the street at night as he scribbles notes under the light of a gas lamp (see the notes on 221 and 241 for more on the moral significance of gas lamps). The image suggests urban authenticity and a certain degree of experience with the literal and figurative nightlife that the book features, and the scattered pages or litter blowing around speak to the unruly out-of-control nature of the book as well. Several of the illustrations, especially in the chapter "As to Adventuresses," are small dramas of detail (see the note on 232). The illustration at the opening of that chapter shows the street scene in which many an adventuress would begin to ensnare her prey (57). Later in that chapter, an encounter in a restaurant or saloon includes two men, one clearly more sophisticated and urbane than the other (note the differences in how each holds his walking stick). Yet it is the sharper of the two who eyes the adventuress, subtly reinforcing the writer's claim that "male vanity" rather than female artifice gives the adventuress her prowess (60). The illustrations also sometimes echo classical illuminated manuscripts updated for a modern age, with initial letters of words formed from the new urban landscape of elevated trains (156). Casual, yet keenly observed and energetic, the illustrations help bring the prose of the book to life.

CHAPTER I. WHERE TO STAY

7   **Michigan Avenue and Congress Street**   As to Chicago's address system: the Brennan Plan of 1908 led to the reform of Chicago's chaotic street naming and numbering system. Due to the annexation of what had been suburbs (Hyde Park, Lake

View, and others), many street names were duplicated. Addresses were based on distance from Lake Michigan or the Chicago River, highly variable starting points for a house numbering system. In the Brennan Plan (so called for its primary supporter, a freelance urban planner of sorts, Edward Brennan) many streets were renamed to eliminate duplication, and the addresses were regularized, with State and Madison Streets as the east–west and north–south zero point of the grid. When the *Pleasure Seeker's Guide* gives locations based on intersections, such locations will still be accurate; when they list addresses, not so much. Consult http://www.chsmedia.org/househistory/nameChanges/start.pdf at the Chicago History Museum's website if you want to convert addresses to contemporary locations; where street names have changed and it's particularly germane, we note it (as in the note for County Jail).

7 **"blooded"** "Bloods" were wealthy young men-about-town; a truncation of "blue bloods." The areas they frequented would have been "blooded districts," just as the city today has its entertainment districts frequented by hipsters, tourists, or clubbers.

7 **habitues** People who can habitually be found somewhere; regulars. As is so often the case, putting a term into French makes it classier. See *demi-mondaines* (page 233).

7 **delicious lays** The sexual double entendre of "delicious lays . . . being caroled forth by the song-birds" would have been as obvious then as now.

7 **A block north of the Auditorium is the Richelieu** While the Auditorium survives today as an acknowledged masterpiece of architects Dankmar Adler and Louis Sullivan, the Richelieu, the "Delmonico of Chicago," which was located at 318 South Michigan Avenue, is no more. It did not long outlive the World's Columbian Exposition and locked its doors in 1895. The *New York Times* noted the hotel's passing and the effect that its short life (1885–1895) had on the dining habits of Chicagoans. Prior to the Richelieu's opening, Chicago was in the "apple-and-beer-for-breakfast stage." The hotel's proprietor, Henry V. Bemis, changed all that by importing French waiters to serve French cuisine and stocking a wine cellar that soon allowed Midwesterners the opportunity to discern whether a

"wine is Chateau La Rose, 1864, or Chateau McGinnis (California) 1896." The Richelieu was the first hotel in the city on the European plan, which meant that the price of meals was not included with the room. In 1891, the finest room at the Richelieu, which included a parlor, two bedrooms, and a private bath, cost $12 to $15 per day, roughly $300 to $375 in 2012 dollars. To roughly calculate the 2012 equivalent of the 1893 prices listed throughout this book, multiply each dollar by twenty-five.

8   **Sara Bernhardt . . . Mrs. Langtry**   Famed actresses of the day (Mrs. Langtry being Lillie Langtry), but not so famous that the typesetter remembered the "h" in Sarah Bernhardt's first name.

10   **"Wayside Inn"**   An establishment operated by a former employee of the Richelieu hotel and, as mentioned in the text, the father of the actress Hattie Harvey, whose photograph appears alongside that of other performers in the chapter devoted to "Special Features of Chicago" (see page 156). Hattie appeared in several popular noted productions from the period, including the first staging in Chicago of *Charley's Aunt* at Hooley's Theater (as described in chapter 2; see page 17) in 1894. Hattie was the protégée of Madame Patti, another popular performer from the period, and sometimes appeared onstage under the name Hattie Patti. A *Tribune* story from June 1890 provocatively describes the performer's history in the context of popular amusements: "Seven years ago Miss Hattie Patti, then Hattie Harvey, started out as a roller-skater in the old rink on the corner of Wabash Avenue and Twentieth Street. She was managed by J. L. Jordan, wore a Highland-fling outfit, cut circles on the asphalt and the hearts of the South Side dudes, lived on a diet of Gunther's candy (see page 151) and popcorn and had herself covered with medals and bangles, with gewgaws she has since put away with her button string. A couple of years ago, Miss Harvey played a little and sung a little, and dressed a little for a part in 'Midsummer Night's Dream.' She is a small, semi-blonde of two dozen years or so, who might have served as a model for Daisy Miller, and who can be trusted to look well after the interests of Miss Hattie Harvey Patti." Daisy Miller was the titular protagonist of Henry James's 1879 novella, a

young American heiress who dies of malaria contracted due to the unforgivable indiscretion of keeping company with Italians at night on the public streets of Rome.

11 **guests of Hebraic extraction** An indicator of taken-for-granted antisemitism and a not-so-subtle warning to anyone who would not want to share quarters with Jewish guests; or, a signal to Jewish travelers that they could get a room at the Palmer House. Most such coded language would have such a double valence, reinforcing the prejudice while also showing a way around it.

11 **the young man lay dead on the floor** When the *New York Times* first reported on the murder of Charles Stiles, caller at the Chicago Stock Exchange, on July 11, 1882, it included some interesting details left out by the author(s) of *Chicago by Day and Night.* According to Teresa, she'd been abandoned the night before at Downings, "a road house north of the city much frequented by fast men and fast women," after her money ran out and had been forced to walk back to Chicago in the rain. For years she'd supported Stiles in his expensive habits, often working at the "establishment" (the polite term of the day for "brothel") of Carrie Watson, the richest and most famous madam in Chicago for over two decades. Watson is a key figure in Stead's *If Christ Came to Chicago,* Asbury's *Gem of the Prairie,* and other exposés of Chicago's vice. *Chicago by Day and Night* suggests that Teresa's "nominal punishment" was partially the result of her "great beauty," but Stead provides the social context to her motives. "Few people realize," he writes, "that a young and pretty woman can make more money for a short time by what may be called a discriminate sale of her person than the ablest woman in America can make at the same age in any profession." Lack of other economic options was one force driving many young women in the city into prostitution.

13 **smaller hotels** Such hotels would have included H. H. Holmes's famed "Murder Castle" on Sixty-third Street, which was under construction while this text was being written.

13 **the Metropole** This hotel was later Al Capone's Chicago headquarters, until his 1928 relocation to the more notorious Lexington Hotel.

14 **one's first thoughts naturally turn to the theaters** Chicago's fame as a theatrical center predates such contemporary companies as Steppenwolf, Lookingglass, Court, Northlight, and Goodman. The emphasis put, throughout this book, on public entertainment reminds us that before the Internet, television, or radio, one's only potential private amusement, when visiting another city, would be reading in one's hotel room. Public entertainment was a necessity.

16 **a party of honest country folks** One wonders if any such putatively naive folks bought this book specifically to find these "leg shows." While Chicago was famed for its population of immigrants from abroad, newcomers from rural America also crowded its streets. Chicago's reputation for wickedness, as expressed in Carl Sandburg's "Chicago," clearly pivots on this fact: "They tell me you [Chicago] are wicked and I believe them, for I have seen your painted women under the gas lamps luring the farm boys." The odds are excellent that some of these painted women were once farm girls come to the big city.

16 **Mr. Hamlin's temple** In 1880 a young Dankmar Adler designed the Grand Opera House, which featured comic operas, minstrel shows, and other popular entertainments, for theatrical manager John A. Hamlin. Hamlin eventually handed off management of the Opera House to his Yale-educated son Fred, who would achieve considerable success with an adaptation of *The Wizard of Oz* and, later still, *Babes in Toyland.*

20 **the Eden Musee** The Eden Musee, also known as Haverly's Casino, located at the corner of Wabash and Jackson, did not long survive the World's Columbian Exposition. In 1897 Pinkerton agents apprehended two nineteenth-century salvagers who had removed from the abandoned museum $3,000 worth of copper wire and plumbing fixtures. Prior to its closure, the Musee offered audiences a mix of waxworks and live performances, in particular minstrel acts, a Hungarian band, and something called "Sousa's Sardine Band." Like today's Madame Tussaud's, the Musee's waxworks mixed contempo-

rary figures such as President Grover Cleveland and historical fixtures such as Queen Elizabeth I. The waxworks reflected advances in science and exploration, with tableaux devoted to Henry Stanley's expeditions in Africa and Louis Pasteur's pioneering work in microbiology, as well as the country's enduring fascination with the American Civil War. The Grand Stereoscopic Hall claimed to have on display "1,000 scenes of Every Famous Place in the World," offering "amusement with instruction," although the emphasis seemed to be decidedly on the former. In 1893, admission cost a quarter, or half the price of admission to the Fair.

Chapter III. The Auditorium and the New German Theater

23 **the tower** Skyscraper technology fundamentally changed the visual relationship people had to the urban landscape. While artists had long imagined bird's-eye views of cities or other landscapes, to be able to actually go 225 feet up in the air and see across the lake to the state of Michigan was a revolutionary spectacle. It is no mistake that one of the most popular sites at the Fair was the Observation Tower on the Transportation Building. We now take skyscrapers utterly for granted, and the Auditorium building is dwarfed by later structures, but for its day it was a wonder.

25 **New German Theater** Better remembered by Chicagoans as the Schiller, later the Garrick, the New German Theater was formally dedicated on September 30, 1892. Designed by Dankmar Adler and Louis Sullivan with a seating capacity of 1,300, the Schiller symbolized the size and success of the German community, which at the time was the largest ethnic group in the city. Rabbi Emil G. Hirsh (see page 44) spoke at the dedication. In describing the ceremony, the *Tribune* proclaimed that the Schiller would, because of its advanced construction, "outlast time." Like many of Adler and Sullivan's creations, the Schiller did not long outlast the first half of the twentieth century. Despite the best efforts of pioneering urban preservationists, including photographer and Sullivan enthusiast

Richard Nickel, the Garrick was demolished in 1960 to make room for a parking lot. Through the work of Nickel and others, fragments of the facade were saved. Some of these details—the faces of four famous German-speaking artists and thinkers—have been incorporated into the facade of the Second City Theater in Old Town on North Wells Street.

26   **the following well-known citizens** Many Chicago histories written during the nineteenth century featured lists naming everyone on various boards of directors or serving in fire companies or other organizations. The fact that some chapters in this book eschew such rosters while others use them is more evidence for multiple authorship.

Chapter IV. Two Unique Playhouses

28   **Sam T. Jack** Sam T. Jack's burlesque was famous enough to still be missed in 1951, when Nelson Algren lamented lost Chicago landmarks in *Chicago: City on the Make.* "What became of Sam T. Jack's Burlesque and the old Globe on Desplaines?" he asked.

29   **Park Theater** Lowest of the lowbrow, the Park Theater encouraged what now might be called "interactive" theater, or extreme heckling. The unfortunate James Owen O'Connor did not long survive his ill-fated performance at the Park in January 1891. O'Connor had been a lawyer and a Baptist preacher, but acting was his true vocation, and he specialized in performing Shakespearean characters, such as Hamlet and Richard III, in vaudeville houses across the country. Responses like the kind he received at the Park apparently drove him insane, and he died while an inmate at the Morris Plains Asylum in New Jersey in April 1894. According to the *Tribune,* O'Connor interrupted the booing and vegetable tossing during his Park Theater performance to ask the audience, "Do you call this fair?" One Chicago wit apparently shouted in response, "Yes, World's Fair," which met with the approval of his fellow audience members.

29   **"Levee," or "Tenderloin" district** Vice area on Chicago's near

South Side, notorious for its countless bars and brothels, including the famed Everleigh Club (see Karen Abbott's *Sin in the Second City*). So called because many of its residents had come to Chicago from New Orleans; "tenderloin" was a common term for such districts in many cities, with its obvious double entendre referencing both food and sex.

30 **stale cats**   We can find no slang interpretation of this phrase, and so must conclude that actual dead felines were sold, along with the more typical stale vegetables, to be thrown at performers whose work hecklers considered unworthy.

Chapter V. Free and Easy Shows

31 **a blot upon the city's escutcheon**   In English heraldry, an "escutcheon" is a shield or shield-shaped image that bears a coat of arms representing a person or family's noble standing. By extension, this term came to mean one's reputation, and a "blot" on one's escutcheon can refer either to an unfair insult or actual ignoble behavior. Given the reality of Chicago's beer dens, in this instance the usage would seem to be the latter.

32 **assassination therein of Jim Elliott**   On March 1, 1883, Jere Dunn walked into the Tivoli Saloon on Dearborn and shot boxer Jim Elliott, killing him. Dunn won at trial by arguing self-defense, claiming that Elliott had threatened to murder him on sight and so, when he happened upon him, Dunn had no choice but to defend himself. Elliott was also armed, and a jury acquitted Dunn after four hours of deliberation. This comment about a saloon that has already been torn down and so could not be visited by the putative audience for this book shows the power of nostalgia in so many Chicago texts. The city has been built and rebuilt so quickly and so frequently that much of its history exists only in such stories of what was once at a given spot. The Fair itself—almost completely burned down or demolished within months of its closing in October 1893—is just such a ghost presence in the urban landscape. The textual city endures longer than the actual city.

32 **Engel's**   Like many of the sites for popular entertainment described in the guide, Engel's Pavilion on North Clark Street

had a relatively short life span. By June 1893, proprietor Adolph Engel had shuttered the doors and was appearing regularly in court to respond to charges being made by various creditors. The *Chicago Tribune* attributed the Pavilion's failure to a larger trend. As a result of the World's Fair with its Midway Plaisance, pleasure seekers were heading south in increasing numbers for their cheap amusements, and North Side establishments suffered as a consequence. This is the exact opposite of the contemporary moment, where venues for popular entertainments—blues and jazz clubs, amusement parks, movie theaters—on the South Side have largely disappeared as a result of deindustrialization, blight, white flight, and the urban renewal policies of the 1950s and 1960s.

33 **soubrette** A stock comic theatrical character, a pert or saucy maid, or an actress who plays one.

35 **Promptly at 12 o'clock** In theory, bars in Chicago at that time had to close at midnight. As much of the information in this book indicates, this law, like so many others, was widely flouted.

36 **coryphees** Ballet dancers who are neither prima ballerinas nor mere members of the corps de ballet but instead tread the middle ground by dancing in small groups.

37 **Baum's Pavilion** According to the guide, Baum's was the South Side analogue to Engel's and, like that establishment, it did not survive the economic upheavals of the early 1890s. By the end of 1892—months before the Fair's opening—Baum's had been torn down and replaced by a four-story brick commercial and residential building named after the owner of the land upon which it stood, Joanna Anderson. One can only wonder if readers of *Chicago by Day and Night* were disappointed; it is not known if this Baum was any relation to Oz author and Fair visitor L. Frank Baum (see note on Baum, page 263).

37 **beer garden** Before air-conditioning was perfected in the 1920s, open-air drinking was the norm in hot-weather months. Beer gardens were also beloved by Chicago's most numerous immigrant ethnic group, the Germans, and despised by Prohibitionists among Chicago's political and business elite, who tended to be "native" Americans—that is, New Englanders,

New Yorkers, or Southerners who settled in the city before the first waves of non-English-speaking immigrants arrived in the mid-nineteenth century. For German Chicagoans, beer gardens maintained old-world and old-country traditions, reinforcing their national identity in resistance to assimilation and Americanization. Beer gardens, especially in residential areas, were considered appropriate family venues by Germans because they offered food and music as well as beer, and entertainment for children as well. The presence of children, the mixing of the sexes, and the public nature of beer gardens made them favorite targets of Prohibitionists, especially since their working-class Catholic clientele favored beer on Sundays (their one day off from work). Conservative Protestants thought Sunday drinking (along with theater, baseball, or any other public entertainment) was inherently sinful and therefore should be illegal. It is noteworthy how much of this chapter describes the ways that social propriety is putatively maintained at beer gardens by proper segregation of the sexes and intolerance of disorder; the writer may be trying to calm the fears of out-of-towners unaccustomed to such places or refute the slanders of temperance forces (see note on Frances Willard and the WCTU, page 243).

41 **Ashland Club Annex** The method to gain entry to such an establishment at any time, if one knows the day's "password," anticipates the Prohibition-era speakeasy, but such methods would have been commonplace for any saloon, then or now, that operated after hours or without a license.

Chapter VI. Churches and Church Services

42 **total Sabbath attendance** The inclusion of this chapter is intriguing and very suggestive of the conflicts extant in Chicago culture at the time. Apart from "foreign" atheistic anarchists, people were assumed to be more or less religious, and visitors to Chicago for the Fair might indeed be in search of services to attend. But the majority of the book is devoted to "entertainments" and "resorts" that would probably be the object of some hellfire-and-brimstone sermons. We can only speculate

about motives for including this information, but along with chapter 16, "The City's Moral Code — A Complete Refutation of the Libelous Assertion that Chicago is the Wickedest City in the World," it could come from the Chicago tendency to want to answer presumed critiques from out-of-towners. Chicago's reputation for vice and crime would, to this way of thinking, be balanced or refuted by emphasis on our many churches and the many people who attend them. As with the description of the materials and physical dimensions of the Auditorium, there is this odd emphasis on numbers: how many attend services, how much the preachers or rabbis are paid, and so forth, as though touting the attendance at a ballgame and the statistics of the players. A sporting attitude toward even divine services is here evident: in Chicago, it seems, we measure everything, even if such numbers seem arbitrary and beyond proof. For the sake of comparison, though, the population of Chicago in 1893 was estimated to be 1,099,850, so 120,000 people attending services would be about 9 percent of the population. Or, to put it another way, more than 90 percent of Chicagoans were otherwise engaged.

42 **Holy Family** This church still stands on West Roosevelt Road, along with St. Ignatius College Prep, formerly Loyola College. Founded in 1857 by Jesuit priest Arnold Damen, for whom Damen Avenue is named, Holy Family's history features a telling anecdote regarding the Great Chicago Fire. The story goes that Damen, in the east raising funds for the parish, got a telegram informing him of the fire; he prayed that Holy Family be spared and promised that if it was, the church would keep seven vigil candles forever lit to the Virgin Mary. The degree to which divine intervention would have been required is debatable at best, as the fire began about a mile east and slightly north of the church, and strong, dry winds from the southwest blew the fire to the north and east, destroying much of the city. But Holy Family did not burn, and those seven candles have been kept lit ever since, though today they are electric. Catherine and Patrick O'Leary, in whose barn the fire began, were parishioners of Holy Family. Like many inner-city parishes, it was nearly closed due to mid-twentieth-century demographic

shifts, but energetic organization and fund-raising have kept the church open, and in 2012 it had largely been restored.

42 **Holy Name cathedral** Still the main office of the Chicago Archdiocese of the Roman Catholic Church.

44 **the most celebrated divines of the city** When Grover Cleveland was in Chicago for the opening of the World's Fair in May 1893, he went to see Reverend S. J. McPherson of the Second Presbyterian Church preach. McPherson was one of the more politically progressive "divines" (clergymen), often using his pulpit to speak out on behalf of striking workers. McPherson, along with Rabbi Emil G. Hirsch, played a part in organizing the World's Parliament of Religions, a major attempt at ecumenicalism and interfaith dialogue, which occurred during the summer of the Fair in the building that currently houses the Art Institute of Chicago. Baptist Poindexter S. Henson occupied a more conservative position, as the author notes, and regarded the nation's economic collapse in 1893 as a sign of God's wrath directed toward Chicago's sinful ways. In a May 1897 article in the *New York Times*, Henson described his method for composing sermons as follows: "I always carry a pocket pistol, by which I mean a notebook, in my hip pocket, loaded with texts, and whenever outlines of sermons come to me, whether it be on the street car or steam car, or anywhere else, I at once make note of them. I think the best work I do is on the railroads in that way. My people tell me that my sermons prepared there are my best, because they have more movement in them and for that reason I always prefer a fast train." The issue of anti-semitism arises here too, as usage of the terms "pastor" and "church" for rabbi and synagogue or temple could be read as either a sign of respect (treating the Jewish clergy and houses of worship as equivalent to Christian ones) or its opposite (disregard for accurate language being one sign of the disrespect inherent in prejudice).

45 **stormy series of events** In 1888 the Reverend J. P. Brushingham went on trial for allegedly fathering a child out of wedlock with a woman who, if newspaper accounts are to be trusted, could be classified as an "adventuress." Both the court and his church exonerated Brushingham, who would go on to write

Catching Men: Studies in Vital Evangelism (1906) and *Spiritual Electrology* (1912), among other religious works. He would also become active in civic affairs, speaking alongside Clarence Darrow on "The Suppression of Vice and Crime in Chicago" in 1901 and decades later championing the notoriously corrupt, but officially "dry," Republican mayor William Hale "Big Bill" Thompson against Democrat Anton Cermak, who favored repeal of Prohibition.

45   **Robey Street . . . Cass Street**   Now Damen Avenue and North Wabash Avenue, respectively.

46   **Prof. David Swing**   By the time of *Chicago by Day and Night*'s publication, the controversial—he was tried for heresy by his own Presbyterian Church—but popular Swing was nearing the end of his life. Swing could be thought of as a more liberal, nineteenth-century version of Billy Graham. Swing's conservative counterpart in Chicago at the time would have been Dwight L. Moody, the popular evangelist who is conspicuously absent in this chapter. The Moody Bible Institute still occupies prominent spaces in the Old Town neighborhood, on Clark Street at North Avenue, and River North, on Chicago Avenue around La Salle Street. One can only speculate as to why Chicago's most famous evangelical preacher would be left out of *Chicago by Day and Night*. Perhaps the writer of this chapter had doctrinal differences with Moody or had been the subject of one of his famed street confrontations, in which Moody would accost passersby with what Nelson Algren called "the simple and terrible question: 'Are you a Christian?'"

Chapter VII. Panoramas and Libby Prison

48   **Panorama Place**   The IMAX theaters of the late nineteenth century, panoramas and cycloramas offered audiences an immersive experience. Detailed paintings of natural wonders or historical events on canvas surrounded the paying audience. The Niagara Falls panorama would have been fairly new at the time of *Chicago by Day and Night*'s publication, having opened its doors in March 1891. In addition to its depiction of the falls, the attraction also contained, somewhat inexplicably, a "real-

istic cotton-picking scene on the Mississippi," which is mentioned in newspaper advertisements from the era. Painter Howard H. Gross proposed creating a fourth panorama that would have depicted the White City on Chicago Day, October 9, 1893, but nothing ever came of the project. By the Fair's close, interest in panoramas and cycloramas was waning. The Chicago Fire cyclorama had been dismantled, and the building became the brief home of actor and impresario Steele MacKaye's Scenitorium. The Scenitorium was a much-reduced version of what was intended to be the premier exhibit at the Fair, the 8,000-seat Spectatorium where MacKaye intended to stage "The Great Discovery, or the World Finder," which would have told the story of Columbus using a cast of thousands; caravels built to three-fourths scale; cloud- and wave-making machines; and a 150-piece orchestra. The Spectatorium represented MacKaye's obsession with "pictorial realism" to erase the boundary between art and reality, which is also reflected in the less ambitious panoramas and cycloramas. MacKaye and his Spectatorium failed as a result of the economic collapse of 1893. The public's fascination with spectacle, satisfied in part by the panoramas, would find a longer-lasting and more economical outlet in the form of the motion picture, which would be established as a popular entertainment by the end of the nineteenth century.

49 **fifty cents** Roughly equivalent to the cost of a 3-D first-run film in 2012.

49 **Libby Prison War Museum** Although the *Pleasure-Seeker's Guide* claims that "Chicago capitalists" transported this Civil War site to the North, confectioner Charles F. Gunther was principally responsible, using the structure to house not only artifacts connected to the war but also his growing collection of curiosities (see note on page 259). By hiring former guards, and inmates, to serve as guides to the exhibits, the Libby Prison museum anticipated contemporary interest in oral histories and living history, as well as the employment of docents to interpret such exhibitions. Public interest waned, and the museum closed in 1895. Gunther eventually donated his artifacts, serious and spurious alike, to the Chicago Historical Society,

now the Chicago History Museum. Parts of the facade of Libby Prison were incorporated into the Chicago Coliseum, constructed in 1899 on the same site in the 1500 block of South Wabash and itself demolished in 1982. The Chicago Coliseum often played host to the First Ward Ball, the annual fund-raiser held by notoriously corrupt aldermen "Bathhouse" John Coughlin and Michael "Hinky Dink" Kenna. "Lollapalooza" is now the name of an annual music festival held in Chicago, but the term originated when Coughlin enthusiastically described the excesses of the First Ward Ball as "A lollapalooza!" The etymology of the word is obscure, but it might be related to "lollypop." This etymology calls to mind an American adage, usually misattributed to P. T. Barnum, from Michael Cassius "King" McDonald, renowned Chicago gambler: "There's a sucker born every minute."

50   **a strong historical interest**   The "fort," in reality a fire engine house, which had been briefly occupied by abolitionist John Brown and his allies during their raid on the Harpers Ferry Armory in 1859, never caught on as a public attraction. Brought to Chicago in anticipation of the Fair and the tourist dollars that would accompany it, the "fort" managed to attract all of eleven guests before shutting down. After moving to several other locations, by 1968 the "fort" eventually ended up close to its original site and is today part of the Harpers Ferry National Historical Park in West Virginia, Virginia, and Maryland.

50   **Enterprise has no compunction in these days**   This complaint regarding how public spectacles are based on bloody or tragic historical events parallels contemporary concern about "reality" TV and other forms of entertainment that might seem to degrade either the exhibitor or the audience. Such concerns are perennial in American culture.

Chapter VIII. Perils and Pitfalls

52   **Such gentry will be well cared for**   Chicago was famed for its high crime rate—violent street crime, corrupt politics, vice, and elaborate con games. Nonetheless, the Chicago-booster tone of "There are probably more 'crooked' people in Chicago

at the present writing than any other city in the Union" is remarkable. The Chicago Police Department did work to run all known "toughs" out of town for the duration of the Fair, but visitors to the Fair provided fresh game to all of Chicago's resident predators and new ones from elsewhere.

53 **"bunco-steerer"**   Someone trying to steer a mark into a confidence game. This term was used in 1896 to signify politicians by Chicago writer Finley Peter Dunne in *Mr. Dooley in Peace and in War*. In "On Reform Candidates," Dooley ("bartender and Doctor of Philosophy," whose stories were written in Irish-American dialect) complains of a voter, Dugan, who's so ignorant that "all he needs is an index and a few illusthrations to make him a bicyclopedja iv useless information." Dooley asks Dugan "which wan iv th' distinguished bunko steerers got ye'er invalu'ble suffrage?" to which Dugan replies that he voted for "Carter Haitch." Informed that Harrison had been assassinated three years earlier, Dugan replies, "He's lived that down be this time. He was a good man."

53 **confidence man**   Confidence men are so named because their schemes required gaining the trust of their victims. Legendary Chicago con man "Yellow Kid" Weil supposedly coined the phrase "You cannot con an honest man" to show that all of his schemes required that his victim knowingly enter into what was presented as a quasi-legal or illegal venture. Only if victims think they are getting inside dope, getting away with something, can the con man safely take them for all they're worth and not expect recriminations, since the victims' own illegal actions make it difficult to bring in the law. Weil's 1948 autobiography, *"Yellow Kid" Weil: The Autobiography of America's Master Swindler*, details many of his schemes, and though he worked after the Fair, the con man's methods were the same in Weil's era, and in ours.

CHAPTER IX. AS TO ADVENTURESSES

57 **adventuresses**   This chapter outlines the three primary methods used by female con artists, and/or crooked prostitutes, to make money, in descending order from genteel blackmail to

the badger game to the panel room. Just as a con man presenting an out-of-town visitor with a chance for some easy money requires his mark to cooperate, a con woman depends on her victim's sexual desire and vanity to put him in a place where he will pay her off or be robbed. The emphasis placed throughout the chapter on not trusting any woman one meets for the first time in a public place continues the theme of gendered spaces in the city: women on their own in public were an erotic opportunity, a physical threat, or both. Blackmail would simply involve threatening to expose a man's indiscretions to his family or business partners back home. The badger game involves a fake husband or other outraged man demanding satisfaction for his dishonor (see Nelson Algren's "Design for Departure" in *The Neon Wilderness* for a story about a couple playing the badger game). The panel game was more straightforward robbery, although the writer here neglects to mention that this last ploy would not happen with a supposed dalliance, but during prostitution. Some brothels were constructed with rooms furnished with only a bed and single chair. The man would leave his clothes on the chair, and as our author delicately puts it, "while the interview between the more or less affectionate lovers is in progress," the woman's compatriot would slide the panel back and steal the man's watch, money, and other valuables. The customer could not complain (if he even noticed before leaving the "establishment") because doing so would mean admitting he'd patronized a prostitute, and the brothel would have both paid-off police protection and on-site bouncers in any case.

57 **demi-mondaines** The demimonde being the world of nightlife and crime, a "demi-mondaine" could be any woman in that world, from a waitress to an actress to a prostitute.

58 **granger** Farmer.

58 **"white wench's black eye"** Quoted from *Romeo and Juliet*, act 2, scene 4. Our writer knows her Shakespeare.

58 **"out of sight"** It might seem as if some 1960s slang traveled back in time to 1892; but the term dates to the nineteenth century and actually appears in Stephen Crane's *Maggie: Girl of the Streets* (1893). It might also signify that the male traveler felt able to indulge in flirtation with random women met on the

street because he is literally out of the sight of anyone from his hometown.

Chapter X. The Tiger and His Haunts

Perhaps the most remarkable chapter in this remarkable book, this guide to gambling in Chicago is distinguished by its inclusion of the Chicago Board of Trade as just another way to lose one's money betting against the house, which always wins. The outline of how the Board of Trade operates is clearer than most economics textbooks and echoes the story told by Frank Norris in *The Pit* (1903). And for all of the book's winking and nodding at vices like gambling, the chapter's admonition—"For, while a few may win, the vast majority lose. Always remember that"—cannot be gainsaid.

65   **proverbial green bay tree**   Psalms 35:37: "I have seen the wicked in great power, spreading himself like a green bay tree." This comment seems to suggest the writer considers the gambling industry, and the corrupt politicians who nurture it, to be destined to fall, as King David's enemies were in the Psalms.

65   **"hells"**   Reformers thus labeled all saloons, gambling dens, brothels, and other sites of vice.

65   **Clark Street**   Clark Street north of the Chicago River has a long history as a red-light district before and after the time of the Fair. Ben Hecht and Charles MacArthur dedicated the book publication of their 1928 play *The Front Page* "To Madison and Clark Streets" for that reason. In the "Shadows" section of *Chicago Poems*, Carl Sandburg describes the realities of urban prostitution, and the second poem is titled "Used Up: Lines based on certain regrets that come with rumination upon the painted faces of women on North Clark Street, Chicago." Nelson Algren set several short stories, including "Katz" and "Design for Departure," in the area. One remnant of this past lingers in the gentrified streetscape, a post–World War II neon saloon sign with the straightforward imperative: Stop and Drink Liquor House. This space, at 742 N. Clark, is currently occu-

pied by the Clark Street Ale House, and its walls feature murals depicting Chicago's brewing history.

65 *croupiers*   The men running various games of chance.

65 **Mr. Washburne's administration**   Hempstead Washburne was a one-term (1891–93) Republican mayor of Chicago. Contrary to this book's claims, Washburne was no more successful than his predecessor, Democrat Dewitt Cregier, in attempts to suppress gambling in the city. Washburne's successor, Carter Harrison Sr., was known for his more tolerant attitude toward vice, stating, "You cannot legislate morality." Harrison Sr. was murdered on October 28, 1893, by Patrick Prendergast, a deranged young man who thought Harrison owed him a job as city attorney. The giant celebration planned for the Fair's last days was canceled for the popular politician's funeral, casting a literal pall over the occasion.

66 **notorious Hankins castle**   George V. Hankins was, along with his brothers Al and Jeff, a prominent gambler and "sportsman" in 1890s Chicago. His interests included horse racing, in particular the Garfield Park and Harlem tracks, as well as his "castle," located originally on Clark Street. The real estate agent for the first property was reputedly W. D. Kerfoot, who'd become famous among Chicagoans as the first businessman to open up shop in the aftermath of the Great Chicago Fire in 1871. Kerfoot denied any association with Hankins. By the end of the Fair, Hankins had tired of his reign as "king of the Chicago gamblers" and announced his abdication in a *Chicago Tribune* article dated October 22, 1894. Such royal titles were generously bestowed by both the mainstream newspapers and the sporting press.

66 **"sporty-looking" gentry**   The term "sport" signified "gambler" before it came to mean the games on which one might bet. In F. Scott Fitzgerald's *The Great Gatsby*, Gatsby's constant use of the term "old sport" to various acquaintances helps signify his criminality.

67 **"wolf"**   Slang term for "cheat"; the more corrupt members of the Chicago City Council were long known as the Gray Wolves. To return to *Gatsby*, the stand-in for the gambler who is re-

puted to have fixed the 1919 World Series, Arnold Rothstein, is named Meyer Wolfsheim.

67 **"brace" game**   Traditional con game, usually the manipulation of faro cards by the dealer, akin to three-card monte or other short cons.

69 **Satellites of the Tiger**   These images reflect an idea, widespread before and after the 1890s, that certain criminal "types" were identifiable by physiognomy and clothes; see also Cheyenne types (147).

71 **lard suddenly declined $3 a tierce**   A tierce is an old imperial liquid measurement, equal to forty-two gallons; so called because it is one-third of another archaic unit of measure, the "pipe." The metric system had not made its way to Chicago yet. Still hasn't, for that matter.

74 **numerous "bucket-shops" all over town**   Essentially a method of gambling on the exchange with limited connection to the actual institution, "bucket-shops" fulfilled the function of the modern-day pyramid scheme in the world of graft. A July 1922 *New York Times* article describes the nineteenth-century version of this con: "In earlier times a bucket shop was a place where stock quotations were shown on a board and the customer usually placed $1 or $2 a share margin against a rise or decline. When he guessed wrong he was wiped out, and the transaction closed automatically. Generally the quotations were inaccurate or wholly false, but the victims were people of small means and easily fleeced. A bucket shop was the one place where they could trade in a few shares of stock, and in the Middle West, where most of the transactions were in grain, a customer could buy or sell as little as 100 bushels, or a 'bucket full.' That was where the bucket shop got its name." A "bucket-shop" plays a part in one of the first serious works of realist fiction set in Chicago, Henry Blake Fuller's novel *The Cliff-Dwellers* (1893).

CHAPTER XI. MASQUERADES AND SIMILAR ENTERTAINMENTS

Here is another chapter outlining public forms of entertainment where the sexes might mix with some anticipation of erotic connection and where drinking and violence would be not-unheard-of. The general anonymity afforded by city life would be exacerbated by the purposeful disguising of identity that masquerades encouraged or required.

77 **Battery D, the roomy building on the Lake Front** Civil unrest in the late nineteenth century led to the creation of National Guard armories close to the city center, but spaces such as Battery D also served as sites for large public events. The first masquerade at the armory occurred in 1889. The space often hosted sporting events as well, including the first organized wrestling match in the city. In 1895, a year after the Pullman Strike, union leader Eugene V. Debs delivered a speech at Battery D to thousands of supporters of the labor movement. The choice of venues was ironic given the role of federal troops in suppressing strikes.

81 **The finest masquerades of all** An article appearing in the *Chicago Tribune* in February 1892 describes the "twenty-seventh annual carnival of the German Mannerchor" as "designed to represent the reception of the Chinese Emperor on a festal occasion." Prominent Chicago Germans played the majority of the roles, including that of the emperor, although a "touch of reality was lent by the presence of a half a dozen bona-fide Chinamen." Costumes of the guests ranged from "Chinese mandarins to American tramps." At the time of the Fair, the Germania Club, which hosted the annual masquerade, found itself involved in a minor controversy when some of its members refused the gift of a portrait of then Governor John Peter Altgeld. The German-born Altgeld had offended some members of the club when, in June 1893, he pardoned the three surviving anarchists associated with the Haymarket tragedy. The club eventually accepted the portrait, and its elegant hall still stands on the west side of Clark Street, just south of North Avenue, now home to a Starbucks, an Ace Hardware, and a catering and reception business.

CHAPTER XII. ON SHOPPING

As argued previously in the note on authors, the tone of this chapter is more than a bit misogynistic. The writer assumes that only women shop and that shopping is a lesser pursuit compared to gambling, theater, or free-and-easy shows.

83   **"special sales"**   The practice of merchants discounting prices for certain periods of time, or on certain merchandise, was unfamiliar enough in the 1890s to require noting by the author.

83   **largest store in the world**   Marshall Field's, Chicago's premier department store, was not the largest, but it was the most influential; it is now a branch of the department store chain Macy's. Founded in 1865 as the Field, Palmer, & Leiter Co., the store catered to the material needs of an emerging business and professional class, particularly women, who could lunch and shop there unaccompanied by a male chaperone. At the time of the World's Fair, a new nine-story "Annex" to the store on the block bounded by Randolph, Wabash, Washington, and State was preparing to open. Daniel Burnham's firm oversaw the construction of a design by Charles B. Atwood. Giving the lady what she wanted earned Field immense wealth and influence, which he mostly used in conservative causes. As a member of the Citizens' Association, which was made up of the city's elite, Field bought the Chicago police a Gatling gun to use on agitating workers, assisted in the acquisition of Fort Sheridan so that federal troops could protect his private property in the case of civil unrest, and publicly celebrated the execution of four of the eight men convicted in connection with the Haymarket bombing. Perceiving no profit for himself in supporting civic institutions, Field had to be persuaded by his friend, railroad-tie magnate Edward Ayer, to found the museum of natural history that, unlike the department store, still bears his name.

And while names like Marshall Field's and the Boston Store still resonate with Chicagoans of a certain generation, other stores are long forgotten. A contemporary of these businesses, the department store established in 1887 and named after founders Henry Siegel and Frank Cooper, specialized in affordable but quality merchandise, making it a sort of Victorian-era Target. A fire, believed by some to have been started intentionally, in 1891 destroyed the original Siegel, Cooper & Co. building that stood on the southeast corner of Adams and State

Streets. Noted architect William LeBaron Jenney designed its successor, an eight-story structure named after Field's co-founder Levi Leiter, which served as Siegel & Cooper's flagship until 1930. Sears then took over the building, using it as its flagship store until 1986. You can still visit the "largest store in the world"; it is the current home of Robert Morris University at 401 S. State Street.

CHAPTER XIII. CARROUSELS

84   **several carrousels in the city**   This chapter features some of the most egregious spelling in this erratic book, with "carou-sel," "carrousel," and "caroussel" all occurring. Nonetheless, as with the chapter on masquerades, this chapter shows how the author, the publisher, and (presumably) the reader are primarily interested in entertainment that features mixing of the sexes in some public place, preferably one that serves alco-hol. Contemporary Chicagoans can visit the AT&T Endangered Animals Carousel in the Lincoln Park Zoo, which currently costs $2.75 a ride. With "48 artisan-crafted wooden animals," all of them endangered species, this attraction is both family-friendly and educational, nothing like its seedier antecedents described in this chapter.

CHAPTER XIV. TURKISH BATHS — MASSAGE — MANICURES

Turkish and other public baths were not just resorts for hung-over travelers to soothe their pains. Housing for most of the population would not have included private baths, and the city itself built and maintained many baths as a public health measure. Private baths also operated for profit, and many were open twenty-four hours a day to serve workers from all three shifts during Chicago's industri-al heyday. Such baths would have had separate facilities for men and women, but the more luxurious ones would have been for men only, as they were more about socializing and less about basic hygiene.

87   **Palmer House baths**   "Bathhouse" John Coughlin, alderman for the First Ward from 1893 to 1938, got his nickname from employment as an attendant in the Palmer House baths as a

young man. The job gave him the opportunity to, quite literally, rub shoulders with Chicago's political and sporting elite. He transformed the "large patronage" of these baths into votes for himself and his partner, Michael "Hinky Dink" Kenna, and thence into political patronage jobs for loyal members of his First Ward Democratic organization.

88 **toper**   Drinker.

88 **"clothed and in his right mind"**   The description, from the Gospels, of a man out of whom Jesus cast a legion of demons. Mark 5:15 and Luke 8:35; our writer knows his Bible.

88 **colored servitor**   "Colored" in this context would denote an African American; Turkish baths were so called not because they were staffed by actual Turks, but because they were often decorated with fashionable Middle Eastern or pseudo-Islamic motifs, and their luxuries called to mind the exotic East in the American imagination. Trades that involved grooming or cleaning other people's bodies were often relegated to African Americans because they were perceived as servile, beneath the purported dignity of white workers. African American barbers actually dominated that industry in northern cities until the late nineteenth century, when Italian immigrants began to take it over, in part by arguing that white men should not want black men touching them at all. Racism works its way out in the urban landscape and its public spaces in many, sometimes diametrically opposite, forms.

90 **massage parlors**   The distinction between legitimate massage parlors and massage parlors that merely front for prostitution goes back at least as far as the nineteenth century. Yet again, this putative warning against vice also directs a visitor how to distinguish which sort of massage parlor to seek out, if one prefers "other entertainment." Such establishments still exist in various Chicago neighborhoods.

Chapter XV. Hackmen and Their Ways

92 **Jehu**   King of Israel who kills Jezebel. In 2 Kings 9:20, he "drives furiously" and so became a nickname for cabdrivers. Archaic. Today if you call a cabbie a "Jehu," no one will

have any idea what you are talking about, but fisticuffs might ensue.

95 **Illinois Central trains** It is remarkable that this chapter does not mention the "Alley El," built specifically to ferry passengers to the Fair. Today's Chicago Transit Authority (CTA) Green Line (the Jackson Park branch) opened in June 1892 to bring fairgoers from downtown to the White City. This El is discussed in chapter 27; this disparity suggests that chapter 15 was written before the El was complete, or that the editor of *Chicago by Day and Night* wasn't paying the closest of attention. The Illinois Central tracks are now used by Metra commuter trains and run from Millennium Park Station to Hyde Park at Fifty-Seventh Street, near the site of the Fair.

CHAPTER XVI. THE CITY'S MORAL SIDE

96 **the wickedest city in the world** Chicago's reputation for wickedness is partially based on reality—Chicago had plenty of wickedness—and partly on representations of the city in various forms of modern media discourse, from newspapers to literature to film. Promoting, while also condemning, such urban wickedness is part and parcel of most of *Chicago by Day and Night*. To reiterate the line regarding Chicago's wickedness from Carl Sandburg's "Chicago": "They tell me you are wicked and I believe them, for I have seen your painted women under the gas lamps luring the farm boys." Note Sandburg's emphasis on the mixing of the sexes in a public space, a constant theme in this book. While the poet's straightforward depiction of prostitution is more daring than anything in this text, it represents the same basic moral drama: big-city women and naive visitors.

97 **Young Men's Christian Association** A nationwide evangelical Protestant organization that provided living quarters, libraries, gymnasiums, and other amenities for single young men living in the city. Attempts to form a chapter of the Young Men's Christian Association in Chicago began in the early 1850s, but it wasn't until 1858 that the organization began offering its services in the city. One of its aims was to provide

housing for men that would preclude the temptations of hotels or boardinghouses, with their mixing of the sexes. Farwell Hall, the building referenced here, named for prominent businessman James V. Farwell, had been helping to strengthen the morals of young men since 1867. A new "Central Y" on Wabash Avenue opened in 1893. Today, the YMCA, and its distaff counterpart the Young Women's Christian Association (YWCA), with more than 60 locations and 100 extension sites, is the fourth-largest charity in Chicago, and still active in urban social justice crusades.

98 **Public Library** The Public Library was founded in Chicago after the Great Fire, when it was assumed by out-of-towners (including Great Britain's Queen Victoria) that Chicago must have suffered the tragic loss of its public library. Well, the city did not have any such institution at the time, but when donations of books and money poured in, the city leaders certainly weren't going to miss the chance to start one. Hence, the Chicago Public Library formed in 1873 and moved into its longtime home, a gift of the Grand Army of the Republic, on Michigan Avenue between Washington and Randolph Streets, in 1897. William Frederick Poole, the first head librarian, left the Public Library to take over the Newberry Library in 1887. He is best remembered for having compiled *Poole's Index to Periodical Literature*, which remains a valuable tool for researchers to this day. In 1991, the main branch of the Chicago Public Library moved from the Michigan Avenue building to the newly constructed Harold Washington Library Center at 400 S. State Street. The newer edifice's namesake was the city's first African American mayor, under whose leadership its design and financing were approved in 1987, but who suffered a heart attack later that year and died before construction began. The old Public Library building became the home of the Chicago Cultural Center, which provides free arts and educational programming to all Chicagoans and is distinguished by its magnificent Tiffany dome and ornate decor throughout its main public spaces. The opulence of the building expresses the same desire to emulate Paris and other world capitals that

drove ambitions of the Fair's boosters and designers. The Chicago Public Library currently has more than 70 branches and more than 5.7 million volumes and is a "good influence" in the communities it serves. Unfortunately, its budget and that of the Cultural Center have been drastically reduced by the current administration, which nonetheless always finds ample funds for any project put forth by large campaign contributors. In this respect, the "wicked city" alluded to throughout *Chicago by Day and Night* continues to this day.

98 **an everlasting monument**   The Woman's Christian Temperance Union (WCTU), which advocated for the prohibition of all alcoholic beverages, got its start in Ohio in the 1870s. In 1879 Evanston resident Frances Willard became the president of the organization, a position she would hold for almost twenty years. During that time, the Woman's Christian Temperance Union Temple was constructed. Designed by Daniel Burnham and John Wellborn Root's architectural firm, the thirteen-story structure had offices and stores that could be rented out to generate funds for the WCTU and featured separate entrances for the respectable public and the wayward drunks in need of the union's services. The building proved to be a financial bust, and the WCTU gave it up after a decade of occupancy. Having achieved its greatest success (along with its masculine ally, the Anti-Saloon League) in 1919 with the ratification of the Eighteenth Amendment, which made the production, transport, and sale of alcohol illegal across the United States, the WCTU began to wane in influence, although it still survives into the twenty-first century. The Frances Willard House is a museum in Evanston, the northern Chicago suburb created as a haven for "Dries" and, incidentally, to house Northwestern University. The WCTU continues its activism today, calling for both a return to the prohibition of alcohol and continued bans of same-sex marriage. At the close of the dedication of the temple, architect Root is alleged to have remarked, rather conspicuously, "Well, that's done, let's get a drink."

99 **Art Institute**   The current building on Michigan Avenue at Adams Street is the structure in question here. Also a product

of the 1870s, the Art Institute moved into its permanent home in 1893 after the conclusion of the Fair. The building, designed by Charles Atwood, had served as the site for the various World Congresses held in conjunction with the Fair, including the World's Parliament of Religions. The Art Institute of Chicago is an internationally famous institution, especially for its collection of French Impressionists, largely donated by Bertha Honoré Palmer, who served as chair of the Board of Lady Managers of the Fair.

Chapter XVII. The Parks and Boulevards

100 **something upon which the city prides itself** The same is true today, especially regarding the lakefront parks. All of the parks mentioned in this chapter are still extant, though the particular amenities described here, such as artesian wells, may or may not remain.

101 **three divisions** The South, West, and North Park Districts, along with other smaller bodies, were unified into the Chicago Park District in 1934. The original divisions reflected the local taxing districts, which built parks in particular parts of the city.

101 **Chicago's boast . . . to be borne out by the facts** Boosterism at its very finest.

102 **Ft. Sheridan** In 1887, in response to the Haymarket riot that occurred the year before, businessmen of the Commercial Club of Chicago donated more than 600 acres of land on the North Shore to the U.S. Army to provide Chicago's municipal government with military support to put down potential labor unrest. Troops from the installation helped quell the Pullman Strike of 1894. Sheridan Road does indeed extend all the way to the former fort (decommissioned in 1993), but Lake Shore Drive terminates at Hollywood Avenue on the north.

102 **water works** Chicago landmarks: the Water Tower (in its pocket park on Michigan Avenue between Chicago Avenue and Pearson Street) and the Pumping Station (on the east side of Michigan), now home to Chicago's famed Lookingglass Theatre Company.

102 **Pine Street** Former name for Michigan Avenue north of the Chicago River.

102 **Palmer castle** This famous residence was under construction during the Fair and was demolished in 1951. The Palmers were Chicago's first family, with Bertha Honoré Palmer as Chicago's social trendsetter. Their relocation north of the river on Lake Shore Drive helped shift Chicago's elite neighborhood from the Prairie Avenue district on the South Side to what became the Gold Coast on the Near North Side.

102 **the sight is a very gay one** While the site of this sight in Lincoln Park is near Chicago neighborhoods that are now populated in part by members of the gay, lesbian, bisexual, and transgender communities, this reference to a "gay" sight does not reference the Gay Pride Parade or the phallic rainbow-themed pillars that officially designate Boystown on North Halsted Street. At the time "gay" still primarily meant "merry" or "lively." As with references in other parts of *Chicago by Day and Night* to "fairies," we should recall that language evolves, and these terms did not yet have their current gendered significance.

102 **tomb of the Couch family** This monument is famed as the last remnant of Lincoln Park's past as the city's cemetery and is still located in Lincoln Park, just south of West La Salle and east of North Clark Street, near the Chicago History Museum.

103 **Grant monument . . . La Salle monument . . . Schiller monument** All of these monuments remain in Lincoln Park, except the Linne Monument, which has been moved to the campus of the University of Chicago, on Midway Plaisance.

103 **new palm house** The Lincoln Park Conservatory, still there today.

104 **the Court House** Before the standardization of Chicago's street numbering system in 1908, noted previously, there were various ways to measure distance from the city center, one being distance from the courthouse.

107 **base-ball, and cricket** "Base-ball" became one word, without hyphen, in the early twentieth century. Cricket was long a popular game in Chicago.

108 **phaetons** Large horse-drawn carriages.

110 **most famous of the three**   Horse racing was one of the three dominant professional sports of the nineteenth and early twentieth centuries, along with baseball and boxing. All three sports were distinguished by their connection with gambling, which put them all in the realm of vice that is so much the subject of this book. Designed by Frederick Law Olmsted in the late 1860s, Washington Park offered sheep grazing in meadows to produce a pastoral effect and to keep the grass in check, but the horses were always the real draw. "Derby day" attracted the respectable and disrespectable alike to the South Side, and the importance of this festivity to Chicagoans can be gauged by the fact that it is one of seven dioramas re-creating important moments in the city's history at the Chicago History Museum. The derby turns up in Dreiser's *Sister Carrie*, and the park itself is a major setting in James Farrell's *Studs Lonigan* trilogy and *Danny O'Neill* pentalogy, together called *The Washington Park Novels*. After the demolition of the racetrack, the White City Amusement Park occupied the site. Today Washington Park is home to the DuSable Museum of African American History. It would have been a primary site for the 2016 Olympics, but Chicago's bid to host the games failed.

111 **dog-carts**   Small horse-drawn carts designed to transport hunting dogs, which could also be used to carry a few people. The other varieties of horse-drawn transportation mentioned here cover the gamut of vehicles, from the expensive to the commonplace, the 1890s equivalent of Escalades to Aveos.

112 **a solid mass of men and women, the toilets of the latter presenting a brilliant picture in the gorgeous sunlight**   The women attending these races did not bring their own Porta Potties or other "toilets" in the modern sense. This term still referred to one's dress, makeup, and hairdo, which an upper- or middle-class woman would prepare in a small private room. Once indoor plumbing became commonplace, often retrofitted into such small rooms or closets, the meaning of the word migrated to apply to these essential fixtures.

114 **"A Night in Pekin"** Along with "The Fall of Pompeii," "A Night in Pekin" was a pyrotechnic extravaganza organized by James Pain and his children. A special performance of "Night" in August 1891, proclaimed "World's Fair Night," included a giant portrait of the Fair's director general, George B. Davis, constructed out of fireworks and a similarly designed "Welcome to All Nations" display. The director of works at the Fair, Daniel Burnham, disdained Pain's pyrotechnic displays and did not want them to be part of the Fair's dedicatory ceremonies but was overruled. Large open-air public spectacles continue to be staged in Chicago today, with the Redmoon Theater company having taken the place of Pain & Sons. Fireworks remain a major attraction at White Sox games and at Navy Pier.

114 **destruction of the city of Pekin by the British** In the Second Opium War, in 1860, British forces destroyed Pekin, which we now know as Beijing.

114 **slack-wire walking** An acrobat's art related to the more famous tight-rope or high-wire walking common in circuses, now usually called "slacklining."

115 **Kiralfys** Brothers Bolossy and Imre Kiralfy staged immense historical spectacles such as "Nero, or the Fall of Rome" and "King Solomon" across the United States and Europe in the last decades of the nineteenth century. For the World's Fair, Imre staged a spectacle dealing with Columbus's voyages, titled "America," at the Auditorium Building.

115 **"guying"** "To guy" is to quiz, chaff, roast, or josh. Pleasant, friendly jiving and mockery.

115 **Barnum & Bailey's** Barnum & Bailey's, which later merged with the Ringling Brothers circus, continues to perform in Chicago, most often at the United Center. Adam Forepaugh was P. T. Barnum's chief rival throughout the nineteenth century. When the Forepaugh circus arrived in Chicago in June 1891, it was celebrating its twenty-eighth season. Starting with a parade on June 15, the circus stayed in town for six days, offering Chicagoans a chance to gawk at African lions, acrobats, Wild

West sharpshooters, Roman chariot races, and, apparently, some educated broncos. General admission tickets cost fifty cents for anyone age nine or older, while children age eight or younger could get in for a quarter. Tickets could be purchased at the Siegel & Cooper department store (see previous note, page 238). In recent decades, when the circus performed at the old Chicago Stadium or the United Center, the parade through town from the train station to the event venue was a highlight of the year for circus-goers—and a target for animal-rights activists. Elephants were led down the streets, awing viewers such as Chicago poet, actor, and artist Tony Fitzpatrick. His drawing collage *Hannibal of Chicago* memorializes the magical sight of young circus workers leading these majestic animals through the mundane city's streets.

116 **bicycle races, cricket and base-ball matches** Bicycle races were all the rage in the 1890s, and many Chicagoans still played cricket. It is also interesting to note that the writers of *Chicago by Day and Night* feel no need to specifically name the Chicago National League Base Ball Club (originally the White Stockings, then the Colts, now the Cubs) as one of the outdoor events a visitor might enjoy. The National League had been founded seventeen years earlier, in 1876, but obviously baseball was not considered a necessary stop for visitors to the city. Today, the home of the Cubs, Wrigley Field, is one of the most visited tourist sites in Illinois; in 1893, the team played at the Second West Side Ballpark, or the West Side Grounds, on a lot bounded by Wood, Taylor, Lincoln (now Wolcott), and Polk Streets. The presence of a psychiatric hospital beyond the left-field wall of the park is reputed to be the root of the phrase "out of left field" for something unexpected or crazy. The park is long gone, but a psychiatric hospital remains. Perhaps the authors were correct to omit baseball from the wayfarer's itinerary: if you were seeking pleasure, you might not find it at the West Side Grounds, as manager Cap Anson's team went 56–71, finishing in ninth place in the twelve-team National League.

116 **"The Coney Island of the West"** Amusements at Cheltenham Beach seemed designed as a lure for increased development in

the area. Despite serving as the site for the World's Pastime Exhibition in 1886, Cheltenham never developed into the assemblage of roller coasters, dance halls, sideshows, and concession stands that eventually made up its New York counterpart. Amusement parks like Coney Island began to appear in Chicago toward the end of the nineteenth century, most notably White City in Washington Park and Riverview on the North Side at Belmont and Western. While Coney Island endures, the Chicago parks shut down long ago, although many living Chicagoans still have fond memories of summer days spent at Riverview.

Chapter XX. An Ideal Afternoon

119 **mammoth viaduct**   Crossing the Chicago River had long been the principal impediment to swift travel around the city. Water traffic, due to federal law, had priority, so any ship coming up or down the river would require that all the drawbridges be raised. Tunnels or viaducts alleviated this problem, and there were three, at Van Buren and Washington to the west and La Salle to the north. One planned for Rush Street was never built. All these tunnels were closed by 1954.

119 **Mr. Yerkes' great electric fountain**   Controversial transit magnate Charles Tyson Yerkes paid $23,000 to have the fountain transported from Coney Island to Lincoln Park. The *Chicago Tribune* expressed some skepticism at the fountain's official dedication in August 1890: "Mr. Yerkes is not only a man of affairs, he is a student of history. The life of Julius Caesar is to him an open book. He well knows how Caesar first acquired popularity among the common people when as consul he inaugurated a series of public spectacles of such magnificence that he became at once the people's idol, rendering the succeeding steps of his career easy. So Mr. Yerkes decided to give the people of Chicago an exhibition the like of which is not anywhere else in this country." Yerkes came to Chicago under a dark cloud, having served a prison sentence in Philadelphia for shady business practices. His attempt to control all transit in Chicago met with general disfavor, and when the first Fer-

ris wheel, the iconic exhibit at the Fair, was later disassembled and moved to a beer garden on the North Side, the venture's failure was often attributed to its association with Yerkes. He did, however, provide the University of Chicago with an observatory in Lake Geneva, Wisconsin, and would serve as the model for the protagonist of three Theodore Dreiser novels. The Yerkes fountain in Lincoln Park no longer exists, although two other fountains he donated to the city, while not in operation, still stand on Sheridan Road and are now used as cache sites by GPS scavenger hunt enthusiasts. Today, Buckingham Fountain in Grant Park, dedicated in 1927, recalls the Yerkes electric fountain with its light shows nightly in season.

121 **a blooded trotter** Here we see the etymology of the young "bloods" whose pursuits shape so much of this book: like a horse whose bloodlines are known, the young man about town whose parents are known to be wealthy is "blooded" as well.

122 **Professor Rosenbecker's orchestra** Adolph Rosenbecker was a popular orchestra leader of the time, who performed not only at Fischer's but also in the Auditorium Building and other venues. Beer gardens attached to such establishments as Happy Village in Wicker Park and Moody's Pub in Edgewater continue to attract a young, pleasure-seeking crowd. Outdoor concerts fill Millennium Park each summer, while Ravinia, on the North Shore, has become a Chicagoland institution.

122 **Evanston Avenue** Now North Broadway Avenue.

122 **Lake View** Now a thoroughly urban enclave, Lake View was originally planned and built as a commuter suburb, as were other formerly independent towns such as Jefferson, Hyde Park, and Rogers Park. Most of these were annexed to Chicago proper around 1890. Lake View, West Ridge, and other outlying neighborhoods still had many working farms as late as the 1920s.

122 **dude town** A dude was a "swell, fop, masher" according to *The Dictionary of Slang and Colloquial English* (1921). Which of course requires further definition. A "fop" was a man who dressed extravagantly; a "masher" was one who was sexually aggressive; and a "swell," just to go one step further, was slang for both a well-dressed man (perhaps one imitating a class

status he did not actually have) and a sexually aroused man's erection.

123 **within comfortable driving distance of the city**   A tract of land near the Sunnyside nearly ended up as the site of the Fair, which no doubt would have affected the fate of the hotel. Businessmen attached to the Graceland Cemetery Association put forth the proposal in June 1890, and had the site been selected, the Fair would have filled an area of about 600 acres north of the cemetery. The fare served by the Dowling family anticipates the current vogue of community gardens, the locavore movement, and farm-to-table restaurants, such as Lula Cafe in Logan Square and Farmhouse in River North. Of course, in an era before reliable refrigeration, most people were locavores by necessity rather than choice.

125 **hostler**   A stableboy or groom.

125 **douceur**   Tip.

Chapter XXI. On the Water

Fairgoers did indeed travel from downtown to the White City via boat, similar to today's water taxis on the river and lakefront. The degree of detailed insider knowledge about Chicago's yachting class demonstrated in this chapter is yet more evidence that *Chicago by Day and Night* has multiple authors.

128 **Chicago Yacht Club**   Founded in 1875, the Chicago Yacht Club still exists, with stations at both Monroe and Belmont Harbors.

128 ***Countess of Dufferin***   This Royal Canadian Yacht Club challenger lost the third America's Cup race, in 1876, to the American defender, *Madeline*.

129 **many boat clubs**   Of the clubs mentioned, the Catlin survived the longest, eventually merging with three others to form the Lincoln Park Boat Club in 1910. Prior to the merger, the clubs combined resources to construct an elegant boathouse in the Prairie School style that remains in use to this day. The beginning of the twenty-first century has seen an increased interest in rowing in Lincoln Park while canoes and kayaks often dot the river during summer months.

131 **excursion steamers** Such lake-boat excursions were often organized by workplaces or ethnic and religious groups as a way to get away from the city during the hot summer months. These vessels were the entertainment parallel to Chicago's shipping industry. Since the relocation of Chicago's industrial port to Lake Calumet on the South Side, the role of the river and the presence of industrial shipping in the city center have largely been forgotten.

Historically, the most famed and forgotten excursion boat was the *Eastland,* which capsized in the Chicago River (between Clark and La Salle Streets) on July 24, 1915. The boat carried 844 people, crew members and employees of the Western Electric Company about to take an outing to South Holland, Michigan, for a picnic, who were trapped belowdecks or thrown into the river and drowned within feet of safety. Entire families died in the disaster. Ironically, the *Eastland* had been fitted with extra on-deck lifeboats in response to the *Titanic* disaster, and the extra weight of those lifeboats helped make the ship more top-heavy and prone to flip over.

131 **St. Joseph and Benton Harbor** These coastal Michigan cities continued to attract Chicago tourists well into the twenty-first century. In *The Adventures of Augie March* (1952), Saul Bellow has his eponymous protagonist embark on one such excursion on *The City of Saugatuck.* "The white-leaded decks had just been washed down and were sparkling with colors of water in a Gulf of Mexico warmth," Bellow writes, "and the gulls let the air currents carry them around." In *Chicago Poems,* Sandburg depicts such an excursion boat in the poem "Picnic Boat": "A big picnic boat comes home to Chicago from the peach farms of Saugatuck. / . . . / Running along the deck railings are festoons and leaping in curves are loops of light from prow and stern to the tall smokestacks. / Over the hoarse crunch of waves at my pier comes a hoarse answer in the rhythmic oompa of the brasses playing a Polish folk-song for the home-comers."

132 **Gretna Green** A village in Scotland, just past the English border, without the impediments to rapid matrimony in English law, where clergy would perform marriages for couples who had eloped.

133 **the commercial side of the Chicago lake marine** More of the bestest boosterism ever.

Chapter XXII. The Restaurants of Chicago

The crowding of modern cities, in part caused by such architectural advances as skyscrapers, required a wide array of places to buy food. The vast crowds of people in city centers like the Loop could not reliably get home to prepare their own meals, and so restaurants catering to all classes of people and levels of income proliferated.

135 **Kinsley's . . . caters to all classes** By the time of his death in 1894, H. M. Kinsley had established himself as one of the premier restaurateurs in Chicago. At various times in his career, he had worked for the Sherman Hotel, the Tremont House, and the Revere House, and first opened a concession stand in the Crosby Opera House in the 1860s. His restaurant at 66 Washington Street changed how Chicagoans dined in much the way that Henry Bemis did at the Richelieu (see earlier note, page 218). The *Chicago Tribune* observed in Kinsley's obituary that he "claimed to have established a new school of cooking, radically different from the French, German, or English schools, which he called American cooking." His chief innovation was the "absence of highly seasoned gravies, smothered in which, by foreign chefs, meats and viands lost their distinctive flavors." One might reply that at Kinsley's, bland Midwestern cuisine was born! The book's insistence that Kinsley's "caters to all classes" makes it the restaurant equivalent of the Siegel & Cooper department store or Hankins's gambling house. Many contemporary restaurants in the Loop, from relatively new ones such as the Mercat to institutions such as Italian Village, also have distinct spaces under a single roof catering to specific dining clienteles.

135 **oyster houses** The popularity of oysters in Chicago seems unlikely, given the city's location so far from salt water. But oysters packed in barrels full of ice had long been shipped to the city, and Chicago saloon culture's legendary free lunch began in the early 1870s when Joseph Chesterfield Mackin gave away an oyster with every beer purchased in his saloon. As a result of

the high tourist trade brought to town by the Fair, waiters at the Boston Oyster House, Rector's, and the Chicago Oyster House went on strike for better wages in May 1893. Oddly enough, the striking waiters held an organizational meeting at Fischer's, the hall and summer garden mentioned elsewhere in *Chicago by Day and Night*. At the meeting they were addressed by prominent labor leader W. C. Pomeroy, who urged them to form a union.

135 **the sporting and professional element**   Again, the confluence of the wealthy and the cutting-edge, as gamblers want the prestige that associating with wealth brings, and the wealthy crave the edginess of sporting life. The same phenomenon informs nightclub culture to this day.

136 **tete-a-tete meal**   A meal served in a private room would be far more conducive to romance, and the soubrettes and bloods would have desired such privacy. Perhaps this practice should be revived, given the way that people now react to overly public displays of ardent affection by telling lovebirds to "Get a room!"

137 *table d'hote*   The Leland Hotel shuttered its doors decades ago, but the form of dining it introduced can still be experienced in restaurants throughout Chicago, such as Nightwood and Publican, where prix fixe menus attract curious epicures. English high tea is still served at the Drake Hotel, named for John B. Drake, who was a contemporary of Leland's and operated the Tremont House, which gave H. M. Kinsley his start in the city.

Chapter XXIII. The Haymarket Monument

140 **Henry Fielden**   The author means Samuel Fielden, who was tried—along with August Spies, Louis Lingg, Albert Parsons, Adolph Fischer, George Engel, Michael Schwab, and Oscar Neebe—for his alleged involvement with the bomb that went off near Haymarket Square on May 4, 1886. The bombing and subsequent violence resulted in the deaths of eight police officers and an unknown number of striking laborers and audience members. Neebe was sentenced to fifteen years in prison;

the other seven, to death. Fielden and Schwab had their sentences commuted by Governor Oglesby to life in prison. Spies, Parsons, Fischer, and Engel would be hanged when their appeals were denied, after Lingg died in prison (see note, page 261). The chapter's conservative political slant should be obvious to contemporary readers, and the bombing continues to be divisive over one hundred and twenty-five years later. In 2004, for instance, the Chicago Park District named a small park on the Northwest Side for Parsons's widow, Lucy Ella Gonzalez Parsons, who had a long and distinguished career as an activist for social justice until her death in 1942. The Chicago Fraternal Order of Police opposed the action, claiming that to do so would be to honor an anarchist and the wife of a cop-killer, despite the fact that even the prosecution during the trial acknowledged that Parsons (who was leaving the speakers' wagon at the moment of the explosion) did not himself throw the bomb. The misspelling of Albert Parsons's name as "Parson" also indicates the author's disdainful attitude toward the workers and activists whose struggle for the eight-hour day came to such a tragic point.

Along with the Great Chicago Fire and the World's Fair, Haymarket is one of the most-written-about events in Chicago history. For a thorough and balanced account, please see James Green's *Death in the Haymarket* (2006). While the Fair was going on in Chicago, Governor Altgeld would pardon Fielden, Schwab, and Neebe. Having reviewed the records attached to the case and the testimony gathered by both the defense and the prosecution, Altgeld, a former federal judge, determined that the trial had been prejudiced against the defendants, whom he believed innocent of the charges against them. A monument to the executed anarchists was unveiled at Waldheim Cemetery, west of the city, one day prior to the pardon being issued.

The police memorial statue, of a police officer with arm upraised to keep the peace, which forms the focus of this chapter, has had a controversial history. The statue was moved multiple times, toppled by a streetcar in the 1920s, and bombed twice in the social tumult that accompanied the late 1960s. It currently resides in the Chicago Police Headquarters at Thirty-fifth Street and Michigan Avenue. A new monument, *The Haymarket Memorial* by Mary Brogger, was installed in 2004 at the precise location of the speakers' wagon and can be seen at Haymarket Square today.

142 **Arbeiter Zeitung** The *Arbeiter Zeitung*, which roughly translates as the "Workers' Newspaper," was a German-language periodical edited by Haymarket martyr August Spies.

144 **the anarchists of Chicago ceased to exist** Anarchists made a return to Chicago in 2012, for the NATO conference, but nothing of the magnitude of Haymarket came to pass. Anarchist graffiti can frequently be found on Brogger's *Haymarket Memorial*.

Chapter XXIV. "Cheyenne"

As discussed in our introduction, the depiction in this chapter of African Americans as animals, and African American women as both exotic and sexualized objects, would have expressed commonplace racist views of the period.

145 **Fifth Avenue** Fifth Avenue was originally called Wells Street for William Wells, a key figure in the events of August 15, 1812—called either the Battle of Fort Dearborn or the Fort Dearborn Massacre, depending on one's political stance toward conflicts between Native Americans and settlers. Wells died, along with most of the residents of what would become Chicago, in the fight between several hundred Potawatomie warriors and Fort Dearborn's soldiers and militiamen at what is now the corner of Roosevelt Road and Michigan Avenue. (Chicago tradition long held that the site of the bloodshed was around Eighteenth Street and South Prairie Avenue, but more recent research suggests the more northerly location.) The vice district on Wells Street was so renowned for its criminal excess that in 1870, the Chicago City Council changed the name of the street to Fifth Avenue, so that the scandalous area would not tar the memory of the heroic Wells. After reforms mitigated the vice somewhat, the street was rechristened for Wells in 1920.

145 **the scum of the large cities of Europe . . . fruit-peddlers and organ-grinders** This sort of rhetoric was commonplace among anti-immigrant "Nativist" American politicians and writers. Also common was the assumption that whites mixing with African Americans was a sign of moral depravity that threatened the city as a whole. Italian immigrants, among the more recent groups to come to the United States in large numbers, were (like immigrants before them and after) often forced by prejudice and economic circumstances to live in crowded, dangerous slums. Italians in particular were stereotyped as fruit sellers and street musicians. This comment also shares the common assumption that cities are inherently immoral, as opposed to the wholesome countryside. The writer assumes that any immigrant who happens to be "scum" must hail from Europe's large cities rather than its rural areas.

Missing from this chapter on "Cheyenne" is its most legendary establishment, for Chicagoans at least: the Workingman's Exchange. It was the saloon run by Michael "Hinky Dink" Kenna, longtime alderman from the First Ward alongside "Bathhouse" John Coughlin (see the note on the Palmer House baths, page 239). At Kenna's saloon, the largely transient clientele could purchase a schooner of beer for a nickel and help themselves to a free lunch. Above the bar was a cage hotel, populated by a portion of the city's immense hobo and tramp contingent, which proved particularly valuable to Kenna on Election Day. As Nelson Algren put it in *Chicago: City on the Make*, Kenna was outraged that urban reformers thought he traded these free lunches for votes. In reality, "He'd paid fifty cents in cold cash for every vote he bought." The building which housed the Workingman's Exchange still stands on the west side of Clark Street, just south of Van Buren, and it still includes a transient hotel. In one of the many ironies Chicago's urban spaces afford, across Clark Street from the site is the Metropolitan Correctional Center, a federal jail where politicians accused of corruption sit in cells awaiting trial. As regards the neighborhood's nickname, residents of Cheyenne, Wyoming, purportedly responded to this "excellent neighborhood to leave alone" by naming their vice district "Little Chicago."

147 **canton**   Neighborhood.

147 **will stop at nothing when booty looms in sight**   Such "booty" would be "loot"—money or other goods to be stolen. "Booty" as a sexual slang term, sometimes associated with African American women like the ones depicted in this chapter, had not yet arisen, but one can see the roots of its evolution here: both definitions of "booty" can be understood as an object of desire, whether criminal or sexual.

148 **Whitechapel of Chicago**   Whitechapel was the horrific East End slum in London where Jack the Ripper committed his brutal murders. Several Chicago journalists, including Finley Peter Dunne and George Ade, founded an association called the Whitechapel Club in the early 1890s and filled the basement of a Calhoun Place saloon with the skulls of criminals, nooses used in executions, and a bloody shirt taken off the back of a ghost warrior at the Battle of Wounded Knee.

CHAPTER XXV. CANDIES AND FLOWERS

150 **gets . . . "the mitten"**   Gets dumped by his girl. This bit is very Chicago for how it characterizes romantic relationships as primarily economic: when a young man is engaged, he has to send flowers and chocolates to his fiancée daily, and when he is dumped and seeking new love, he has to . . . send flowers and chocolates to whomever he is wooing. Daily. Either way, the florists and chocolatiers make out like bandits. Chicago had long been a center of the confectionery business, but in recent decades most of the candy industry has been offshored to countries with cheaper labor and cheaper sugar. The Blommer Chocolate Company on West Kinzie Street is one of the few remnants of this once thriving industry, and when a sufficient breeze blows north-by-northwest, sometimes the atmosphere of the Loop and River North smells delightfully of chocolate.

150 **new Masonic Temple building**   This structure is described further in chapter 27 (page 159) and an accompanying endnote (page 261).

150 **best-known florist in Chicago**   Michael Gallagher made his

name, in part, by claiming multiple prizes at the annual Battery D flower shows (see previous note, page 237). He would receive the concession to sell floral arrangements at the Fair but like many of the people and businesses profiled in the guide would be undone by the nationwide economic collapse in 1893. Less than a year after the Fair, Gallagher appeared in bankruptcy court.

151 **first challenges attention**   As mentioned earlier, caramel manufacturer Charles F. Gunther brought Libby Prison to Chicago and opened it as a museum. His "curios of all sort" eventually ended up in the possession of the Chicago Historical Society, today's Chicago History Museum. For the Fair, Gunther purchased the sixteenth-century Moro portrait of Christopher Columbus and later balked when he had to pay $647 in duties on it, believing that the tariff laws of the time exempted paintings of that age.

CHAPTER XXVI. SUMMER NIGHT CONCERTS

153 **"Music hath charms to soothe the savage breast," said Shakespeare**   Actually, said William Congreve, in the poem "The Mourning Bride." This passage is also often misquoted, substituting "beast" for "breast." At least the *Chicago by Day and Night* author of this chapter got it half right.

153 **shriek of a locomotive on the Lake Front**   While today Chicago's waterfront is almost entirely parkland, industrial trains ran right down the Chicago waterfront well into the twentieth century. Were it not for the many lawsuits of A. Montgomery Ward, Chicago's waterfront would probably be an industrial site; the Metra tracks that run south from the Millennium Park Station remind us of that fact.

153 **Seipp or Bass**   Conrad Seipp operated what was once one of the largest breweries in the United States, dominating the Chicago market for lager in the late nineteenth century. After Seipp's death in 1890, the brewery was bought by British investors. Bass Ale began to be brewed in the late eighteenth century and became one of the first international brands, the red

triangle on its label recognizable to European and American imbibers around the globe. A bottle of Bass is clearly visible in Édouard Manet's *A Bar at the Folies-Bergère* (1882). While the Conrad Seipp Brewing Company did not survive Prohibition, the emergence of smaller craft breweries such as Goose Island, Metropolitan, Half Acre, Revolution, Five Rabbit, and the Haymarket Pub & Brewery demonstrates that Chicago is once more becoming a center for beer production. Like the locavore or sustainable food movement, what sometimes seems new and very twenty-first-century is actually a return to nineteenth-century cultural and business models. The 2011 corporate takeover of Goose Island, bought out by international conglomerate Anheuser Busch-Inbev, shows that history can repeat itself in several ways.

155   **Thus all tastes are catered to and all desires satisfied.** One definition of an ideal city.

CHAPTER XXVII. SPECIAL FEATURES OF CHICAGO

156   **the elevated railroad** The fact that the elevated has been mentioned only twice to this point—and was not included in the chapter advising visitors how to get to the Fair—shows that this book was written by multiple authors relatively rapidly. This El is still extant, the Green Line Sixty-third Street branch, formerly the Jackson Park/Englewood line. The stations closest to the former Fairgrounds have been demolished.

157   **demi-toilette** Half-dressed. As always, our writers are interested in the salacious possibilities of anything in the urban landscape, including a promising new vantage point for Peeping Toms.

157   **the county jail** Tours of jails and other public facilities were a commonplace entertainment for tourists and locals alike. The verb "slumming" comes from this practice. The current Cook County Jail has been located at 2700 S. California since the late 1920s. It houses, on average, 10,000 inmates. Public tours are no longer offered. "Murderer's Row" also no longer exists. In 2000 Republican Governor George Ryan instituted

a moratorium on capital punishment in the state of Illinois. Ryan, like Kenna and Coughlin before him, confirms Nelson Algren's claim that "always our villains have hearts of gold and all our heroes are slightly tainted." His rejection of the death penalty has earned Ryan a Nobel Peace Prize nomination, but he was convicted on corruption charges after serving one term and was released in early 2013 from the federal penitentiary in Terre Haute, Indiana.

158 **in lieu of a better explanation**   Some historians of Haymarket believe Louis Lingg was murdered by a guard.

158 **north side on Michigan Street, close to Clark**   Michigan Street is now Hubbard Street; the jail and courthouse were located in the block bounded by Clark, Hubbard, Dearborn, and Illinois. The jail, on the north half of that block, was demolished, but the courthouse is extant and has been converted to condominiums.

158 **Home Insurance Building**   Designed by William LeBaron Jenney, the Home Insurance Building was the first skyscraper to use steel frame construction and began what came to be known as the Chicago school of architecture. It opened in 1884 and was demolished in 1931.

159 **Rookery, Royal Insurance . . . Pontiac building**   Of these structures, the Rookery, Monadnock, Manhattan, Insurance Exchange, and Pontiac buildings survive. The others have been demolished.

159 **Masonic Temple**   Designed by Daniel Burnham and John Wellborn Root, the Masonic Temple was erected in 1892. It was demolished in 1939, in part due to its relative inefficiencies and in part due to the construction of the State Street Subway, which would have undermined its foundation. At twenty-two stories, the temple was the tallest building in the city for a time. The site is now occupied by Joffrey Tower, home to the Joffrey Ballet.

159 **if indeed, in the entire universe**   Our author once again exceeds the norms even for Chicago boosterism, with a claim that would be difficult to substantiate concerning extraterrestrial architectural rivals to Chicago's great buildings.

Chapter XXVIII. A Few Final Words

161   **to tell facts and to tell them briefly**   This final chapter before the description of the Fair is one last attempt to assert that *Chicago by Day and Night*, despite its attention to burlesques, leg shows, gambling, drinking, and other diversions which so many Chicagoans and visitors would disdain, is just stating the facts. It's up to the individual reader, and visitor to the city, to behave appropriately. Oddly, this attitude parallels Theodore Dreiser's approach to realism, expressed in his 1903 essay "True Art Speaks Plainly." Dreiser claimed his goal was simple: "The sum and substance of literary as well as social morality may be expressed in three words—tell the truth." Dreiser, however, did not share *Chicago by Day and Night*'s concern with brevity.

The Great World's Fair

Part I. The Project for the World's Columbian Exposition

The World's Fair of 1893 is one of the most-written-about events in Chicago history, from contemporary accounts to recent best sellers such as Erik Larson's *The Devil in the White City*. For this reason, we only annotate this section slightly; the description of the anticipated Fair itself is relatively accurate and self-explanatory, with the usual flourishes of boosterish braggadocio. And so much has been written on the Fair that any attempt at annotation seems inadequate compared to what a diligent reader can find through a little research. Important period sources include *A History of the World's Columbian Exposition Held in Chicago in 1893* (1897–1898), edited by Rossiter Johnson, and *The Book of the Fair* (1893) by Hubert Howe Bancroft. Slightly more idiosyncratic are *Midway Types* (1894), a series of photographs of the various entertainers and ethnographic village inhabitants appearing on the Midway Plaisance; *Humors of the Fair* (1893), a somewhat farcical account of the experiences in Chicago of Nathaniel Hawthorne's son, Julian; and *Two Little Pilgrims' Progress: A Story of the City Beautiful* (1895), by Frances Hodgson Burnett, which in terms of plot and characters is more or less a prototype of her better known *The Secret Garden* (1911). Chicago's own Neil Harris contributes to *Grand Illusions: Chicago's World's Fair of 1893* (1993), which does a good job of situating the Fair historically, although Chris Ware's *Jimmy Corrigan: The Smartest Kid on Earth* (2000) is perhaps the best contemporary attempt to capture what it was like to have actually been at the Fair.

The White City also inspired one of fiction's most famous cities, L. Frank Baum's Emerald City of Oz. Baum, a Chicago native, attended the Fair, as did his illustrator, W. W. Denslow. Denslow had moved to Chicago to work illustrating the Fair for the Chicago *Herald*, and various aspects of the Fair and Chicago seem to have influenced Baum's depiction of Oz in the many novels he wrote. Instead of a White City, it's an Emerald City; but like the Fair, the Emerald City was built very rapidly in the first Oz book, *The Wonderful Wizard of Oz*. Chicago's motto, *Urbs in Horto* (City in a Garden), might also come into play, as the emphasis urban planners put on such green spaces as parks, beaches, and boulevards, as well as the common practice of families having their own gardens, could be a source for the greenness of Oz's capital city.

Edgar Rice Burroughs, creator of Tarzan, also attended the Fair. In June 1893, he worked driving a demonstration model of one of the first "horseless carriages" that would evolve into the automobile. Besides whatever influence the White City might have had on the futuristic and fantastical worlds he imagined, from Mars to Venus to the interior of the Earth, Burroughs was also well grounded in his criminal Chicago lore. The hero of his 1914 adventure novel *The Mucker*, Billy Byrne, is from the slum district just north of Cheyenne. The book begins:

BILLY BYRNE was a product of the streets and alleys of Chicago's great West Side. From Halsted to Robey, and from Grand Avenue to Lake Street there was scarce a bartender whom Billy knew not by his first name. And, in proportion to their number which was considerably less, he knew the patrolmen and plain clothes men equally as well, but not so pleasantly.

This odd novel in many ways resembles the Fair, as it tried to be all things to all readers. Burroughs combined every popular fictional genre of the day: it was an urban crime narrative, a boxing novel, an "adventure on the high seas" story, an "explorer of lost civilizations" epic, and finally a "rough man redeemed by the love of a good woman" story. To make this romantic redemption as dramatic as possible, Burroughs had Byrne begin in the roughest place imaginable, Chicago's West Side.

Another creator of American popular culture who was influenced, albeit more remotely, by the Fair was Chicago native Walt Disney. While he wasn't born until 1901, Disney attended the 1933–34 Century of Progress Fair; but more directly, the culture of the Midway led to the creation of the American theme park. "Midway" became shorthand for any such carnival attraction with rides, food, and exotic shows. Disneyland and Disney World are direct cultural descendants of the Fair's Midway. "Karnival Kid" (1929) was one of the earliest Mickey Mouse cartoons, when the character was still more of a rogue rather than the goody two-shoes he was later reduced to. This black-and-white cartoon depicts just such a midway, with carousel and Ferris wheel in the background. Mickey pursues "shimmy dancer" Minnie, who performs her "hoochie-coochie dance" for the crowds. Mickey was a hot dog vendor, and the cartoon abounds with visual double entendres that would satisfy any viewer with Freudian inclinations.

166 **it was a case where "money talked"** Money is often the language spoken most fluently in Chicago.

168 **The principal officers** . . . As noted previously (page 223), the lists of important personages that occupy the next few pages were commonplace in newspapers and histories of the period.

177 **Art Palace** Most of the buildings for the Fair were built to last as long as the Fair did and no longer; the exception was the Palace of Fine Arts (or Fine Arts Building), which had a brick structure under its white plaster facade. After the Fair, this building housed the Field Museum, until that institution's present building was constructed in 1920. It now houses the Museum of Science and Industry, located at Fifty-seventh Street and Lake Shore Drive.

181 **willow-ware** A popular china pattern of the period, willow-ware typically consisted of white dinnerware with a royal blue design featuring a willow tree in a Chinese-style setting including other images such as a bridge over a river, a pagoda, and flying birds; it depicted icons of a Chinese legend of star-crossed lovers parallel to Shakespeare's *Romeo and Juliet.*

182 **the marvelous power, electricity . . . advancements in which are destined ultimately to revolutionize the world** One boosterish prophecy from the Fair which has turned out to be entirely correct.

183 **double-eagles** Twenty-dollar gold coins, so called not as a vernacular nickname, but due to Acts of Congress in 1792 and 1849 authorizing their minting, along with eagles, half- and quarter-eagles.

185 **war department** Now the Department of Defense, though the title may be a distinction without a difference.

186 **relics of the war** Casual references to "the war" in this period would have meant the American Civil War of 1861 to 1865.

Part III. The Dedicatory Ceremonies

188 **Benjamin Harrison** Harrison did not attend the dedication due to his wife's illness. Instead, Vice President Levi Morton fulfilled the various ceremonial duties. The fascinating thing about this chapter is the detailed account it provides of an event that had yet to occur. The writer clearly had great faith in the best laid plans of mice and men coming to pass. The president would have received a forty-eight gun salute because the Union at the time consisted of 44 states and 4 territories.

189 **Miss Harriet Monroe** Harriet Monroe (1860–1936) would, some twenty years later, found *Poetry* magazine, one of the English-speaking world's most influential literary journals, still going strong in 2013. *Poetry* helped establish the Chicago literary renaissance of the early twentieth century (it published Carl Sandburg's "Chicago" and other poems) and,

along with Margaret Anderson's *Little Review*, promoted modernist writers such as James Joyce and Ezra Pound. Monroe's "Columbian Ode," judged purely on its literary merits, might not be the greatest work of art ever, but it was significant in another way. The *New York World* newspaper republished the poem without even crediting Monroe as the author, much less paying her. The lawsuit that Monroe pursued and won helped establish modern American copyright laws.

PART IV. THE CHICAGO HUSSARS

192 **regiment of volunteer cavalry**   The Chicago Hussars, an affluent collection of citizen-soldiers, remained active throughout the 1890s and briefly considered using the former Libby Prison (see note, page 230) as their headquarters. They played an active role in preserving law and order during the labor struggles, particularly the Pullman railway strike, that followed the conclusion of the Fair. Such independently organized military outfits were common in the nineteenth century.

PART V. WORLD'S CONGRESS

194 **exclusive use of the world's congresses**   One of the key events at these World's Congresses was the World's Parliament of Religions, which helped introduce Hinduism and Buddhism to the United States. The "Permanent Memorial Art Palace" is today's Art Institute of Chicago. At the meeting of the American Historical Association, one of the congresses, University of Wisconsin historian Frederick Jackson Turner first delivered his famous talk on "The Significance of the Frontier in American History," in which he argued that the frontier, perhaps the most significant factor in shaping American identity through the nineteenth century, had closed.

PART VI. THE FAIR ITSELF

This chapter also repeats and slightly recasts material from various earlier chapters, further evidence of multiple authorship.

197 **Edwin Lee Brown**   Born in Maine in 1827, Edwin Lee Brown settled in Chicago in the 1850s and made his money in iron. In addition to championing the Fair, he proposed building a gigantic obelisk as a memorial to the police officers who died at Haymarket. Brown may not have cared much about workers and labor rights, but his sympathies did extend to books and animals. He was active in the Chicago Library Association and served as the first president of the Illinois Humane Society.

198 **"everything went," so to speak**   We imagine that this might've been current slang in response to a query along the lines of "How did everything go?" It would also connect with the idea that at an outrageous party, "anything goes," so at this one, "everything went."

199 **the most wonderful exhibition in all history . . . mild language indeed.**   Indeed.

PART VII. SPECIAL FEATURES OF THE FAIR

One of the odd features of the Fair was the division between the Fair proper and the Midway Plaisance and its various shows. The writer of this chapter seems especially fascinated with foreign contributions and with the idea of replicating things: a "Street in Cairo" on the Midway or a model of the Agricultural Building done up by a Mexican silversmith. In some sense, the Fair could be understood as a collection of such copies, inauthentic simulacra, anticipating the postmodern world of endless replication.

201 **sliding railway**   Like Steele MacKaye's Spectatorium (230), the Sliding Railway was an entertainment at the World's Fair that never achieved completion. Had it been finished, it would have run the length of the mile-long Midway Plaisance and would have functioned much like "log rides" at contemporary amusement parks.

202 **Mrs. Stowe's literary works**   Harriet Beecher Stowe's 1852 novel *Uncle Tom's Cabin* was the best-selling American book of the nineteenth century (other than that perennial favorite, the Bible), and beyond its legions of readers, audiences across America thronged to stage adaptations as well. It made Stowe

one of the most famed women in the world, a natural to be featured at the Fair, and her home state of Connecticut sent a custom-made bookshelf full of rare editions of her books for the Woman's Building. A bust of Stowe was featured there as well, and according to the *Chicago Record* of May 25, 1893, African American abolitionist and author Frederick Douglass was to play the role of Uncle Tom when Stowe's sister, Isabella Beecher Hooker, unveiled it. Other historical accounts of the event make no mention of Douglass, who attended the Fair as representative of Haiti and supported African American participation in the controversial "Colored American" Day that the Fair organizers had set aside, doing any such thing. This assertion may be a hoax or a joke; then as now, perhaps one shouldn't believe everything one reads in the papers.

204 **Princess Christian** This oddly gendered name refers to Queen Victoria's daughter Helena, who was married to Prince Christian of Schleswig-Holstein. Princess Louise was Victoria's sixth child (or perhaps her daughter-in-law, Louise Margaret of Prussia, who married Victoria's son Arthur). Princess Beatrice was her ninth and final offspring.

205 **Cape Colony** British colonial possession in what is now the Republic of South Africa.

205 **has already begun to assume the character** Much to landscape architect Frederick Law Olmsted's dismay, the wooded island would serve as the site of the Japanese Ho-o-den and the Hunter's Cabin, also known as the Davy Crockett Cabin. The Osaka Japanese Garden, a gift from Chicago's sister city, is on the island today.

PART VIII. ABOUT THE CITY DURING FAIR TIME

This chapter summarizes much of the first two-thirds of the book, with its roster of hotels and advice about theaters.

208 **Pain & Sons** See the previous note on "A Night in Pekin" (page 247).

208 **Micawber-like** Wilkins Micawber was a character in Charles Dickens's popular novel *David Copperfield*. Despite his eco-

nomic and legal travails (which included debtor's prison) he would repeatedly assert that he wasn't worried about the future because "something will turn up." Our author knows his Dickens as well as the Bible and Shakespeare.

208 **to catch the nimble dollar . . .** The actual aim of the entire book and most of the entertainments featured therein.

208 *"saloonish,"* **. . . Hannah & Hogg's saloons** A. D. Hannah and David Hogg, both natives of Scotland, joined forces in the early 1870s to open a series of highly successful saloons and a wholesale business in Chicago. The saloon "on Madison Street, under the Madison Street Opera House" served as the model for the establishment where George Hurstwood is employed in Theodore Dreiser's *Sister Carrie* (1900) and is, in fact, referred to as "Hannah & Hogg's" in the original manuscript before Dreiser changed it to "Fitzgerald and Moy's in Adams Street."

The disclaimer here that no one would ever go to a saloon except to investigate vice is a standard moralist's dodge, but the emphasis on the art on the walls is important. One attraction of saloon culture to city dwellers was aesthetic: the mirrors, the glassware, the lighting, and the art. "Saloonish" art is a polite way of saying "pictures of naked women," as many saloons would hang the image of an odalisque behind the bar for diversion of their male clientele and to scandalize the Prohibitionists. But such pictures could also be found in the Art Institute, supporters of saloons argued. It seems that where a work of art is displayed figures crucially in its cultural capital. "The Indestructible Masterpiece" in Ben Hecht's *1001 Afternoons in Chicago* tells the tale of one such painting. To view modern versions of such "saloonish" art with a contemporary political edge, see Bruce Elliott's work on display at the Old Town Ale House, at North Avenue and Wieland Street.

209 **principals in the old-time "boodle" sensation** Harry Varnell spent his entire life in Chicago, where he was a sort of cross between a celebrity gambler like George V. Hankins and a corrupt politician like "Bathhouse" John Coughlin. While serving as the warden at the Cook County Insane Asylum in Dunning, he used county funds to entertain his friends and associates.

According to his obituary in the *Chicago Tribune* from September 1898, at Dunning, Varnell hosted "dances for the patients every night with impromptu spreads for the commissioners in the infirmary drug store every few minutes." In 1887 he was brought to trial by Julius Grinnell, the same state's attorney who prosecuted the eight anarchists connected to the Haymarket affair. After serving time in Joliet, Varnell returned to Chicago and opened the saloon mentioned in the guide.

209 **the personality of its chief proprietor**   William J. McGarigle was brought down in the same scandal that ruined Harry Varnell and, like Varnell, opened a saloon upon his release.

210 **touts**   Touts were horse-players, or men who solicited customers for gambling dens or brothels.

211 **closed on Sundays**   Despite opposition from some religious figures, the Fair and the Midway did open on Sundays, allowing the pleasure seeker to chase after his thrills any day of the week. Some aspects of anti-Sunday opening laws linger to this day, though, as it's illegal in Chicago to sell alcohol before 11 A.M. on the Lord's Day, while the rest of the week you can start at 7 A.M. Even pleasure seekers, it seems, need at least a morning of rest.

FINIS—AN ANNOTATOR AT REST.

Bibliography

Since this is a book aimed at a pleasure-seeking audience, we have not cluttered up the text with footnotes for our sources. The following are texts we consulted in the process of our research. Should you also seek knowledge about Chicago (some of it, perhaps, not entirely accurate, although entertaining) as well as pleasure, please continue by reading these texts.

Abbott, Karen. *Sin in the Second City*. New York: Random House, 2007.

Ade, George. *The Old-Time Saloon*. New York: Long and Smith, 1931.

Algren, Nelson. *Chicago: City on the Make*. Sixtieth anniversary edition, ed. David Schmittgens and Bill Savage. With an introduction by Studs Terkel. Chicago: University of Chicago Press, 2011. First published 1951.

———. *The Neon Wilderness*. Reprint, New York: Seven Stories Press, 1999. First published 1947.

Arthur, T. S. *Ten Nights in a Bar-Room*. Boston: L. P. Crown, 1854.

Asbury, Herbert. *Gem of the Prairie*. New York: Alfred A. Knopf, 1940. Reissued as *Gangs of Chicago*. New York: Basic Books, 2005.

Bancroft, Herbert Howe. *The Book of the Fair*. Chicago: Bancroft Co., 1893.

Baum, L. Frank. *The Emerald City of Oz*. Chicago: Reilly and Lee, 1910.

———. *The Annotated Wizard of Oz,* Centennial Edition. Ed. Michael Patrick Hearn; preface by Martin Gardner. Illustrations by W. W. Denslow. New York: Norton, 2000.

Bell, Ernest. *Fighting the Traffic in Young Girls, or, War on the White Slave Trade*. N.p., 1910.

Bellow, Saul. *The Adventures of Augie March*. New York: Viking, 1952.

Brushingham, J. P. *Catching Men: Studies in Vital Evangelism* (Cincinnati: Jennings and Graham, 1906).

———. *Spiritual Electrology* (Cincinnati: Jennings and Graham, 1912).

Burnett, Frances Hodgson. *Two Little Pilgrims' Progress: A Story of the City Beautiful*. New York: Charles Scribner's Sons, 1895.

———. *The Secret Garden*. New York: F. A. Stokes, 1911.

Burnham, Daniel, and Edward Bennett. *Plan of Chicago*, 1909. Centennial Edition. Chicago: Great Books Foundation, 2009.

Burroughs, Edgar Rice. *The Mucker*. New York: Ace Books, 1974. First published 1914.

Chicago: The City Beautiful. Chicago: Curt Teich and Co., 1943.

Chicago Record. http://utc.iath.virginia.edu/articles/n2ar73at.html

Chicago Tribune Internet archive. Accessed via Proquest.com

Colbert, Elias, and Everett Chamberlain. *Chicago and the Great Conflagration*. New York: C. F. Vent, 1871.

Crane, Stephen. *Maggie: Girl of the Streets*. New York: Bantam Books, 1986. First published 1893.

Dreiser, Theodore. *Sister Carrie*, ed. Donald Pizer. Norton Critical Edition. New York: Norton, 1991. First published 1900.

———. "True Art Speaks Plainly." *Booklover's Magazine*. February 1903. In Pizer.

Duis, Perry. *Challenging Chicago: Coping with Everyday Life*. Chicago: University of Illinois Press, 1998.

———. *The Saloon: Public Drinking in Boston and Chicago, 1880–1920*. Chicago: University of Illinois Press, 1983.

Dunne, Finley Peter. *Mr. Dooley in Peace and in War*. Reprint, Chicago: University of Illinois Press, 1988. First published 1898.

Farmer, John S. and W. S. Henly, eds. *A Dictionary of Slang and Colloquial English*. London: Routledge, 1912.

Farrell, James T. *The Face of Time*. Champaign: University of Illinois Press, 2008.

———. *Father and Son*. Champaign: University of Illinois Press, 2008.

———. *My Days of Anger*. Champaign: University of Illinois Press, 2008.

———. *No Star is Lost*. Champaign: University of Illinois Press, 2008.

———. *The Studs Lonigan Trilogy*. New York: The Library of America, 2004.

———. *A World I Never Made*. Champaign: University of Illinois Press, 2008.

Fitzgerald, F. Scott. *The Great Gatsby*. Corrected Edition. Ed. Matthew Bruccoli. New York: Scribners, 1995.

Fitzpatrick, Tony. "Hannibal of Chicago" (drawing collage) in *The Wonder: Portraits of a Remembered City*, Vol. 1. San Francisco: Last Gasp Press, 2005.

Flinn, John J. *Chicago: The Marvelous City of the West; A History, An Encyclopedia and Guide*. Chicago: Flinn and Shepherd, 1891.

Fuller, Henry Blake. *The Cliff-Dwellers*. New York: Harper and Brothers, 1893.

Goodspeed, E. J. *History of the Great Fires in Chicago and the West*. New York, 1871.

Green, James. *Death in the Haymarket*. New York: Anchor, 2007.

Grossman, James R., Ann Durkin Keating, and Janice L. Reiff, eds. *The Encyclopedia of Chicago*. Chicago: University of Chicago Press, 2004.

Harris-Lacewell, Melissa Victoria. *Barbershops, Bibles and BET: Everyday Talk and Black Political Thought*. Princeton: Princeton University Press, 2004.

Hayner, Don, and Tom McNamee. *Streetwise Chicago: A History of Chicago Street Names*. Chicago: Loyola University Press, 1988.

Hecht, Ben. *1001 Afternoons in Chicago*. Introduction by Bill Savage. Illustrations by Herman Rosse. Chicago: University of Chicago Press, 2009. First published 1922.

Hecht, Ben, and Charles MacArthur. *The Front Page*. New York: Covici and Friede, 1928.

Johnson, Rossiter. *A History of the World's Columbian Exposition Held in Chicago in 1893*. New York: Appleton, 1897–98.

Jones, Judy, and William Wilson. *An Incomplete Education*, 2nd edition. New York: Ballantine Books, 1995.

Lait, Jack, and Lee Mortimer. *Chicago Confidential*. New York: Vintage, 1950.

Larson, Erik. *The Devil in the White City*. New York: Vintage, 2003.

Lewis, Lloyd, and Henry Justin Smith. *Chicago: The History of Its Reputation*. New York: Harcourt, Brace, 1929.

Lincoln Park Zoo carousel information, accessed at http://www.lp-zoo.org/

Midway Types. Chicago: American Engraving Co., 1894.

New York Times Internet archive. Accessed via Proquest.com

Norris, Frank. *The Pit*. Reprint, New York: Penguin, 1994. First published 1903.

Pacyga, Dominic A. *Chicago: A Biography*. Chicago: University of Chicago Press, 2009.

Reed, Christopher Robert. *"All the World is Here": The Black Presence at White City*. Bloomington: Indiana University Press, 2000.

Sandburg, Carl. *Chicago Poems*. Introduction by John Halwas. Champaign: University of Illinois, 1992. First published 1914.

Sinclair, Upton. *The Jungle,* ed. James Barrett. Chicago: University of Illinois Press, 1988. First published 1906.

Skilnick, Bob. *The History of Beer and Brewing in Chicago, 1833–1978*. Chicago: Pogo Press, 1999.

Smith, Carl S. *Urban Disorder and the Shape of Belief: The Great Chicago Fire, the Haymarket Bomb and the Town of Pullman*. Chicago: University of Chicago Press, 1995.

Stead, William T. *If Christ Came to Chicago*. Chicago: Laird and Lee, 1894.

Ware, Chris. *Jimmy Corrigan: The Smartest Kid on Earth*. New York: Pantheon, 2000.

Weil, J. R., and W. T. Brannon. *"Yellow Kid" Weil: The Autobiography of America's Master Swindler*. Reprint, Oakland, Calif.: Nabat/AK Press, 2011. First published 1948.

Weimann, Jeanne Madeline. *The Fair Women: The Story of the Woman's Building, World's Columbian Exposition, Chicago 1893*. Chicago: Chicago Academy Press, 1981.

Acknowledgments

We would first like to thank Colleen Kelly, who transformed a garbled scan of *Chicago by Day and Night* into a workable manuscript. As deadlines loomed, her editorial labor made this book possible. The book would also not exist were it not for the patience, friendship, and support of Sarah Crawford.

We would also like to thank people at an institution that has long been central to our research and teaching, both independently and together on this project—The Newberry Library of Chicago—including Rachel Bohlmann, Diane Dillon, Rachel Rooney, and Danny Greene. We owe special thanks as well to John Powell, director of Digital Imaging Services, and Catherine Gass, photographer, who produced the amazing scans of the full-page images in this book, on very short notice. The beautiful image on the cover is courtesy of the Chicago History Museum, another invaluable resource to anyone interested in Chicago. We also relied upon the libraries at Northwestern University and the University of Chicago. We'd like to thank our students at Northwestern, the Newberry Library Seminar Series, and the University of Chicago. Their intellectual curiosity helps fuel research like this.

Chicago has inspired a vast community of scholars, writers, researchers, and students with whom we are lucky to associate. Our work here has been assisted greatly by the scholarship, journalism, and creative writing done by Carl S. Smith, Henry Binford, Perry Duis, Carlo Rotella, Dominic Pacyga, Erin McCarthy, Ellen Skerrett, Neil Steinberg, Jim Lonergan, Alex Stathakis, Chris Ware, John Musial, Andrew White, Liam T. A. Ford, Dmitry Samarov, Paul D'Amato, John Greenfield, Larry Bennett, Pete Crowley, Steve

Mosqueda, Fred Sasaki, Stuart Dybek, Tony Fitzpatrick, Studs Terkel, J. C. Gabel, Russell Lewis, John Russick, Jill Austin, Ann Durkin Keating, James Grossman, Elizabeth Garibay, David C. Schmittgens, John Lillig, Salli Berg Seeley, Emily Ponder, and Rick Kogan. At the website forgottenchicago.com, Jacob Kaplan, Serhii Chrucky, Daniel Pogorzelski, Patrick Steffes, Mike Damien, and Corinne Aquino exemplify passion for Chicago history, dedication to rigorous research, and imaginative engagement with urban spaces and city audiences.

We'd also like to thank the Internet.

Research originally conducted for various Pocket Guide to Hell tours and reenactments made its way into this book, and Paul would like to thank the many, many people who made those events a success, especially Jamie Albert, Martin Billheimer, Jerry Boyle, Mairead Case, Tim Dashnaw, Michelle Faust, Nick Fraccaro, Ingrid Haftel, Adam Hart, Matt Hauske, Jim Hodge, Jon Langford, Meghan McGrath, Matt Malooly, Liz Mason, Meredith Milliron, Kenneth Morrison, Tim Newberg, Scott M. Priz, Elisa Schoenberger, Sayward Schoonmaker, Sally Timms, Katie Tuten, Tim Tuten, Brant Veilleux, Nat Ward, L. Wyatt, and Nicki Yowell.

Operating in the spirit of *Chicago by Day and Night*, we often met to discuss our work (or conduct it) in various contemporary "resorts," where we took advantage of wi-fi and historically well-informed clientele and staff, along with coffee, food, and drink. These venues include the Clark Street Ale House, the Unicorn Café, The Skylark, Hopleaf, Maria's Community Bar, Pleasant House Bakery, Bleeker's, the Hideout, Bruno's, Cunneen's, the Old Town Ale House, Sky Ride Tap, New Wave Cafe, the Billy Goat, Celtic Crossings, the Celtic Knot, the Haymarket Pub and Brewery, Simone's, and Jimmy's Woodlawn Tap. We recommend them all very highly to any contemporary pleasure seekers among our readership.

At Northwestern University Press, we would like to thank Sara Dreyfuss, Anne Gendler, Marianne Jankowski, Gianna Mosser, Katherine Woodrow, and everyone else involved with this project, especially freelance copy editor Lori Meek Schuldt. Her substantive suggestions improved the introduction and notes, and she heroically saved us from several blunders. She also distinguished herself with a counterintuitive ability to resist the copy editor's inevitable and admirable urge to correct all mistakes and irregularities in the mistake-ridden and highly irregular original text. Her work enabled us to strike the balance between preserving the original eccentricities and flavor of *Chicago by Day and Night* as a historical document, while also making it readily readable for a twenty-first-century audience. Finally, we would like to thank Mike Levine of Northwestern University Press. This whole thing was his idea, but he pretty much let us do it our way. So, as is customary, we will take responsibility for any errors in the text proper (or improper), our introduction, and the notes, except for those introduced by the spirits of Chicago's bunco steerers, adventuresses, or wayward denizens of Little Cheyenne.

—PAUL DURICA AND BILL SAVAGE